Does Environmental Policy Work?

NEW HORIZONS IN ENVIRONMENTAL ECONOMICS

Series Editors: Wallace E. Oates, *Professor of Economics, University of Maryland, USA* and Henk Folmer, *Professor of General Economics, Wageningen University, The Netherlands and Professor of Environmental Economics, Tilburg University, The Netherlands*

This important series is designed to make a significant contribution to the development of the principles and practices of environmental economics. It includes both theoretical and empirical work. International in scope, it addresses issues of current and future concern in both East and West and in developed and developing countries.

The main purpose of the series is to create a forum for the publication of high-quality work and to show how economic analysis can make a contribution to understanding and resolving the environmental problems confronting the world in the twenty-first century.

Recent titles in the series include:

Pollution, Property and Prices
An Essay in Policy-making & Economics
J.H. Dales

The Contingent Valuation of Natural Parks
Assessing the Warmglow Propensity Factor
Paulo A.L.D. Nunes

Environmental Policy Making in Economics
with Prior Tax Distortions
Edited by Lawrence H. Goulder

Recent Advances in Environmental Economics
Edited by John A. List and Aart de Zeeuw

Sustainability and Endogenous Growth
Karen Pittel

The Economic Valuation of the Environment and Public Policy
A Hedonic Approach
Noboru Hidano

Global Climate Change
The Science, Economics and Politics
James M. Griffin

Global Environmental Change in Alpine Regions
Recognition, Impact, Adaptation and Mitigation
Edited by Karl W. Steininger and Hannelore Weck-Hannemann

Environmental Management and the Competitiveness of Nature-Based
Tourism Destinations
Twan Huybers and Jeff Bennett

The International Yearbook of Environmental and Resource Economics 2003/2004
A Survey of Current Issues
Edited by Henk Folmer and Tom Tietenberg

The Economics of Hydroelectric Power
Brian K. Edwards

Does Environmental Policy Work?
The Theory and Practice of Outcomes Assessment
Edited by David E. Ervin, James R. Kahn and Marie Leigh Livingston

Does Environmental Policy Work?

The Theory and Practice of Outcomes Assessment

Edited by

David E. Ervin

Professor of Environmental Studies, Portland State University, USA

James R. Kahn

Director of Environmental Studies and John Hendon Professor of Economics, Washington and Lee University, US and Collaborating Professor, Centro de Ciências Ambientais, Universidade do Amazonas, Brazil

Marie Leigh Livingston

Professor of Economics, University of Northern Colorado, US

NEW HORIZONS IN ENVIRONMENTAL ECONOMICS

Edward Elgar

Cheltenham, UK • Northampton, MA, USA

Published by
Edward Elgar Publishing Limited
Glensanda House
Montpellier Parade
Cheltenham
Glos GL50 1UA
UK

Edward Elgar Publishing, Inc.
136 West Street
Suite 202
Northampton
Massachusetts 01060
USA

A catalogue record for this book is available from the British Library

Library of Congress Cataloguing in Publication Data
Does environmental policy work? : the theory and practice of outcomes assessment /
    edited by David E. Ervin, James R. Kahn, and Marie Leigh Livingston.
        p. cm.— (New horizons in environmental economics)
    Includes bibliographical references and index.
    1. Environmental policy—Evaluation. 2. Environmental policy—Social
aspects—Evaluation. I. Ervin, David E. II. Kahn, James R. III. Livingston, Marie Leigh.
IV. Series.

GE170.D64 2004
363.7'056—dc21

                                                                    2003049218

ISBN 1 84064 170 3

Printed and bound in Great Britain by MPG Books Ltd, Bodmin, Cornwall

Contents

v

List of figures

List of tables

List of contributors

Sandra Archibald
Hubert H. Humphrey Institute of Public Affairs, University of Minnesota, USA
Edward B. Barbier
Department of Economics, University of Wyoming, USA
Dan Biller
World Bank Institute, USA
Zbigniew Bochniarz
Hubert H. Humphrey Institute of Public Affairs, University of Minnesota, USA
Alex Dubgaard
Department of Economics and Natural Resources, Royal Veterinary and Agricultural University, Denmark
David E. Ervin
Environmental Sciences and Resources Program and Sustainability Programs, Portland State University, USA
Nick Hanley
Department of Economics, University of Glasgow, UK
James R. Kahn
Environmental Studies Program and Department of Economics, Washington and Lee University, USA
Marie Leigh Livingston
Department of Economics, University of Northern Colorado, USA
David S. McCauley
Environmental Studies, East-West Center, USA
Peter F. Smith.
Resource Economics and Social Sciences Division, Natural Resource Conservation Service, US Department of Agriculture, USA
Martin Whitby
Emeritus Professor of Countryside Management, University of Newcastle upon Tyne, UK

PART I

Introduction

1.   Introduction

David E. Ervin, James R. Kahn
and Marie Leigh Livingston

1.1   INTRODUCTION

By most markers, the age of environmental policy began in the late 1960s or early 1970s. In the US, this period saw the publication of Rachel Carson's *Silent Spring*, the publication of John Krutilla's *Conservation Reconsidered*, the revelation of the Love Canal, the fire on the Cuyahoga River and the first Earth Day. Similar events occurred in other countries.

At the same time, we began to see the development of legislation to regulate environmental degradation. This legislation had very broad goals, such as to protect public health with an adequate margin of safety. Support for this legislation was strong, because people felt that environmental problems had been ignored for years, and that the environment was degraded to the point that the costs of environmental protection could be ignored. Public approval was based on an implicit assumption that the current situation was so bad that the benefits of environmental improvement were surely greater than the costs.

More than 30 years later, we have addressed the most egregious problems, and we are not so quick to leap at new opportunities for environmental regulation. First, we want to make sure that the social benefits of a policy are greater than the costs. Second, we want to make sure that the proposed policy is the best alternative possible. This is particularly important because in our haste to address the most egregious environmental problems three decades ago, we did not choose the most effective policies and built many inefficiencies and inconsistencies into our environmental regulatory system. Third, we need to consider additional criteria, such as the fairness of the distribution of environmental benefits across social groups and across time, aspects that were neglected in early policy choices.

Now, as a global society, we want to look before we leap and recognize the need for developing systems of environmental policy assessment that focus on outcomes. This is important both in terms of understanding the potential impacts of proposed new policies and in terms of evaluating the actual impacts of existing policies. There may be several advantages for environmental policy in placing more emphasis on outcomes:

- It facilitates accountability to the public by management agencies.
- It assists with benefit valuation.
- It helps design policies that avoid production and trade distortions.
- It signals the R&D process for innovations to foster such outcomes.

Yet, as we see below, there are also several serious challenges in shifting to an outcomes assessment for environmental policy. First, as will become abundantly clear, our environmental and social science theory and methods are immature on many aspects of outcomes. Second, we often have partial or no monitoring of actual environmental impacts with which to conduct the assessments. Third, even if we could measure the various impacts with acceptable precision, we have difficulty in entering the multiple outcome criteria in a consistent manner in the environmental policy decision-making process. In short, we do not have clear theory and methods about how to combine them in consistent ways. Finally, bureaucratic impediments can stymie well-intentioned outcomes assessments, and even turn them into regulatory mechanisms, contrary to their intent.

This book reflects an effort to further the development of the assessment process for identifying and measuring outcomes. Much of the book has a decidedly economic orientation, focusing on issues such as economic efficiency, cost-benefit analysis and economic valuation of environmental resources. Even though the book has an economic focus, it does not ignore other assessment or decision-making criteria and uses additional criteria both in conceptual discussion and actual implementation of assessment projects.

Before moving on to discuss each chapter and its focus, a short discussion on assessment and decision-making criteria is warranted. The first question that should be addressed is: what is the difference between an assessment criterion and a decision-making criterion? The answer is that they are largely the same and any distinction between the two is really a matter of timing. In the true sense of the word, an assessment criterion is used to evaluate past decisions. However, when one then re-evaluates these decisions and makes new decisions, the assessment criteria become decision-making criteria. Similarly, decision-making criteria are used to inform a decision before the decision is made. However, these same criteria will be used to evaluate the success of the decision some time in the future, as these decision-making criteria then become assessment criteria. Thus, there is a sort of cyclical equivalency between assessment criteria and decision-making criteria. Accordingly, we will treat the two as synonyms.

The development of a set of criteria on which to base public policy decisions is very much like selecting the football players for a country's World Cup competition. Everyone agrees on a few key players, but as one moves past the celebrated stars, there is considerable disagreement on who should fill the remaining places on the team. This analogy holds for decision-making criteria as well. For example, almost everyone agrees that economic efficiency is an important criterion, and some people think it should be the only criterion, but what of equity issues, ethical considerations, public participation and environmental stewardship?

Despite the potential for lack of consensus, this chapter suggests a set of criteria, with full knowledge that there will be disagreement about and further discussion of the included criteria, as well as the omitted criteria. However, we hope that the demarcation developed in this chapter will accelerate the debate about decision-making criteria, and emphasize the important point that one must include a wide set of criteria in the decision-making process. The following criteria are suggested for consideration and inclusion, and the intention is to extend this list as this line of research is further developed.

Table 1.1 Decision-making criteria

- Economic efficiency
- Equity
- Sustainability
- Ecological impact/environmental stewardship
- Environmental justice
- Public participation
- Ethics
- Advancement of knowledge

1.2 ECONOMIC EFFICIENCY

The criterion of economic efficiency has to do with the maximization of the difference between the social benefit and social cost of an economic activity, policy or project. In theory, all social benefits and all social costs over the life of the activity, policy or project could be incorporated into the measure of economic efficiency. However, in common practice, only benefits and costs that are readily measured in monetary terms are incorporated into the measure. Hence, there is the desire to develop additional criteria, since 'measurable' economic efficiency will inadequately incorporate environmental impacts, equity and other important societal consequences.

Economic efficiency is usually measured using one of two different concepts. The first of these is the idea of net economic benefit, which is generally measured as the total willingness to pay for a good or activity, less the costs of providing the good or activity. This is the measure preferred by economists. The second measure is that of Gross Domestic Product (or Net Domestic Product), which is a measure of the value of market output. This is the measure generally preferred by international development and lending agencies. It should be noted that these two measures are alternative measures of economic benefit and, as such, should not be added together.

1.2.1   Net Economic Benefit

Net economic benefit can be measured as the area under a demand curve, and above a supply curve, for a particular good or service. The demand curve can be interpreted as a marginal willingness to pay function, so the area underneath it (CBQ0) can be interpreted as the total willingness to pay for the activity, or the total social benefit of the good or activity. The short-run supply curve can be interpreted as the marginal opportunity cost of producing the good or service, so the area underneath it (ABQ0) can be interpreted as total social cost. Hence, the difference between the two, or area ABC in Figure 1.1, is the measure of net economic benefit for that period. This measure does not include the cost of market failures associated with the good. The net economic benefit is the discounted sum of net benefits over the relevant life of an activity, good or project.

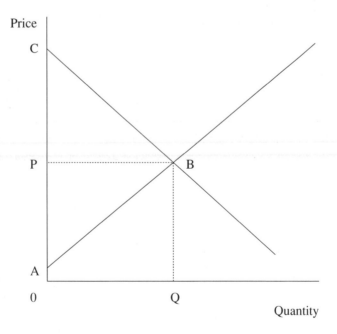

Figure 1.1   Net economic benefits

1.2.2 Gross Domestic Product

Gross Domestic Product is a measure of the total value of all goods and services produced in an economy. It replaces the old measure of Gross National Product. Since expenditures become income for the persons receiving the funds, Gross Domestic Product is also a measure of national income.

Every single economics principle textbook stresses the fact that GDP is not a measure of social welfare (it is not even truly a measure of economic efficiency), yet many policy makers, especially those with international funding agencies, view it as such and incorrectly use it as such.

It is very easy to understand GDP as a potential measure of economic efficiency by looking at Figure 1.1. The contribution of this particular good to GDP is simply its market value, or price multiplied by quantity. This is equal to the area of rectangle 0PBQ. As can be seen in this diagram, GDP is not based on behavioral functions, but merely multiplies equilibrium marginal benefit (price) times equilibrium quantity. Note that the opportunity costs of producing GDP are not subtracted from the measure.

As mentioned, GDP is not a measure of social welfare, as it does not measure other dimensions of the quality of life, such as health, environmental quality, social justice, freedom from crime, access to education and so on. Moreover, as GDP fails as a measure of social welfare, it also fails as a measure of economic efficiency. The important failure of not taking costs into account has already been mentioned. The importance of this failure can be noted by the following example: increased presence of HIV/AIDS will increase GDP because so much more is being spent on health care. However, social welfare will not increase as a result of an increased incidence of HIV/AIDS, because the costs to human health, family stability and economic productivity are not counted. GDP also fails as a measure of economic efficiency because GDP is based on market goods, it does not include production in the subsistence or informal sector. This can lead policy based just on the performance of GDP to favor formal economic activity over informal activity. In turn, this can lead to the displacement of small subsistence farms by commercial export-oriented agriculture. It is possible that this can actually reduce total social output, even though the formal measure of GDP increases. Blindly pursuing growth in GDP can actually lead to the impoverishment of large segments of the rural population.

Although GDP is not an adequate measure of either economic efficiency or social welfare, it is often incorrectly used to measure both. It should be noted that GDP measures the income associated with output, not the net benefit of the output. When using the criterion of economic efficiency, it should be measured using the methodology portrayed in Figure 1.1. Decision-makers must resist the temptation and political pressure to base decisions on a GDP criterion.

1.3   EQUITY

The level of net benefits is not the only criterion associated with benefits and costs. Another important aspect is the fashion in which the costs and benefits are distributed among the members of society. The equity criterion relates to these distributional criteria, and is multi-dimensional. One has to be concerned about the distribution of costs and benefits across various components of contemporary society, including socio-economic groups within a country, regions of a country, gender and age. As the recent collapse of the Hague round of negotiations on the Kyoto Protocol suggests, an extremely important aspect of equity is the fairness of the distribution of participation and outcomes across countries. Of particular note is the impact of decisions on the distribution of costs and benefits between developing and developed countries.

One additional dimension of equity merits consideration and that is equity across generations. This is an important impetus behind the development of an increasing concern with the sustainability of our actions, for example reducing the effects of climate change on future generations.

Although income is only one component of the equity issue, decisions related to environmental policy can have important impacts on the distribution of income. The distribution of income has received much attention in the economics literature, and a set of measures has been developed to measure the inequality of the distribution of income. The primary measures for this are the Lorenz Curve and the Gini Coefficient.

Figure 1.2 contains an illustrative example of a Lorenz Curve. The curve shows the percentage of income received by a given percentage of the society. In this example, the poorest 50 per cent of the population receives only 20 per cent of the nation's income. The diagonal line, where the two percentages are

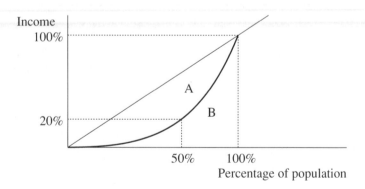

Figure 1.2   Equity and the Lorenz Curve

equal, represents a perfectly equitable distribution of income. The further the Lorenz Curve is skewed away from the diagonal line, the more inequitable is the distribution of income. The curve can be transformed into a single variable called the Gini Coefficient. The Gini Coefficient is equal to A/(A+B), where A is the area between the diagonal and the curve, and B is the area underneath the curve. With a perfectly equitable distribution of income, A is equal to zero and the Gini Coefficient is equal to zero. With a perfectly inequitable distribution of income, B is equal to zero and the Gini Coefficient is equal to one. Gini coefficients can be used to describe the distribution of wealth as well.

Of course, as already indicated, income and wealth are not the only aspects of equity of fairness. Equal access to the law, education, employment opportunities, education and health are among the many dimensions of the quality of life that are important. Of particular importance is equal access to environmental quality. This issue has become known as the environmental justice issue, and forms one of the criteria this chapter suggests is important in assessing environmental policy.

1.4 ENVIRONMENTAL JUSTICE

The criterion of environmental justice has taken on increasing importance in the last decade, as studies have suggested that certain segments of the population face disproportionate exposure to environmental risk. This is true both in developed and developing countries. For example, it has been found that in the United States, minorities, especially low income groups living in rural areas, face a disproportionate level of exposure to environmental hazards, particularly carcinogenic and mutagenic hazardous chemicals.[1] Of course, those living in inner cities face disproportionate exposure to air pollution, as well as hazards from brownfields and from the lead paint in old buildings.

The same pattern holds in developing countries, with the giant cities such as Mexico City, São Paulo, Beijing, Cairo and Calcutta having levels of air pollution that surpass those of any city in the developed nations, as well as exposure to toxic waste. In fact, whole cultures have developed on waste sites, where families actually live in the waste dump and generate income by recovering and selling useful material from the waste sites. While this recycling activity may seem environmentally beneficial at one level, it generates incredibly high exposures to harmful substances for the residents, many of whom are children.

Environmental justice is an issue in the rural areas of developing countries as well. Farm workers at industrial agricultural sites such as large banana plantations are exposed to high levels of pesticides, as are the villages downwind and downstream. Informal mining activity exposes workers and nearby populations to mercury, cyanide and other toxic hazards. In addition, there is the issue of contaminated drinking water, perhaps the most significant environmental problem in the world.

1.5 SUSTAINABILITY

The decision-making criterion of sustainability has received increasing attention since the Brundtland Commission Report. Although many definitions of sustainability and sustainable development have been offered, the most widely accepted definition of sustainable development is that it is a process that improves the well-being of the current generation without constraining the well-being of future generations.

Economists' discussions of sustainability generally focus around the accumulation of capital. These early discussions focused primarily on artificial capital and natural capital. Artificial (or human-made) capital consists of human-made structures and goods that are used to produce other goods and not consumed in the process. Artificial capital includes factories, the machines in factories, other buildings, highways, bridges, trucks, computers, and so on. Natural capital consists of renewable and non-renewable natural resources such as oil, wood, coal, minerals, and fish.

Early discussions of sustainability focused around whether sustainability could occur in the presence of a finite amount of natural resources (Pezzey 1997, Hartwick 1993). In fact, Hartwick derived an axiom known as the Hartwick Rule which suggests that sustainability is possible provided that the economic rents (the difference between revenue and the cost of extraction) are reinvested in artificial capital. The mathematical model they use to derive the result is based on the assumption of substitutability between artificial capital and natural capital in the production of output. The Hartwick article has been frequently cited as an argument that we do not need to be concerned about sustainability, as if there is sufficient investment in artificial capital that will guarantee sustainability. Unfortunately, this work neglected two important types of capital, human capital (the quantity and quality of the labor force) and environmental capital. (It also ignores social/cultural capital such as legal systems, non-government organizations and other social institutions essential to assure sustainable development.) Environmental capital refers to renewable resource systems that provide a flow of ecological services. For the purposes of our discussion, environmental capital is the most important, as the importance of environmental capital implies that the Hartwick rule cannot be true in the real world.[2] The reason is that the Hartwick rule (and other neo-classical economic treatments of sustainability) are dependent on the assumption that the different types of capital are complete and perfect substitutes for each other. This assumption is appropriate when looking at only human capital, artificial capital and natural (exhaustible or extractive) capital.

The assumption works well in this model, because these types of substitutions are possible. If oil becomes increasingly scarce, other types of capital can be substituted, such as developing more energy-efficient cars and appliances, developing alternative fuels, and so on. On the other hand, it is not possible to make this assumption when talking about environmental capital in general, as it is not possible to produce these ecological services on the same scale as provided by ecosystems.

A classic example of this is the provision of flood control services, which are often provided by ecosystems. Historically, the vast wetlands of the huge floodplain of the upper Mississippi River provided a tremendous amount of flood control services, but these wetlands were largely converted to farmland. Artificial (human-made) capital was substituted for these ecological services, in the form of levees and other flood control structures. However, the human capital could not duplicate the complexity of the ecologically provided services, in particular it did not remove the sediments from the river system, allowing the river bed to grow to be above the surrounding land, necessitating even higher levees in a non-ending cycle. The inadequacy of the human engineered system was demonstrated in 1994, when a '25 year' rain caused a '100 year' flood.

Similarly, it would be absurd to think that human engineered systems could sequester carbon on the scale of tropical rainforests, produce oxygen on the same scale as the phytoplankton layer and forests, create soil on the same scale as ecosystems, and maintain hydrological cycles on the same scale as forests and other natural ecosystems.[3]

Franceschi and Kahn (forthcoming) show that if one drops the assumption of the substitutability of other types of capital for environmental capital, then the Hartwick rule no longer holds. Sustainable development then requires the maintenance of a minimum stock of (non-substitutable) environmental capital, plus growth in the stocks of other types of capital.

Indicators of sustainability therefore must focus on the development of indicators of our stocks of capital. Stocks of artificial capital are measured in the national income and product accounts, stocks of human capital can be measured by the level of education and productivity of the labor force, and stocks of natural resources can be measured by a variety of techniques, such as stocks of 'proven reserves'. However, the same progress has not been made in the development of indicators of our stocks of environmental capital, either with regard to quality or quantity aspects. Thus indicators of sustainability require indicators of our stock of environmental capital and their ability to provide ecological services. Therefore, the development of indicators of scarcity requires developing indicators that reflect the quantity and quality of environmental capital.

1.6   ECOLOGICAL CRITERIA

At the outset, it should be said that there is no consensus of how to develop measures of the quality or functionability of an ecosystem or ecosystems in aggregate. In fact, little progress has been made in terms of developing an ecological indicator that can be used to guide policy. This section discusses several alternatives for assessing the status of ecosystems and their ability to contribute to social welfare.

The first question that needs to be addressed is how to define a desirable state of an ecosystem. Two primary concepts have been advanced, namely, ecosystem health and ecosystem integrity. Ecosystem health has to do with a system's ability to provide a flow of ecological services while ecological integrity measures the closeness of the system to a hypothetical reference system that is completely unperturbed by human activity.

Ecosystem health is a controversial topic, because it can be difficult to define the counterfactual, or what would constitute a healthy ecosystem in terms of the flow of ecological services if human development had not altered the system. For example, you could get a set of services flowing from a southern pine or eucalyptus plantation, but not the full suite of ecological services that would be found in an Amazonian rainforest or Siberian boreal forest. This leads to the questions of what level of ecological services is sufficient to conclude that an ecosystem is healthy?

Schrader-Frechette (1998) addresses this issue, arguing that ecosystem health can be measured with an extension of the traditional ecological risk assessment paradigm. She finds the original brand of risk assessment, focusing on animal risk assessment, an unproductive avenue to follow. That paradigm looks at toxicity research, and incorporates such research into an assessment of risks of exposure from human activity. As Schrader-Frechette notes, this method is particularly inappropriate for most types of ecological risk, such as those that involve land use change and other environmental threats unrelated to toxic chemicals. Although many aspects of materials and mining do involve toxic substances, this is not a promising road for developing an indicator of the full set of effects of ecosystem impacts on social welfare.

Shrader-Frechette also discusses the 'wholistic[sic] health approach' to ecosystem management and risk assessment. She notes that many proponents of the concept of ecosystem health believe it is related to at least three ecosystem characteristics:

- an ecosystem's ability to maintain desirable vital signs;
- an ecosystem's ability to handle stress; and
- an ecosystem's ability to recover after perturbations.

She notes that the controversy about the use of this method is that there are no non-normative or value-free ways to make this concept operational. In fact, she notes that in the human medical arena, we do not have a general holistic measure of human health related to the status of the entire being. In fact, it would be easier to do this for a human than an ecosystem, because we know more about the relation between subsystems and the overall being for humans than we do for ecosystems. For example, if a person's arteries become clogged with plaque, we can make predictions about future heart attacks, longevity and related outcomes. However, if an ecosystem loses 20 of 45 species of freshwater mussels, what does this mean for ecosystem health?

Cairns (1995) cites several definitions of ecological integrity that he has previously developed and that have been developed by others. He advances the definition by Karr as particularly noteworthy, where biological integrity is defined as: 'The capability of supporting and maintaining a balanced, integrated, adaptive biological system having the full range of elements (genes, species, assemblages) and processes (mutation, demography, biotic interactions, nutrient and energy dynamics and metapopulation processes) expected in a natural habitat of a region.'[4]

Any attempt to make this concept operational is very difficult because the definition has nine components, each of which is multidimensional. Although some attempts have been made to develop such an index, such as the Index of Biological Integrity, the concept has largely been unoperationalized.

It should also be noted that for many urbanized, industrialized or highly agricultural areas the concept of ecological integrity may be inappropriate. A good case in point is the Tennessee River Valley, which has over 50 dams on the tributaries and main stem of the river. In a highly engineered system such as this the concept of ecological integrity may not be applicable, since much of the valley is an engineered ecosystem rather than a naturally occurring ecosystem. For this reason, the concept of ecosystem health and looking at the flow of services from the human-made reservoirs should be stressed, rather than comparison to the historic ecosystem which no longer exists, except above the most upstream reservoirs. The same theory would be true with regard to the decision of whether or not to breach existing dams in the Pacific Northwest. Neither the existing system nor the proposed breached system would resemble the 'untouched' system viewed by Lewis and Clark in the early nineteenth century. Instead of making a comparison to this standard, the decision could focus on the flow of ecological services (including the ability to support salmon reproduction) of these two alternatives.

It is important to understand that any notion of a measure of ecosystem health or integrity would involve development of an aggregate measure by building up from measures of components or characteristics. Aggregation systems take on a life of their own, and have distinct properties associated with the method of aggregation.

At least four methods have been suggested or employed to develop operational indicators of environmental quality. These include:

1. the use of 'representative' environmental variables;
2. the development of satellite accounts for the national income and product accounts;
3. green GDP/NDP; and
4. indices of sets of environmental variables.

These alternative methods are discussed in James Kahn's contribution to the book, Chapter 3.

1.7   ETHICS

Ethical dimensions are particularly important in decision-making, but are also difficult to quantify into indicators. In fact, each method used to develop indicators has ethical implications associated with it. Even the idea of using social welfare as the primary objective of decision makers has ethical implications. For example, 'deep ecologists' would argue that it is simply unethical to manage ecosystems for human benefit, as ecosystems have inherent rights that do not originate from human concessions.

A firm or government agency may find itself confronted with certain ethical decisions regarding the environment. For example, if the opening of a mine were to threaten to cause the extinction of a species, but the species seems relatively unimportant to social welfare due to redundancy of species, should the mining company go ahead and allow the species to become extinct? While this decision is obviously going to be influenced by the provisions of national environmental codes involving endangered species, it represents the type of ethical choice that firms or agencies may face. This is a very interesting issue. Are there some cases where it would be unethical to cause an environmental impact that in all other facets seems to improve social welfare? In other words, does the firm or agency have an ethical obligation for environmental stewardship independent of the impact of the environment on social welfare? This is obviously a decision that cannot be made by analysts, but must be decided by society through deliberative processes within and among all the relevant stakeholders of the social system.

Ethical considerations are not amenable to the development of indicators. Rather than developing indicators related to ethics, we recommend that ethics screens be treated as constraints to the decision-making process and be used in assessment in a qualitative sense.

1.8   PUBLIC PARTICIPATION

Public participation is a very different type of decision-making criterion from the six criteria discussed above, as it relates more to process than outcome. This is not incongruous, however, as experience has shown that some people are willing to accept an inferior outcome if they have been actively involved in the process of developing the outcome. In other words, the fairness and appropriateness of the process of arriving at the outcome are also considered to be important and people do not focus exclusively on the desirability of the outcome.

Public participation is more of an *ex ante* than *ex post* criterion. Before the decision-making process even begins, decision-makers must make sure that they have appropriate levels of public participation. Of course, public participation is a ubiquitous concept, difficult to define and difficult to measure.

There are four major approaches to incorporating public participation into the decision-making or assessment process. These include processes which:

- incorporate information about stakeholder preferences in the decision-making process;
- allow stakeholders to negotiate a solution amongst themselves;
- allow stakeholders to arrive at a solution through role playing; and
- empower a representative group of stakeholders to hear the evidence and make a decision, jury style.

There are serious ethical issues associated with the last three methods, as the stakeholders must be chosen in some fashion, and all citizens might not approve of the manner in which stakeholders are selected, or they might not feel that these stakeholders are entitled to represent them. For this reason, the first method, of incorporating information about stakeholder preferences, may be preferable. Of course, the stakeholder information may be incorporated in a variety of ways, including survey research, focus groups, public meetings and web-based interchanges.

Because public participation is more related to a process than an outcome, it is recommended that firms and agencies focus on the development of indicators of the success of this process. This emphasis is likely to be more successful and more meaningful than trying to include indicators of public participation success as an indicator of the impact of a firm or agency's action on social welfare. In addition, information derived in the public participation process will help decision-makers understand how changes in the indicators for other criteria impact social welfare.

1.9 ADVANCEMENT OF KNOWLEDGE

The advancement of knowledge contributes indirectly to social welfare by creating new possibilities for increasing it. For example, research that contributes to the basic understanding of the properties of a material can result in future products and applications that reduce waste. Greater understanding of the process of nutrient cycling in tropical rainforests can lead to the development of more effective sustainable forestry management methods. An increased knowledge of the human genome will lead to future cures and treatments of disease.

These three examples have been chosen to show the advancement of knowledge criterion is extremely diverse and has multiple attributes. All the arguments that were made in Section 1.5 about how difficult it is to develop an indicator for ecological criteria apply to the advancement of knowledge with greater force. Nonetheless, the advancement of knowledge is an important criterion and care must be taken to include this in the decision-making process. This is best done in a qualitative fashion, as experts in the field and related fields of knowledge qualitatively evaluate the importance of potential gains in knowledge associated with a project or decision.

1.10 OUTLINE OF THE BOOK

This book is based on two sessions on environmental outcomes assessment that were organized by the Resource Policy Consortium at the 1997 World Congress of Environmental and Resource Economists in Venice, Italy. The papers were subsequently updated and revised and have been incorporated into this book. We would like to thank the sponsors of the Resource Policy Consortium for providing financial support. These sponsors include the Farm Foundation and the US Department of Agriculture's Natural Resources Conservation Service.

The papers in the volume address three basic questions:

1. *What* outcomes should be measured?
2. *How* can these outcomes be accurately measured?
3. How can the indicators of the outcomes be *used* in policy and program decision-making?

The book is organized into one section of chapters that are primarily conceptual contributions and one section of chapters with primarily applied contributions, although most chapters have both conceptual and applied facets. The primarily conceptual contributions include those by Archibald and Bochniarz, Dubgaard, Kahn, and Hanley and Whitby. The primarily applied contributions include Biller, Barbier, McCauley and Smith.

A common theme of the conceptual chapters is that they all focus on extending the assessment process to multiple criteria. Each chapter focuses on a different subset of criteria and different methodologies for measuring progress with respect to these criteria.

Archibald and Bochniarz focus on developing a set of sustainability criteria, which they apply to the six Central European Countries of Bulgaria, the Czech Republic, Hungary, Poland, Romania and the Slovak Republic. Their chapter examines reported changes in environmental quality (as measured by key environmental pressure indicators) that have occurred following the major economic and political restructuring of the past decade. The chapter not only measures the changes, but goes an important step further by employing an econometric analysis to sort out the degree to which observed changes in pressure indicators can be explained by the movement of critical economic and institutional variables of significance to the environment.

Dubgaard looks at the issue of physical indicators versus value indicators in terms of informing policy decisions. He uses the Danish pesticide program as his laboratory, and tests the ability of indicator indices – such as an environmental impact quotient – to assess environmental programs. He develops a number of innovative indices of physical change, as well as techniques for integrating the set of indices. He then tests his method by applying it to the Danish Pesticide Program.

Hanley and Whitby also look at environmental assessment in the context of European agriculture. They identify a set of criteria against which agricultural and environmental policies can be judged, articulating the primary and secondary benefits associated with each of the criteria. They then look at efficiency-based methods, effectiveness-based methods and combined methods for assessing progress in attaining these criteria. A set of empirical studies is examined to develop insights about program efficiency and efficacy.

Kahn explores a discrete choice-based method, conjoint analysis, for its potential in developing an index of environmental quality. One aspect of the type of analysis that Kahn stresses is that since the derived index is based on willingness to make trade-offs, it is congruent to measures of economic efficiency such as willingness to pay or GDP. An advantage of his approach is that the same methodology can be used to produce both monetary and non-monetary measures.

The applied chapters tend to focus on case studies and use them to actually assess past policies. Of course, in doing this, the authors not only shed light on the success of the policies, they also illuminate strengths and weaknesses of the assessment process.

Several of the chapters focus on the formal process of environmental impact assessment and its ability to assess potential outcomes and contribute to the decision-making process. Dan Biller focuses on the EIA process in Brazil, reaching an important conclusion that the Brazilian EIA has become a tool for regulation rather than a technique to discover and ensure improved environmental performance. David McCauley looks at the EIA process and its application in Asia. He criticizes EIA for its lack of economic content and focus on physical change, rather than the societal consequences of the physical change. Then he discusses the efforts of the Asian Development Bank to develop methods for monetizing the costs and benefits of environmental change.

Edward Barbier also looks at the issue of monetizing the costs and benefits of environmental change in developing countries. His focus is on Africa, where he has developed case studies in Nigeria and Sudan that look at our ability to value the environment as an input to economic production processes.

Finally, Peter Smith looks at the processes used to assess the performance of conservation projects sponsored by the US Department of Agriculture. He discusses the significance of the Government Performance and Results Act of 1994 and how the US Department of Agriculture has responded to this legislative requirement by articulating a set of goals and operational indicators of success in the pursuit of these goals.

The concluding chapter of the book looks at unanswered questions in terms of our ability to assess environmental performance and the success of environmental and natural resource policies. We articulate a set of areas where intensified research efforts could significantly advance our assessment capabilities.

In concluding this introductory chapter, we would like to thank the people who helped make it possible. In particular, we would like to thank the editorial and production staff at Edward Elgar, and Helen Downes and Carol Karsch at Washington and Lee University for their editorial assistance.

NOTES

1. See Bullard (1993).
2. See Franceschi and Kahn (2001) for a discussion of this point.
3. The non-substitutability of other types of capital for natural capital is discussed by Pearce and Warford (1993), Franceschi and Kahn (forthcoming), and Kahn and O'Neill (1999).
4. Cairns, 1995, p. 314.

REFERENCES

Bullard, Robert D. *(1993), Confronting Environmental Racism*, Boston: South End Press.

Cairns, John Jr. (1995), 'Ecological integrity of aquatic systems,' *Regulated Rivers: Research and Management*, **11**, 313–23.

Carson, Rachel (1962), *Silent Spring*, New York: Houghton Mifflin Press.

Franceschi, D. and James R. Kahn (forthcoming), 'Beyond strong sustainability', *International Journal of Sustainable Development and World Ecology*.

Hartwick, John (1993), 'The generalized R% rule for semi-durable exhaustible resources', *Resource and Energy Economics* **15**, 147–52.

Kahn, James R. and Robert O'Neill (1999), 'Ecological interaction as a source of economic irreversibility', *Southern Economic Journal*, **66**(2), 381–402.

Krutilla, John (1967), 'Conservation reconsidered', *American Economic Review*, **57**, 777–87.

Pezzey, John (1997), 'Sustainability constraints', *Land Economics*, **73**(4), 448–66.

Schrader-Frechette, Kristen S. (1998), 'What risk management teaches us about ecosystem management', *Landscape and Urban Planning*, **40**, 141–50.

PART II

Theory

2. Improving environmental impact assessment through outcomes valuation: experience from Asia

David S. McCauley

2.1 INTRODUCTION

Environmental impact assessment, or EIA, has become an important policy tool worldwide to ensure that proper account is taken of the environmental outcomes associated with development projects. Many countries have incorporated this approach into their national environmental regulations, giving EIAs the force of law in project approval. Even with implementation weaknesses, the use of this approach has resulted in greatly improved attention being given to the assessment of environmental outcomes associated with project investments.

As currently practiced, however, EIA lacks economic content. This has limited its ability to link with project economic appraisal and the economic dimensions of project design and implementation. Recent developments in the field of environmental economics have improved the methods of environmental outcomes valuation, and several attempts are under way around the world to tie together improvements in EIA with environmentally 'extended' benefit-cost analysis.

This chapter reports on one such effort in the Asia-Pacific region. The Asian Development Bank has been in the forefront of both EIA development and the encouragement of new methods for monetizing the environmental benefits and costs associated with project investments. The Asia-Pacific Regional Environmental Economics Technical Assistance (APREETA) Project was the latest in these efforts, seeking to build regional capacity in this field. The author served as Team Leader for the project, and its activities and results serve as the basis for this chapter. It illustrates an important emerging approach to generating information for improved decision making, and the efforts undertaken under this project have documented remaining weaknesses as well as opportunities for expanding applied environmental economics beyond project-level analysis to the analysis of environmental outcomes from policy and institutional reforms.

2.2   ENVIRONMENTAL ECONOMIC ANALYSIS IN THE ASIA-PACIFIC REGION

Beginning in the 1970s, countries around the world began passing legislation to require that an EIA be conducted for all public and most large private investment projects posing significant risks to the environment. This initiated a global trend toward the use of EIA as a policy tool to better incorporate environmental considerations into project design and the development process. By the 1980s the movement had expanded to many Asian and Pacific nations as newly formed environmental management agencies seized on EIA policies to draw attention to the environmental dimensions of economic development.

Several regional development and academic organizations have played important roles in furthering this process within the Asia-Pacific region. One of the most influential and pervasive has been the Asian Development Bank (ADB), adopting its own strict EIA requirements in the early 1980s and promoting the use of EIAs in project design through grants to nearly all of its member countries in the region. The Bank invested millions of dollars in capacity-building efforts throughout the Asia-Pacific region to help establish appropriate EIA oversight institutions and otherwise to strengthen in-country skills needed to conduct sound environmental analysis of development projects.

By the mid-1980s, however, it was increasingly apparent that the most commonly employed EIA methods fell short of generating sufficient information to economically evaluate the benefits and costs of environmental consequences. In the standard EIA process, little or no attempt is made to place economic values on a project's environmental impacts. EIA methods generally involve the screening of potential impacts through a checklist approach, resulting in the identification of those effects that warrant specific mitigatory measures, and scant attention is paid to positive environmental outcomes resulting from projects. The analysis also has tended to be largely subjective in nature, with few EIAs calculating in quantitative terms the effects of environmental change on natural systems or human health.

For those seeking information on the full economic and environmental outcomes of project investments, this posed a problem. It became the impetus for an ADB-led effort to encourage the development of methods and approaches capable of placing values on the environmental benefits and costs associated with project investments. Drawing upon advances in the field of environmental economics, in 1985 the ADB sponsored a groundbreaking study conducted in cooperation with the East-West Center in Hawaii that reviewed available methods for the economic assessment of environmental impacts. The resulting book (Asia Development Bank, 1986) was widely recognized at the time as the best available guidance on this subject.

Despite the inclusion of several case studies and other efforts to make the book accessible to a wide audience, the Dixon et al. book's treatment of the subject did not lend itself to use by EIA and project benefit-cost analysis practitioners. The ADB began to think about producing a more detailed handbook on the subject for its own staff and others in the region who could use such methods. Concern about the need for better economic evaluation of environmental impacts in the region was further reinforced by the findings of a review of 33 sample projects conducted by the ADB's Environment Division in 1994 (Asian Development Bank, 1994). It concluded that economic assessment in the Bank's EIAs remained.

In an effort to address these shortcomings, the ADB commissioned the development of a more user-friendly handbook entitled *Economic Evaluation of Environmental Impacts: A Workbook* (Asian Development Bank, 1996). This document (hereafter referred to as the *ADB Workbook*) provides a set of guidelines for those conducting project economic and environmental analyses that may be used to take EIAs a step further by placing monetary values on the environmental damages and benefits associated with projects. The intent is that these values be incorporated into the economic analysis of the project to gain a much fuller understanding of its overall benefits and costs, including those of an environmental nature (sometimes referred to as 'extended' benefit-cost analysis).

The *ADB Workbook* recognizes that according to this development bank's policies, the EIA – and its precursor, the Initial Environmental Examination (IEE) – serve as the primary mechanisms for considering environmental impacts during project design. If the IEE determines that a more detailed EIA is needed to look into potentially significant environmental impacts, then the Bank requires that an EIA be conducted by project proponents before the project undergoes economic analysis. This is a pattern common to the environmental laws of Asia-Pacific nations as well as those of the United States. When responsibly applied, the IEE/EIA has become an effective tool for assessing the potential environmental impacts associated with large development projects.

2.3   LIMITATIONS OF EIA

Despite the successes of EIA as a policy approach, in practice there have been two important shortcomings in its use as a planning tool in the Asia-Pacific region. First, severe problems have often arisen with the objectivity of EIA reports. Second, preparatory work by regulatory authorities, primarily prior agreements on the scope or terms of reference for EIAs, has often missed opportunities for directing sound analysis towards the major environmental problems or opportunities associated with a given project.

The issues associated with corruption or conflict of interest in the conduct of EIAs lie beyond the scope of this chapter. Suffice it to say that, though EIAs are meant to improve project design and decision making, this is often overlooked in practice. They too frequently are seen only as a stumbling block to investment. Furthermore, it has become common for oversight of the EIA process to be vested in the same line department responsible for promoting development of that sector. This often places environmental staff at odds with others in the department whose principal objective is to encourage investment in, for example, mining, agriculture, or transportation. Project proponents – public or private – normally contract directly with environmental consulting firms or university centers to conduct EIAs, and it is easy to see that such groups may be reluctant to severely criticize project design if the proponent is paying their bills and government oversight is weak.

The second major shortcoming in the application of EIA policies in the Asia-Pacific region relates to their scope of analysis. As mentioned, the most common methods employed are based on a checklist approach wherein a pre-set range of potentially negative environmental impacts – sometimes refined according to the sector involved – is reviewed and the likelihood of adverse outcomes assessed. EIAs rarely attempt to fully quantify the environmental effects of project-induced change (for example, the numbers of people with specific types of adverse health conditions resulting from air pollution or the reductions in crop yields due to erosion). They almost never describe these impacts in monetary terms.

2.4   APPROACH TAKEN IN ADB GUIDEBOOK

The *ADB Workbook* was prepared to address this latter shortcoming and to support a new Bank policy recommending that environmental outcomes (damages and benefits) from projects not only be quantified but also monetized to the greatest extent possible. As noted, the intent of this policy is to generate values for damages or benefits that can be incorporated into the economic appraisal to produce a better estimate of the project's net benefits to society. This may even include benefits to the global environment if the investing country agrees that these should be counted.

To provide the foundation for an economic evaluation of a project's environmental impacts, both the actual and potential impacts must first be identified and screened for their significance and amenability to monetization. After values have been assigned and their likely distribution over time determined, these results can be incorporated into the project economic analysis. Figure 2.1 shows the impact screening process advocated in the *ADB Workbook*, and Figure 2.2 illustrates the steps involved in valuing environmental impacts.

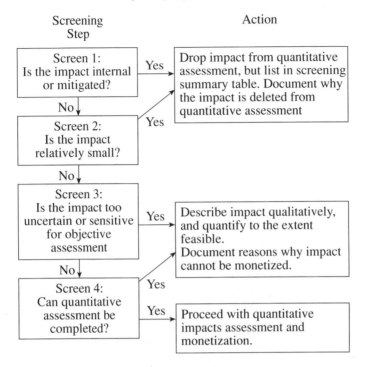

Screening Step   Action

Source: ADB (1996)

Figure 2.1   The impact screening process

Physical, physiological and psychological impacts must first be identified, screened and quantified. If quantitative estimates are not available from the EIA, then they must be generated as a part of the environmental valuation exercise (adding time and expense to the process).

Once a magnitude has been determined for each outcome, then this must be converted into an appropriate monetary unit. Sometimes there are readily accessible market prices that reflect the marginal social value of the environmental good or service that has changed as a result of the project. If so, these may be used to assign monetary values to the impacts. Several 'primary' methods for estimation of environmental values have been developed for situations in which prices are either distorted or absent. However, these require research that entails considerable effort and economic expertise. They also can be costly and time-consuming.

Since there is strong motivation to generate reliable estimates of environmental values quickly as a means for improving the information on which

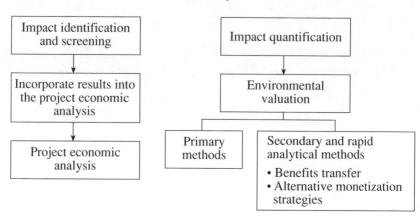

Source: ADB (1996)

Figure 2.2   Valuing environmental impacts

project decisions are based, there has been tremendous interest in identifying reliable rapid and 'secondary' methods of analysis.

Rapid methods of valuation include a range of techniques and practices that can be used when time, data and budgetary constraints make more detailed and robust primary research infeasible. The basic approach is to deal first with impact quantification and valuation data that is readily available and to then to estimate values in a logical and well-documented manner. The quantitative data used in rapid valuation techniques can come from a variety of sources. If it is not already available from the EIA (the preferable situation), it can sometimes be obtained during a short field visit to the project site. This information can then be analyzed through a variety of estimation techniques to obtain rough values for environmental damages and benefits resulting from the project.

Data also can be obtained and analyzed using secondary valuation methods. These may be used in concert with, or in lieu of, a rapid analysis. The most widespread approach (and that most strongly advocated in the *ADB Workbook*) is commonly referred to as the 'benefits transfer method' (or BTM). Using BTM, monetary valuation data are obtained by carefully reviewing and interpreting the existing environmental and resource economics literature that reports the findings of primary research on environmental outcomes valuation. Plausible monetary values are approximated through various adjustments of the unit values given in the primary research to the project impacts at hand.

The reliability of BTM estimates is heavily dependent upon the degree of similarity between the project site and impacts and those that are the subject of the reference study. The larger the differences in terms of their physical, social and economic characteristics, the greater the likelihood that the approximate values derived will be weak or even misleading. Thus, while rapid and secondary methods often present the only practical course available to assess the value of a project's environmental impacts, these approaches must be used with great care if inaccuracies or distortions are to be avoided.

2.5 FIELD-TESTING THE APPROACH

It was within this context that ADB launched the APREETA Project.[1] Having produced the *ADB Workbook*, the Bank set out – in cooperation with six of its member countries in the region – to expand awareness of and test this new approach to generating economic values for environmental benefits and costs. The APREETA Project also used the *ADB Workbook* as a basic text for training programs meant to build in-country capacity needed to apply these methods.

The overall goal of the project was to strengthen institutions and to develop associated training and reference materials that would improve project analysis in the region through better incorporation of environmental considerations into project design and decision making. The specific objectives centered on the following:

- *training* for national officials and analysts on how to use the tools of environmental economics in EIAs, project analysis and policy formulation;
- *capacity building* for the executing agency (a local university) in each country to carry on training beyond the life of the project;
- *preparation of case studies and course materials* to demonstrate the use of valuation techniques, to support future capacity building efforts, and to supplement the *ADB Workbook*; and
- *review of environmental economics literature* in each country to update and augment valuation reference materials presented in the *ADB Workbook* for use in the Asia-Pacific region, especially to apply the BTM approach to economic evaluation of environmental impacts.

The six countries chosen for participation in the APREETA Project were: Bangladesh, Indonesia, Pakistan, the Philippines, the People's Republic of China and Sri Lanka. Representatives of these countries gathered in Manila at the ADB for an Inception Workshop in August 1996. They developed a rationale and strategy for the project comprising three themes:

- *bridging between economics/planning authorities and environmental management agencies* by linking project benefit-cost analyses and EIAs and by using economic valuation of environmental impacts as a common language to bring the two groups together;

- *economically extending EIAs* to encourage the quantification of impacts in ways that lend themselves to subsequent valuation of associated benefits and costs; and
- *environmentally extending project economic analysis* to calculate more comprehensive project net present values taking into account all significant environmental benefits and costs.

2.6   PROJECT RESULTS

The APREETA teams produced three main types of outputs: course materials; case studies; and reference/literature materials. The original expectations were that the course materials to be produced would be in such a form that they could readily be used across countries; largely based on and limited to the information contained in the *ADB Workbook*. At least one case study was anticipated from each country team, with the objective that this document would serve both as a training resource and, where possible, an illustration of the efficacy of environmental economics as an aid to decision making. The main objective of the valuation literature reviews was to update and expand the Asia-Pacific coverage of Appendix J to the *ADB Workbook*, a matrix of environmental economic studies providing reference environmental values that can be used in BTM to estimate project environmental benefits and costs. The country-level literature review was also meant to enrich the relevance of materials and information available in each Asian country participating in the APREETA Project. In several cases there also were unanticipated outputs.[2]

Generic materials were produced as guidelines for the country teams at the APREETA Inception Workshop. These covered national five-day training programs targeted to economists and EIA practitioners using the *ADB Workbook* as the principal text. Each country then adapted and expanded upon these materials to suit their individual needs. Because of the variety of circumstances faced in the six countries – including language differences – the goal of producing easily transferable course materials was not realized. As a training document, the six country teams fully tested the *ADB Workbook* and found it to be a useful addition to available materials on economic analysis of project environmental impacts. An unanticipated further output was the translation of the *ADB Workbook* into the Chinese and Indonesian languages (a parallel effort is under way to translate the document into the Thai language).

The quality and coverage of the case studies produced was mixed. This reflected variations in the data available – particularly the scarcity of good quality EIAs with environmental impacts well quantified – as well as differences in the interests and skills of the country teams.[3]

There also were significant differences in approach and outputs of the country teams with respect to the environmental valuation literature reviews, but these were largely attributable to the range of references available across the six countries. Despite shortcomings, the teams were able to provide 84 new citations that were added to the matrix of environmental economic valuation studies previously presented as an Appendix to the *ADB Workbook*.[4]

2.7 BUILDING A REGIONAL ENVIRONMENTAL ECONOMICS NETWORK

Carrying out the APREETA project produced a range of other advances in applied environmental economics within the six cooperating countries and the region. It is clear that awareness has been raised – amongst policy makers and practitioners alike – about the usefulness of economic evaluation of environmental impacts as an aid to decision making. This should be very helpful as further needed capacity-building efforts move forward, and the increased capacity of both institutions and individuals should assist those seeking to conduct such analyses in these countries.

At the regional level, there now exists a latent network of environmental economists, development planners and environmental professionals who can assist each other in staying abreast of and generating further developments in the field of environmental economics. Many in this group have now worked together and share common experiences in both the conduct of training in this field and the application of environmental economic concepts and methods to project and policy analysis.

They are also increasingly in touch with other regional efforts with similar interests. Of greatest note in this regard is the Environmental Economics Programme for Southeast Asia (EEPSEA) led by the Canadian International Development Research Centre. It has been proposed that a more formal APREETA Secretariat be formed – perhaps to be based at the East-West Center where this regional effort began – that can sponsor a regular newsletter and further information exchange within an APREETA Network. Requests also have been received from other organizations in the six cooperating APREETA countries as well as from Nepal and several other countries expressing an interest in joining the network. This represents an important resource at the regional level for those encouraging further capacity-building efforts.

2.8 LESSONS LEARNED FOR FURTHER CAPACITY-BUILDING EFFORTS

As a result of this project and information drawn from other environmental economics capacity-building efforts in the region,[5] a fairly clear picture is now emerging with respect to current environmental economic skills as well as the prospects for effective strengthening of individual and organizational capacities.

Despite the efforts of the APREETA Project and others, environmental economics skills in the region remain generally weak. The theoretical underpinnings of the concepts and methods employed require strong training in neo-classical economics, and it is difficult for the environmental economics field to compete with finance, trade and other interests for the best-trained people in the region. Likewise, degree training in this field is new to the region, so most Asia-Pacific environmental economists were educated outside of the region at graduate level.

The APREETA Project initially thought to target mainstream economists involved with traditional project appraisal (benefit-cost analysis). However, efforts to environmentally 'extend' project appraisal methods through the training of such individuals or work with organizations known for such analysis proved frustrating.

On the other hand, APREETA's work with economically 'extending' EIAs met with a far more receptive audience and bore more fruit. The APREETA team members were pleasantly surprised to find EIA practitioners largely unthreatened by the proposal that their analysis dig deeper into quantifying the physical and health impacts of environmental change and that these numbers be used to help in placing economic values on the associated costs and benefits. Capacity of this kind created through the APREETA Project should improve the overall quality of EIAs in the participating countries and it also helps to build common ground for the inherently interdisciplinary nature of environmental analysis.

One somewhat troubling problem this raises is that the training of non-economists in the methods such as those embodied in the *ADB Workbook* does not address the limitation of too few trained environmental economists in the region. It is vital that there be sufficient numbers of economists capable of understanding how and when the benefits transfer method can and cannot be prudently applied in a rapid valuation exercise. Without such sound advice, the risks of misapplying BTM increase substantially.

An important lesson from this experience is the power behind the basic concept of placing economic values on environmental impacts. The APREETA courses – whether at the awareness level or geared to more intensive training – consistently elicited a positive reaction to the idea that the consequences of environmental change resulting from development activities should be translated into economic terms. It was felt that this would serve as an important and new source of information for decision makers, despite the obviously young and uncertain science of environmental economic valuation.

The APREETA experience also showed the benefits of building capacity within the context of key institutions rather than focusing only on the training of individuals. However tempting it may be to work only with the most highly skilled researchers or analysts, the situation in the Asia-Pacific region dictates that many others must patiently be brought along with the concepts and found useful roles to play in their application. Good environmental economic analysis is very challenging, but through the establishment of mentoring relationships and other approaches, a critical mass of trained individuals within key institutions can be established.

2.9 REFERENCE MATERIALS DEVELOPMENT

As noted above, there was some disappointment with the quality of the case studies and other training materials produced. This is partly the result of the high diversity of interests and backgrounds among the six participating countries. It also reflects the young state of the environmental economics profession in the region.

Demand for good region-specific case study and training materials remains high. All six APREETA country teams are now fully capable of conducting good quality awareness-level and basic training (of three to five days' duration) on the subjects covered in the *ADB Workbook*. They have country-specific materials in hand, and some have carried on with such training beyond the life of the APREETA Project. They also now have at their disposal an improved set of Asia-Pacific environmental economic valuation references as produced under the project. These have already been put to use in limited cases, and they deserve wider dissemination.

Despite the challenges of producing good case study materials, it seems worthwhile to invest further in this area. Greater attention and direction should be given, however, to the choice of sector and environmental problems addressed. Though attempts were made under APREETA to do so (encouraging both pollution and natural resources management cases, for example), this was not handled in a systematic fashion. It would not be too difficult to identify the sectors in key countries likely to see the greatest volume of investment and/or to produce the largest potential for generating negative environmental consequences. With sufficient resources devoted to sound analysis of such cases, a useful set of reference documents could be produced to guide future project and policy analyses.

There are two logical extensions of this analysis. The first relates to project evaluation and outcomes assessment, and the second to broader application of environmental economics methods to policy analysis. EIAs typically have some form of monitoring plan, in which certain key parameters are supposed to be measured over the life of the project, to ensure that measures to mitigate adverse environmental impacts are successful and to aid the *ex post* evaluators of project outcomes. If the expected environmental benefits and costs are monetized during the project design stage, this would add further information of tremendous use to those conducting outcomes assessment. Unfortunately, even the most traditional of monitoring schemes are rarely kept up to date in Asia-Pacific EIA practice. Nevertheless, the potential application of valuation methods to project (and other development) outcomes assessment merits further work.

Another potential expansion of applied environmental economic work in the region would be to move from a project orientation to broader analysis of anticipated environmental outcomes from policy and institutional reforms. In fact, APREETA training participants generally drew only scant distinctions between these two subjects despite the *ADB Workbook*'s clear bias towards project-level analysis. Most of the same analytical principles apply, but further specific guidelines for such policy review and associated training would be extremely useful.

2.10   FURTHER CAPACITY-BUILDING OPPORTUNITIES

The previous section has shown that valuable lessons may be drawn from the APREETA experience with regard to training programs, materials development and regional networking. This final section examines the implications of these lessons for future environmental economics capacity building in the Asia-Pacific region. These recommendations cover measures to improve both EIA and the economic evaluation of environmental impacts and relate to both country and regional level capacity building. It is suggested that a next stage of environmental economics capacity building in the region be centered on how to improve the analysis and role of environmental policy and institutional reforms as an integral part of development assistance programming.

Information gathered on current EIA practices in the six APREETA countries confirms the strong need for better quantitative estimation of project effects on natural systems and human health. Such information would greatly improve the basis upon which the magnitude of environmental impacts – positive or negative – may be assessed in EIAs. This will be useful even in the absence of further economic analysis to value the associated benefits and costs.

However, either through EIAs or by some other means quantitative measures must be calculated for the physical, physiological and psychological impacts of environmental changes wrought by projects if they are to be valued. It is not possible to conduct economic evaluation of environmental impacts without such information. This economic analysis will be most efficient if the quantitative impact estimates are routinely generated by EIAs, as it may otherwise be too costly and time consuming to collect and organize this data.

The ability to apply rapid valuation approaches and BTM wisely depends on having access to the valuation literature, and particularly to studies in which unit values are derived from sound economic analysis with all conditions and assumptions made clear. The *ADB Workbook*'s now updated Summary Value Tables are an attempt to make this information more readily available and relevant to the region. The Bank has been encouraged to place this information on its website, and it would be helpful to have the *ADB Workbook* Executive Summary placed there as well.

None of the APREETA case studies would yet appear to merit wide dissemination, though several are not far from becoming highly useful reference documents. This further effort to refine these cases – and to supplement them with others that either have been prepared already within the Bank or could be commissioned in the near future – would be a good investment to build on APREETA's work. As noted, the subjects and countries chosen should take into account their potential influence over investments and major environmental concerns.[6]

It is also important that ADB and other regional organizations and interested donors continue to encourage further developments in this field. The APREETA team found that the prospect of environmental economic analysis of project outcomes becoming an ADB requirement attracted considerable attention; much the way multilateral banks previously encouraged the use of EIA by mandating that it be used to screen the projects they financed. A forum is needed for collaboration among international financial institutions and environmental organizations to share lessons learned and promote wider application of the analytical techniques described and advocated in the *ADB Workbook*.

The Workbook and other applied environmental economics texts and guidebooks like it also could be improved. Since the APREETA Project primarily used the *ADB Workbook* as a training tool rather than a guidebook for project evaluation, no systematic critique by APREETA team members of its contents was conducted; but this should be done. For example, one comment received by many of those who used the *ADB Workbook* was that the approach it outlines is more readily applicable to pollution problems than to other disruptions of natural systems. Another common piece of feedback was that the book over-emphasized environmental damages and costs relative to the potential environmental benefits of projects. This may reflect some remaining misperceptions among Asia-Pacific practitioners regarding valuation principles; for example, the symmetry between benefits and costs, in which a benefit foregone is a cost and a cost avoided is a benefit. But it also points to a strong underlying interest in using environmental valuation as a means for boosting the economic case for project approvals. Care must be taken by ADB and others active in this field to guard against such biases.

2.11 FROM PROJECT TO POLICY ANALYSIS

As noted, despite APREETA's project-oriented approach, most of the country-level activities did not draw a strong distinction between applying environmental economic principles and methods to the analysis of decisions regarding projects versus broader choices among policies or programs. Together with the possible application of environmental values to monitoring and project evaluation, this would seem to be the next logical step in terms of both materials development and capacity building.

There is a rapidly growing applied environmental economics literature that addresses the efficiencies of alternative environmental policy measures and uses many of the same valuation techniques utilized in project outcome assessment to evaluate policy choices. Either an efficiency framework (benefit-cost) or a cost-effectiveness perspective lies at the heart of much of this work. But there are many more dimensions and nuances to policy analysis – such as the availability of fiscal measures and a host of institutional issues – that go far beyond project-level extended benefit-cost analysis.

The advocacy of multilateral development banks such as ADB of environmental policy adjustments – whether tied to traditional development projects or to sector or program lending – is becoming increasingly common. This is partly in response to a growing appreciation of the effectiveness of well designed and implemented policy measures to address environmental problems. Taking ADB as an example, there is growing interest and understanding of the possibilities. As reflected in several recent publications on the use of market-based incentives[7] and an in-house training program on this subject,[8] the ADB is rapidly coming to terms with both the difficulties and opportunities this presents. Although environmental policy formulation and choice will remain something of an art, there appears to be strong demand for additional applied reference materials on this subject. If the record of recent advances in project analysis is any guide, such an effort will be both challenging and rewarding as part of ongoing efforts to improve capacity in the Asia-Pacific region for better informed decision making.

NOTES

1. Officially known as Regional Technical Assistance for Capacity Building in Environmental Economics (RETA 5669), implemented by International Resources Group, Ltd.
2. A fuller description of the project organization and its results may be found in International Resources Group (1999).
3. The case studies, including an overview discussing their strengths and weaknesses, appear in Volume 3 of the APREETA Final Report.

4. This updated summary table of environmental values may be found as Annex 5 of the APREETA Final Report (main report).
5. See, for example, International Development Research Centre (1998), and McCauley and Sedjo (1997).
6. The ADB is publishing a useful compilation of case studies based on its experience with the environmental economic evaluation of its own projects (see Abeygunawardena et al., 1999).
7. See Asian Development Bank (1997a), Asian Development Bank (1997b), Asian Development Bank (1999a).
8. Training program on '*Emerging Policy Instruments for Environmental Management*', conducted by ADB in cooperation with Resources For the Future and International Resources Group (see Asian Development Bank 1999b).

REFERENCES

Abeygunawardena, P., B.N. Lohani, D.W. Bromley and R. Barba (1999), *Environment and Economics in Project Preparation: Ten Asian Cases*, Manila: Asian Development Bank.
Asian Development Bank (1986), economic staff paper No. 31, subsequently revised for publication, the latest edition being: Dixon, John A., Richard A. Carpenter, Louise F. Scura and Paul Sherman (1995), *Economic Analysis of Environmental Impacts of Development Projects*, London: Earthscan.
Asian Development Bank (1994), *Evaluation Study of the Bank's Experience in the Preparation and Review of Environmental Assessment Reports*, Manila: ADB.
Asian Development Bank (1996), *Economic Analysis of Environmental Impacts: A Workbook*, produced by a Hagler Bailly team under the oversight of an international panel and funded through ADB Regional Technical Assistance (RETA) no. 5515, Manila: ADB.
Asian Development Bank (1997a) 'Potential uses of market-based instruments for environmental management in the Philippines – the essentials', report for the ADB Office of Environment and Social Development, Manila: Philippines.
Asian Development Bank (1997b), 'Strategies for the use of market-based instruments in Indonesia's environmental management', report for the ADB Office of Environment and Social Development, Manila: Philippines.
Asian Development Bank (1999a), *Emissions Trading in the Energy Sector: Opportunities for the People's Republic of China*, Manila: ADB.
Asian Development Bank (1999b), http://www.rff.org/proj_summaries/99files/bell_training.htm.
International Resources Group (1999), *APREETA Project Final Report*, vols 1–3, Washington, DC: IRG.
International Development Research Centre (1998), *EEPSEA 1993–1998: The Economy and Environment Program for Southeast Asia*, Ottawa: IRDC.
McCauley, D. and R. Sedjo (1997), 'Evaluation of the USAID–Harvard Institute for International Development Asia Environmental Economics and Training Program', mimeo.

3. Trade-off based indicators of environmental quality: an environmental analog to GDP

James R. Kahn

1.1 INTRODUCTION

Every student who takes the first course in principles of economics learns that GDP is not a measure of social welfare. However, sometimes by default and sometimes by intent, GDP is used as a measure of social welfare in a variety of policy contexts. Of course, this has led to a significant discussion of the problems associated with using GDP as a measure of social welfare. At the same time, increasing concern with the environment and sustainable development have led to criticisms of GDP and traditionally measured NDP, as these measures do not capture the consumption of environmental capital which occurs during the process of generating current income. Many authors have suggested ways of 'greening' measures of GDP and NDP to better capture the loss of environmental capital, and have a measure of economic performance that is better related to the concept of sustainable development.

However, it is important to recognize that the environment contributes to social welfare independent of its contribution to GDP or green GDP. If one is to embark on a set of environmental and economic policies to improve social welfare, a mechanism is needed to ascertain all the impacts of the policies on social welfare. In an ideal world, one would endeavor to estimate a social welfare function to forecast these impacts, but this process is exceedingly difficult in terms of both data requirements and specification.[1] In the absence of a social welfare function (and as a precursor to attempts to estimate a social welfare function), an operational indicator of environmental quality can give insight into the impacts of policies on social welfare, just as GDP is an operational indicator of the health of the economy.

The development of such an operational indicator of environmental quality is the question that this chapter addresses, by developing an environmental analog to GDP. This indicator focuses on the measurement of elements of the stock of environmental capital (and services flowing from the capital) that directly impact social welfare. It is not an attempt to follow in the footsteps of Daly and Cobb (1989), Moffat and Wilson (1994) and others in redesigning GDP and NDP to account for the depreciation of income-producing environmental capital. Section 3.2 of the chapter explains this distinction in greater detail, by diagramming the relationships among the economy, the ecosystem and social welfare. Section 3.3 of the chapter discusses other efforts to develop indicators of environmental quality, while Section 3.4 discusses the approach suggested in this chapter, a trade-off weighted index of environmental quality. The fifth section presents a discussion of how the index can contribute to the policy-making process.

3.2 THE RELATIONSHIP BETWEEN THE ENVIRONMENT AND SOCIAL WELFARE

Figure 3.1 illustrates the relationships between four different aspects of the quality of life and social welfare. These facets of the quality of life include the health of the economy, the health of the population and the health of the environment. Although there are many other important influences on social welfare, this chapter diagrams only these four factors in an effort to focus on the direct and indirect impacts of the environment on social welfare. Direct impacts are depicted by the thickest solid arrow (B) and represent environmental resources

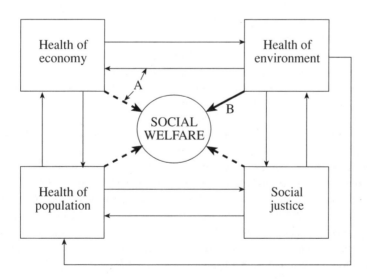

Figure 3.1   Selected determinants of Social Welfare

(or services flowing from environmental resources) that appear as individual arguments in an individual's utility function.[2] In addition, environmental quality also indirectly impacts social welfare through its effects on the economy, health of the population, and social justice.

It is important to note that we have already developed operational indicators associated with non-environmental direct impacts (thick-dashed arrows). For example, GDP, green GDP, unemployment rates and inflation rates are all operational indicators of the health of the economy. Similarly, infant mortality, birth weights and longevity are used as operational indicators of the health of the population, while variables such as the inequality of income distribution (Gini Coefficient), literacy rates and incarcerated proportion of the population are used as indicators of social justice.

One can use these indicators to evaluate policy, even in the absence of a social welfare function. For instance, ceteris paribus, if longevity or literacy rates increase, social welfare will be increasing. The difficult policy question arises in terms of trade-offs, for example, if reducing infant mortality rates requires a sacrifice in terms of potential GDP. Methods for examining this trade-off will be further discussed in Section 3.5, but for now the crucial point is that we have not developed a corresponding environmental indicator for the health of the environment.

Again, it is emphasized that this chapter is not suggesting a new green method for measuring GDP, which incorporates environmental influences on GDP. The arrows labeled 'A' in Figure 3.1 show the influence of the environment on the health of the economy and the subsequent impact on social welfare. These impacts are the subject of focus for improved measures of green GDP or green NDP such as those suggested by Daly and Cobb and Moffat and Wilson. This chapter focuses on developing an operational indicator of the health of the environment that focuses primarily on the solid thick arrow (B), but can also encompass some aspects of the indirect impacts associated with the chain involving the health of the environment, the health of the population and social justice.

It should be noted that any choice of an operational indicator of the environment will have both advantages and disadvantages and will not be an 'ideal indicator'. For example, the unemployment rate is an operational indicator of the health of the economy, but it has flaws. It does not include those who are so discouraged that they are not actively seeking work, and aggregate unemployment rates understate the true unemployment rates for some sectors of society, such as young people in the inner cities. However, if one understands the idiosyncracies of an operational indicator, it can be used in the policy formulation process.

3.3 A DISCUSSION OF PAST EFFORTS TO DEVELOP AN OPERATIONAL INDICATOR OF ENVIRONMENTAL QUALITY

At least four methods have been suggested or employed to develop operational indicators of environmental quality. These include use of 'representative' environmental variables, the development of satellite accounts for the national income and product accounts, green GDP/NDP and indices of sets of environmental variables.

3.3.1 Representative Environmental Variables

Measures of individual species of pollution have been used in many studies, with the underlying assumption being that the trends associated with these individual pollutants are somehow representative of environmental quality. For example, sulfur dioxide pollution has been used as an indicator of overall environmental quality in the estimation of 'environmental Kuznet's curves', which purportedly show a u-shaped relationship between environmental quality and income (an inverse u-shaped relationship between income and concentrations of pollution). The use of particular pollutant to proxy for environmental quality in general is conceptually similar to using output in the steel industry as a proxy for GDP or incidence of lung cancer as a general indicator of the health of the population, and has been criticized by Arrow et al. (1995) and O'Neill et al., (1996), among others. In particular, the measure is completely unrelated to land use changes (such as deforestation and desertification) and to water quality changes (with the exception of acidification of water bodies). In addition, sulfur dioxide is a fund or flow pollutant which does not accumulate over time, unlike carbon dioxide, chlorofluorocarbons, or heavy metals.

3.3.2 Green GDP

Many economists, including Daly (1991), Peskin (1976), Prince and Gordon (1994), and Repetto (1989) have argued that disastrous consequences can occur when macroeconomic policy is based on promoting the growth of GDP. They argue that not only does this ignore other aspects of the quality of life, but that GDP has a serious flaw as a measure of economic progress.

This flaw has to do with the fact that measures of Net Domestic Product (NDP) subtract the depreciation of human-made capital, but do not subtract the depreciation of natural capital. Thus, when a machine is too worn out to produce current income, the loss in income-producing ability is subtracted from the measure of current income. The consumption of human-made capital is subtracted from GDP to give NDP, a more accurate measure of the current economic well-being of a nation. However, when a forest is clear-cut, soil degraded, or stocks of minerals depleted in order to produce current income, a similar debit is not made.

Although one can argue that this is just a definitional issue, and that all definitions are arbitrary in nature; there are serious implications when national economic policy is based on this flawed measure of NDP. If increasing current NDP is a primary policy goal, then natural capital and its ability to produce future income (or other services) may be expended even if this is detrimental to producing future social welfare. Although this is a crucial problem in developed countries such as the United States, it is perhaps even more important in developing countries where pressing needs to increase current income have caused catastrophic deforestation, pollution, soil erosion and desertification.

As Repetto et al. (1989) indicate, this difference in the treatment of natural capital and human-made capital

> reinforces the false dichotomy between the economy and the 'environment' that leads policy makers to ignore or destroy the latter in the name of economic development. It confuses the depletion of valuable assets with the generation of income. Thus, it promotes and seems to validate the idea that rapid rates of growth can be achieved and sustained by exploiting the resource base. The result can be illusory growth and permanent losses in wealth.

Therefore, Repetto and others argue that the depreciation of natural capital should be factored into GDP in a fashion analogous to the depreciation of human-made capital. Repetto recomputes Indonesia's national income and product accounts making corrections for deforestation, soil erosion and oil reserves. Repetto found that the measured 7.1 per cent annual growth rate of GDP is actually only 4 per cent when these corrections are made.

Although this type of analysis can aid in the formulation of macroenvironmental policy, it does not give complete information about the relationship between the health of the environment and social welfare. As stated above, this measure only takes into account one pathway for the environment to affect social welfare and, most importantly, it ignores the direct effect of the health of the environment on social welfare. Although the value of these direct effects or non-pecuniary environmental services could be incorporated into national income and product accounts, this would be difficult, if not impossible to do. It is much more difficult to monetize these other aspects of environmental quality than it is to monetize environmental effects such as oil depletion and soil erosion. Thus, the monetary conversion problem associated with willingness-to-pay measures is not eliminated with national income and product accounts, it has simply been transferred to the national income and product accounts.

This chapter is not intended to provide a discussion of the pros and cons of contingent valuation.[3] However, it will be noted that there is such controversy associated with measuring the willingness to pay for individual environmental resources, that it is likely to be some time before the method progresses to the point where there are generally accepted estimates of the willingness to pay for environmental quality in general. It should be noted that in terms of other indicators of social progress, we do not necessarily use willingness to pay measures as a guide for measuring progress. For example, when we look at reducing infant mortality rates, we are conscious of the cost effectiveness of programs, but do not attempt to measure progress in this social arena through willingness to pay to reduce infant mortality.

An additional problem with these macroeconomic approaches is that there is a tendency to focus on environmental resources that are part of the economic production process and focus less on environmental resources that contribute more basic life support services or amenity benefits. More importantly, GDP and NDP are measures of the health of the economy, not the health of the environment. Separate measures of the health of the environment must be developed to better understand the relationship between environmental quality and social welfare.

Even though the greening of the national income and product accounts cannot create an operational indicator of the health of the environment, it should be pursued to give a more accurate indication of the health of the economy. Prince and Gordon provide a detailed discussion of this type of modification of the US national income and product accounts.

3.3.3 Satellite Accounts

In addition to the types of modifications of GDP discussed above, the UN Statistical Division recommends the development of a system of environmental satellite accounts, to monitor environmental change.

> Satellite Accounts try to integrate environmental data sets with existing national accounts information, while maintaining SNA concepts and principles as far as possible. Environmental costs, benefits and natural resource assets, as well as expenditures for environmental protection, are presented in flow accounts and balance sheets in a consistent manner. That way, the accounting identities of the SNA are maintained. One of the values of the SEEA framework compared to more partial approaches is that it permits balancing, so that rough monetary estimates can be made for residual categories (Hamilton and Lutz, 1995, p. 5).

However, satellite accounts (by intent) represent a disaggregation of measures of environmental change, rather than an aggregation. They could serve as inputs for developing operational indicators of environmental change, but as an independent set of indicators they would suffer from the same problem as the indicators that EMAP collects. This problem revolves around the large number of measures which make the examination of trade-offs and overall trends more difficult. However, these satellite accounts could serve as a basis of an aggregate measure, in which the individual variables categorized in the satellite accounts are aggregated into a more general index.

3.3.4   Aggregate Indices

The Environmental Monitoring and Assessment Program (EMAP) of the US Environmental Protection Agency represents an effort to develop indicators of environmental quality.

EMAP attempts to develop overall indicators for individual ecosystems (such as forests, wetlands or estuaries). In the case of estuaries, EMAP develops a series of over 20 indicators, but creates an aggregate index by summing the indicators based on water clarity, the benthic index and the presence of trash (Schimmel et al., 1994). This is indicative of a general procedure employed by natural scientists to create aggregate indicators by summing all individual environmental indicators and dividing by the number of indicators to create an unweighted index. This unweighted index is virtually meaningless, because it implicitly and arbitrarily uses equal weights for each individual indicator. For instance, why should a 10 per cent increase in the benthic index and a 10 per cent increase in the presence of trash receive the same weight in the index? Additionally there is a potential problem of the level of the index being a function of the choice of the unit of measurement of each of the individual variables. For example, if one variable is measured in parts per million and another is measured in parts per billion, they will have very different impacts on the index. One way to get around this measurement problem is to normalize each variable by dividing by its maximum level, so that all the variables are then numbers between zero and one.

While normalization solves the unit of measurement problem, it does not solve the problem associated with an arbitrary choice of equal weights for each variable. One way of developing more meaningful weights is to base them on expert opinion. This could be done through a Delphi process or through averaging the weights that each expert has assigned. While this is certainly an improvement over the arbitrary choice of equal weights, the following section outlines a more formal procedure for defining weights that is consistent with the way decisions are made with respect to private goods, by examining individuals' willingness to make trade-offs.

3.4   THE TRADE-OFF WEIGHTED INDEX OF ENVIRONMENTAL QUALITY

An operational indicator – *consistent with the economic paradigm* – can be developed by looking at how people prefer one state of the world to another. While it is a difficult task to ask people to place a value on a state of the world, stating a preference for one state over another is consistent with the way people make many decisions such as locational choice, whether to get married and/or have children, or which political party to vote for. It should be noted that people do not contemplate the marriage decision by asking themselves about their willingness to pay for being married to one potential spouse versus another potential spouse versus being single, but which choice gives them the highest quality of life. These optimizing choices may be constrained by ethical or moral rules that people have imposed upon themselves.

A choice, or trade-off based indicator, can be developed by using discrete choice-based conjoint analysis to present alternative states of the environment to the individual.[4] The alternative states would be defined by different levels of physical characteristics of the environment, including the characteristics of important sub-systems of the environment. These include, but are not limited to, characteristics of the state of forests, estuaries, rivers, wetlands, atmospheric chemistry, ambient air and water quality and presence of toxic sites.[5]

Indices could be established to account for those environmental resources which directly impact social welfare (thick arrow in Figure 3.1) and those that impact it through human health and social justice (outer chain of arrows in Figure 3.1). Presumably, a properly constructed green GDP would appropriately account for many of the relationships which comprise the arrows labeled 'A' in Figure 3.1. Moreover, a 'sustainability index' could also be developed, incorporating those environmental resources which provide ecological services. Some of these resources would be easy to incorporate into a green GDP, such as soil fertility, since it is relatively easy to measure the marginal value of declining soil fertility. In addition, environmental resources such as stocks of timber, reserves of fossil fuels and minerals and the impact of tropospheric ozone on agriculture can be easily computed from studies published in the peer reviewed literature.

However, other ecological services such as biodiversity, watershed protection, production of oxygen, habitat, primary productivity and so on have important but more difficult to measure links to future social welfare, both directly and indirectly through future impacts on GDP. A separate sustainability index would allow us to track these important ecological resources and ecological services to see if current actions are increasing or reducing our ability to develop in a sustainable fashion.

Whether one was developing an environmental index or a sustainability index, people would be asked to choose which set of physical environmental characteristics they prefer, with each person presented with several different choice sets to evaluate. One could conduct this choice process with either ordinary citizens or experts in environmental sciences (both social and natural sciences). The level of the physical environmental characteristics in the choice sets would be varied both within the choice sets presented to individuals, and across individuals. This variation in the level of the characteristics of the alternative states of the environment would allow the estimation of a preference function. In this preference function, the probability of preference is estimated as a function of the levels of the physical characteristics. The derivatives (with respect to each physical characteristic) of the preference function can then be used as weights to aggregate the physical characteristics into a single index or set of indices. In other words, if the estimated preference function was of the form,

$$PROB = \theta(C_1, C_2, C_3,...C_n) \qquad (3.1)$$

where the C_i's refer to the levels of the environmental characteristics that define the alternative states of the world, the index could be computed as

$$I = \sum_{i=1}^{n} \frac{\partial \theta}{\partial C_i} C_i \qquad (3.2)$$

At first glance, this method for deriving these weights may seem to be a recast version of contingent valuation, as both this method and contingent valuation ask the respondent hypothetical questions about willingness to make trade-offs concerning environmental quality. However, the two are based on fundamentally different mental models. Contingent valuation asks people to state a willingness to pay for a non-market good, but people are not accustomed to purchasing non-market goods. This forced employment of an unfamiliar mental model may be what gives rise to the biases which many people argue are associated with contingent valuation. However, conjoint analysis asks people to choose among alternative states of the world. Even though these alternative states may involve non-market goods, people are accustomed to making this type of choice. For example, the choices of whether to get married or stay single, have children or not have children, vote Republican or Democrat, live downtown versus the suburbs, or go into academics versus consulting, are all alternative states of existence which are associated with different bundles of non-market goods. (They may also be associated with changes in income and bundles of market goods.)

Although conjoint analysis remains largely untested with respect to environmental goods, its performance with market goods indicates a high degree of internal and external validity. In particular, in comparisons of hypothetical and actual responses, conjoint analysis has been a good predictor of actual responses.[6] In comparison, in many experimental studies, contingent valuation has been a poor predictor of actual responses (see Cummings, 1996).

Even though the method proposed for deriving indexes is not based on willingness to pay, one of its attractive features is that it is still based on the willingness of individuals to make trade-offs. In contrast, the Environmental Monitoring and Assessment Program (EMAP) of EPA has developed indices of physical characteristics that are unweighted indices. In addition to the inherent desirability (at least from the point of view of an economist) of basing the indicators on willingness to make trade-offs, the trade-off based foundation of the indicators would make the measures of the health of the environment analogous to the primary measure of the health of the economy (GDP), as GDP is a set of physical quantities which are weighted by people's willingness to make trade-offs, which in the case of GDP are measured by prices. An indicator of the health of the environment which is based on 'trade-off weighted' physical quantities would be completely analogous to GDP, except in this case, the trade-offs are measured through a survey process, since market prices do not exist for the physical characteristics of the environment.[7]

One of the major criticisms by non-economists of willingness to pay measures and other methods which are based on individual choice is that they do not take into account expert knowledge of the consequences of environmental change. It is possible to incorporate expert knowledge into the trade-off based indicator of environmental quality (or indicator of sustainability) by implementing a parallel choice process and separate index among a sample of experts.

An important policy consideration is the determination of how much importance to place on the expert index in comparison to the ordinary citizen index. This expert index could be kept separately and then policies could be evaluated with respect to both indices. Alternatively, the indices could be merged into one index. One way to do this would be to include a statement in the survey to which citizens respond. This statement would indicate that experts are being asked to state preferences for alternative states of the environment in the same fashion. The citizens could then be asked (as part of the survey questionnaire) how much weight in the decision-making process expert opinion should be given relative to citizen opinion.

This chapter has illustrated that a trade-off weighted index of environmental quality has the potential to meet many needs in understanding the relationship between the health of the environment and social welfare. However, outside of discussing conjoint analysis as a general framework in which the index could be estimated, the chapter has not discussed the nuts and bolts of the estimation process. A comprehensive discussion of all the estimation issues is beyond the scope of this chapter, but it is important to point out that the estimation process is quite complex. A schematic of the process for developing this indicator is contained in Figure 3.2. Each step of the process indicated in Figure 3.2 must be researched to determine the best means of implementation.

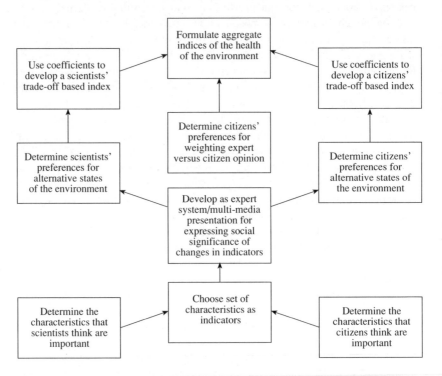

Figure 3.2   The process for developing a trade-off based indicator of environmental quality

3.5   THE TRADE-OFF BASED INDEX AND POLICY EVALUATION

3.5.1   Evaluating Efficiency

The trade-off based index is not measured in dollar terms, so it cannot be exactly determined if the benefits of a set of policies which are based on the index exceed the costs of the policies. However, the trade-off based index can still be used to shed light on the efficiency question. For example, assume that a particular set of policies only affect the health of the economy and the health of the environment. In Figure 3.3, each set of policies is associated with an environmental outcome and a GDP outcome, and the outcomes are plotted. An outer envelope can be constructed which would reveal that for any set of social indifference curves with the usual properties, the policies associated with interior outcomes are inferior to those associated with outcomes on or near the frontier. Potential Pareto improvements, such as movements from point E in the north-easterly direction can also be identified. Trade-offs between environmental quality and the health of the economy are explicitly defined by the slope of the frontier. This analysis can be extended to multiple dimensions, to include social justice, the health of the population and other social objectives.

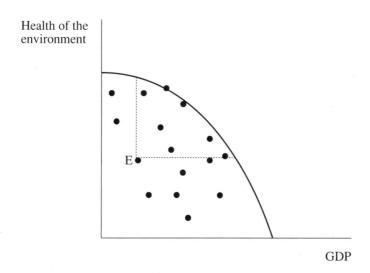

Figure 3.3   Technically efficient and inefficient sets of policies

Of course, if the health of the economy is a function of the health of the environment, the production possibilities frontier might not have the characteristic shape associated with Figure 3.3. The shape of the frontier in Figure 3.3 assumes that promoting the health of the economy must always reduce the health of the environment and vice versa. If GDP is functionally dependent on environmental quality, where environmental quality is an input to the production process, then the production possibilities frontier could have the shape illustrated in Figure 3.4. Many developing countries are likely to be in the backward bending portion of the function, where environmental quality has become so degraded that further degradation unambiguously lowers GDP.[8] Of course, the location of a particular country on the frontier, and its proximity to the backward bending portion of the frontier, is an empirical issue, but it underlines the importance of having an operational indicator of the health of the environment which can be used in empirical studies of the relationship between environmental quality and economic productivity.

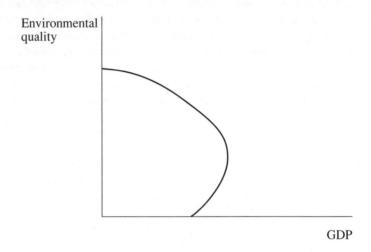

Environmental quality

GDP

Figure 3.4   Backward bending production possibilities frontier

3.5.2   Evaluating Sustainability

Sustainability has become a much talked about goal, with many definitions as to what constitutes sustainability. The general thrust of many of the definitions is that sustainable development is a pattern of development which meets the needs of the current generation without diminishing the prospects of future generations. However, less has been done in terms of measuring sustainability. Many case studies have been conducted of projects and policies which are shown to be unsustainable, however, there is currently no accepted standard by which it can be determined whether an entire economy is on a sustainable path. The trade-off based index of environmental quality offers an opportunity to quantify the concept of sustainability.

If sustainability is related to the maintenance of our environmental assets,[9] then a sustainable set of policies can be defined as one in which the index of the health of the environment is non-declining. Note that since the index is a composite of physical characteristics, some characteristics could be declining as long as other characteristics increase sufficiently to compensate for the declining characteristics. This allows considerably more flexibility in economic development than a constraint which implies that no physical characteristics may be declining and it also avoids the arbitrariness associated with unweighted indices. An examination of sustainability in the absence of an aggregated index would require one to look at the entire set of physical characteristics, and either impose a non-negative change constraint on each characteristic or attempt to look at trade-offs. However, trade-offs are difficult, if not impossible, to examine in an ad hoc comparison when there are literally thousands of environmental indicators. In terms of sustainability and whole ecosystem effects, the only analysis possible is to impose a non-negativity constraint on all relevant environmental variables. In other words, this type of analysis allows only 'no decline' changes in environmental endpoints. Almost every feasible policy option or project will violate at least one of the individual non-negativity constraints.

An alternative way to use the index to measure the sustainability of outcomes is to estimate the previously discussed relationship of green GDP or NDP as a function of the trade-off based index, among other variables. A sustainable outcome could then be estimated as one in which the predicted national income variable was non-decreasing in every time period or over some selected time path, where the effect of changes in the environment on future GDP was explicitly considered. However, since this would not take into account the direct effect of the environment on social welfare and other aspects of the quality of life, it could only be considered sustainable in a narrow GDP-related context.

3.5.3   The Trade-off Based Index and Equity

The trade-off based index may be a more equitable way of setting policy goals because it is less dependent than other methods on ability to pay. Willingness to pay measures and cost-benefit analysis are based on the principle of 'one dollar, one vote', and the willingness to pay is a function of the ability to pay. In contrast, as long as the survey sample which is used to estimate the index is representative of the population as a whole, the trade-off based index is based on the principle of 'one person, one vote', which is the principle upon which the US constitutional democracy (and most other democracies) is based. This consistency with constitutional democracy is not obtained by abandoning the economic paradigm, as the trade-off based index is still based on people's willingness to make trade-offs. Of course, people at different income levels may have different preferences for environmental quality, but the aggregation of these preferences into the index gives each person an equivalent weight, provided the sampling process includes all preference groups.

Of course, other dimensions of equity, such as who pays for environmental improvements, whether some people have less access to environmental quality than others and whether some people are disproportionately exposed to environmental hazards, must still be addressed. Trade-off based indicators developed on a more local basis (in addition to the national indices) can help determine the 'environmental justice' implications of alternative policy outcomes.

3.6   CONCLUSIONS

Since GDP is not a good measure of social welfare and since not all aspects of environmental quality and sustainability can be incorporated into GDP, it is important to develop an independent operational indicator of environmental quality. Various methods have been employed in an effort to do this, including the use of representative environmental variables, satellite environmental accounts and unweighted indices of environmental variables. Each of these methods has shortcomings that makes it less than ideal for formulating environmental and economic development policy.

However, a set of trade-off based operational indicators can be developed that are still consistent with the economic paradigm and that can be used to measure the efficiency and sustainability of alternative outcomes. In addition, these measures are more consistent with the principles of constitutional democracy and are more equitable, since they are based on one person, one vote, rather than one dollar, one vote. Although the proposed method would require a substantial research effort to develop it to the point where one could contemplate implementation, there are significant potential welfare gains associated with the evaluation of environmental policy with such a measure.

NOTES

1. See Boadway and Bruce (1984) for a discussion of the Arrow Impossibility Theorem and the practical implications of the theory for the identification and estimation of social welfare functions.
2. If one were looking at this problem in a household production function approach, then these environmental resources and services would be inputs to the production of a final service flow.
3. This discussion is provided in many places including Portney, Hanneman, Diamond and Hauseman, and Bjornstad and Kahn.
4. See Louviere (1988, 1996) for a general discussion of conjoint analysis.
5. It is not the purpose of this chapter to define which characteristics should be included, that is a topic of further research. Rather, this chapter focuses on the development and justification of a method with which to develop an indicator of the health of the environment.
6. See Louviere and Hensher 1982; Levin, Louviere, Schepanski and Norman 1983; Louviere and Woodworth 1983; Louviere 1988; Horowitz and Louviere 1993; Elrod, Louviere, and Davey 1992; Louviere, Fox, and Moore 1993; Adamowicz, Louviere and Williams 1994.
7. The same procedures could be used to develop a single indicator variable for the other areas of social concern. For example, this process could be used to aggregate longevity, infant mortality and other health indicators into a single indicator variable of the health of the population.
8. A few examples of such countries would include those where massive (or complete) deforestation has lead to declining soil fertility and agricultural productivity (such as Haiti), countries where overgrazing has led to desertification (such as the African countries in the Sahel region) and countries where air pollution has significantly impacted the health of the labor force (central Europe).
9. Environmental assets are broadly defined here to include those assets which are directly used in production activities (such as timber, clean water, fertile soil and so on), those which are indirectly used in production activities, and those which contribute to social welfare either directly or indirectly through some mechanism other than the economy.

REFERENCES.

Adamowicz, W., J.J. Louviere, and M. Williams (1994), 'Combining revealed and stated methods for valuing environmental amenities', *Journal of Environmental Economics and Management*, 26: 271–92.

Arrow, Kenneth, Bert Bolin, Robert Castanza, Partha Dasgupta, Carl Folke, C.S. Holling, Bengt-Owe Jansson, Simon Levin, Karl-Göran Maler, Charles Perring and David Pimentel (1995), 'Economic growth, carrying capacity and the environment', *Science*, 268: 520–21.

Bjornstad, David and James R. Kahn (eds) (1996), *The Contingent Valuation of Environmental Resources: Methodological Issues and Research Needs*, London, Edward Elgar Publishing.

Boadway, Robin W. and Neil Bruce (1984), *Welfare Economics*, Oxford, Blackwell.

Cummings, Ronald (1996), 'Relating stated and revealed preferences: challenges and opportunities', in Bjornstad, David and James R. Kahn (eds), *The Contingent Valuation of Environmental Resources: Methodological Issues and Research Needs*, London, Edward Elgar Publishing.

Daly, Herman E. (1991), 'Towards an environmental macroeconomics', *Land Economics*. 67: 255–59.

Daly, Herman E. and John B. Cobb Jr (1989), *For the Common Good: Redirecting the Economy Toward Community, the Environment and a Sustainable Future*, New York: Beacon Press.

Diamond, P.A. and J.A. Hauseman (1994), 'Contingent valuation: is some number better than no number?', *Journal of Economic Perspectives*, 8: 45–64.

Elrod, T., J.J. Louviere and K.S. Davey (1992), 'An empirical comparison of ratings-based and choice-based conjoint models', *Journal of Marketing Research*, 29: 368–77.

Hamilton, Kirk and Ernst Luntz (1995), 'Accounting for the future', working paper, Environment Department, World Bank.

Horowitz, Joel. L. and Jordan. J. Louviere (1993), 'The external validity of discrete choice models based on laboratory choice experiments', *Marketing Science*, 12: 270–79.

Levin, I.P., J.J. Louviere, A.A. Schepanski and K.L. Norman (1983), 'External validity tests of laboratory studies of information integration', *Organizational Behavior and Human Performance*, 31: 173–93.

Louviere, J.J. (1988), 'Conjoint analysis modeling of stated preferences: a review of theory, methods, recent developments and external validity', *Journal of Transport Economics and Policy*, pp. 93–119.

Louviere, J.J. (1996), 'Relating stated preference methods and models to choices in real markets: calibration of CV responses', in Bjornstad, David and James R. Kahn, (eds), *The Contingent Valuation of Environmental Resources: Methodological Issues and Research Needs*, London, Edward Elgar Publishing.

Louviere, J.J. and D.A. Hensher (1982), 'On the design and analysis of simulated choice or allocation experiments in travel choice modeling', *Transportation Research Record*, 890: 11–17.

Louviere, J.J. and G.G. Woodworth (1983), 'Design and analysis of simulated consumer choice or allocation experiments: an approach based on aggregate data', *Journal of Marketing Research*, 20: 350–67.

Louviere, J.J., M.F. Fox and W.L. Moore (1993), 'Cross-task validity comparisons of stated preference choice models', *Marketing Letters*, 4: 205–13.

Moffat, I. and M.D. Wilson (1994), 'An index of sustainable economic welfare for Scotland, 1980–91', *International Journal of Sustainable Development and World Ecology*, 1: 264–91.

Neill, Helen R., Ronald Cummings, Phillip Ganderton, Glenn Harrison and Thomas McGuckin (1994), 'Hypothetical surveys and real economic commitments', *Land Economics*, 70: 145–54.

O'Neill, R.V., J.R. Kahn, J.R. Duncan, S. Elliott, R. Efroymson, H. Cardwell and D. Jones (1996), 'Economic growth and sustainability: a new challenge', *Ecological Applications*, **26**(3): 23–4.

Peskin, Henry M. (1976), 'A national accounting framework for environmental assets', *Journal of Environmental Economics and Management*, 2: 255–62.

Portney, P.R. (1994), 'The contingent valuation debate: why should economists care?', *Journal of Economic Perspectives*, 8: 1–18.

Prince, Raymond and Pratice L. Gordon (1994), 'Greening the national accounts', *CBO Papers*, Congressional Budget Office, Washington DC.

Repetto, Robert, W. Magrath, M. Wells, C. Beer and F. Rossini (1989), *Wasting Assets: Natural Resources in the National Income and Product Accounts*, World Resources Institute, Washington DC.

Schimmel, Steven C., Brian D. Melzian, Daniel E. Campbell, Charles J. Strobel, Sandra J. Benyi, Jeffrey S. Rosen and Henry W. Buffum (1994), Statistical Summary: EMAP – Estuaries, Virginia Province – 1991, USEPA, EPA/620/R-94/005, March.

4. Environmental project evaluation in developing countries: valuing the environment as input

Edward B. Barbier

4.1 INTRODUCTION

Natural resource management is crucial to the developing economies of the world. These economies, especially the lower-income countries, are highly dependent on primary production as the source of long-term, sustainable economic development (Barbier 1994). Successful exploitation of primary production agriculture, fishing, forestry and minerals, in turn depends on efficient and sustainable management of the resource base supporting primary productive activities. Moreover, as developing countries industrialize and as their populations concentrate in urban settlements, the role of the environment in assimilating waste products and providing life-support amenities will become increasingly important. Protection and conservation of key natural systems and important ecological functions will also be essential, not only in terms of their potential value for recreation and tourism but because these systems and functions may provide invaluable support and protection for economic activity and human welfare.

Any analysis of the contribution of environmental resources to development must invariably involve valuing the key economic functions performed by these resources, and in turn, the impact of economic activity on the environment. Valuation of environmental resources and impacts is the starting point for the application of environmental economics in developing countries, and is essential for comparing the economic and social returns to economic activities and projects that involve the use of environmental resources.

This chapter examines the critical valuation issue of assessing the role of ecological resources and services in supporting and protecting economic activity in developing countries. This valuation issue is important for two principal reasons. First, as the economic contribution of environmental resources and systems is often nonmarketed, it is generally ignored in investment decisions and policies that affect the allocation of these resources and systems. Second, failure to take into account such environmental values may distort development and investment decisions, leading to unnecessary and inefficient depletion, degradation and over-exploitation of natural resources and environments. The result can be a net loss of economic welfare to a developing country.

However, assessing the role of the environment as an input into economic activities in developing countries raises some interesting methodological challenges. The direct exploitation or use of environmental resources is often fairly straightforward to value, but valuing the indirect use of ecological resources and services in terms of providing external support and protection of economic activities elsewhere can be more problematic. To illustrate the various approaches and issues involved, this chapter draws on several case studies, such as allocating land among competing uses (for example, gum arabic versus annual crops in Sudan), diversion of water from downstream flood-plains for upstream water developments (such as the Hadejia-Jama'are floodplain, northern Nigeria) and evaluating the benefits of ecological services in support of economic activity (for instance mangrove–fishery linkages in Campeche, Mexico).

4.2   COMPARING RETURNS FROM COMPETING ENVIRONMENTAL USES

Many large-scale investment projects and programs, such as hydroelectric dams, irrigation schemes, commercial agricultural development schemes, road building, and so on, have significant environmental impacts. Some of these impacts may impose additional costs or benefits on society. In recent years, advances have been made in applying economic valuation techniques to analyzing the environmental impacts of investment projects and programs in developing countries (Barbier et al. 1997; Dixon et al. 1988).

Failure to account fully for the environmental impacts of an investment project or program means that its net economic worth is being misrepresented. Often, when significant external environmental costs are present, the result is a misallocation of resources and excessive environmental degradation. These additional costs must be included as part of the costs of the development investment.

For example, assume that there is an upstream development project on a river that is providing water for agriculture. Given direct benefits (for example, irrigation water for farming), B^D, and direct costs (costs of constructing the dam, irrigation, channels, and so on), C^D, then the direct net benefits of the project are:[1]

$$NB^D = B^D - C^D \qquad\qquad (4.1)$$

However, by diverting water that would otherwise flow into downstream wetlands, the development project may result in losses to floodplain agriculture and other primary production activities (such as fishing, fuelwood or livestock grazing), less groundwater recharge and other external impacts. Given these reductions in the net production and environmental benefits, NB^E, of the wetlands, then the true net benefits of the development project (NB^P) are $NB^D - NB^E$. The development project can therefore only be acceptable if:

$$NB^P = NB^D - NB^E > 0 \qquad (4.2)$$

Thus, in the presence of significant environmental impacts, the net benefits of a development project or programme cannot be appraised in terms of its direct benefits and costs alone. The forgone net costs of disruption to the natural environment and degradation must also be included as part of the opportunity costs of the development investment.

4.3   VALUING THE ENVIRONMENT AS INPUT

Assessment of the net production and environmental benefits, NB^E, is of course critical to implementing the above decision rule (Equation 4.2). However, the analysis of such benefits is not always so straightforward. Although many production and environmental benefits directly or indirectly support economic activity, there are many ways in which such use values occur.

For example, direct uses of the environment would include both consumptive uses of resources (such as livestock grazing, fuelwood collection, forestry activities, agriculture, water use, hunting and fishing) and non-consumptive uses of environmental 'services' (for example recreation, tourism, *in situ* research and education and navigation along water courses). Direct uses of natural resources and systems could involve both commercial and non-commercial activities, with some of the latter activities often being important for the subsistence needs of local populations. Commercial uses may be important for both domestic and international markets. In general, valuing the marketed products (and services) of the environment is easier than valuing non-commercial and subsistence direct uses.

When the environment is being indirectly used, in the sense that the ecological functions of the environment are effectively supporting or protecting economic activity, then the value of these functions is essentially nonmarketed. This value arises out of the natural 'interaction' between different ecological systems and processes; in particular, the ecological functioning of one ecosystem may affect the functioning and productivity of an adjacent system that is being exploited economically. As a result, the overall productivity and stability of the latter ecosystem may be critically dependent on the maintenance of a few key external support functions provided by the neighbouring ecosystem. Examples include the role of coastal marshland and mangrove systems as breeding grounds and nurseries for offshore fisheries; flood and sedimentation control provided by upper watershed and montane forest systems; sediment and nutrient retention by riverine wetlands; and semi-arid and arid brush forests protecting against desertification of rangelands. As the economic contribution to production activities of these external ecological support functions are non-marketed, go financially unrewarded and are only indirectly related to the economic activities that they protect or support, the indirect use values of external ecological support functions are often extremely difficult to value. They are also good examples of how the existence of ecological externalities also gives rise to economic externalities (Barbier 1998).

In recent years, our understanding of the direct and indirect use of the environment for economic activities and our valuation techniques for assessing these economic contributions have improved greatly. In particular, economists have demonstrated that it is possible to value nonmarketed environmental resources and services through the use of surrogate market valuation, which essentially uses information about a marketed good to infer the value of a related nonmarketed good (Freeman 1993). Travel cost methods, recreational demand analysis, hedonic pricing and averting behaviour models are all examples of surrogate market valuation that attempt to estimate households' derived demand for environmental quality.

However, this chapter describes another type of surrogate market valuation that is particularly useful for the valuation of nonmarketed values associated with biological resources and ecosystems that make a direct or indirect contribution to economic activity. This is often referred to in literature as either the production function approach or valuing the environment as input (Aylward and Barbier 1992; Barbier 1994; Freeman 1993; Mäler 1991).[2] This approach recognizes that ecological resources and functions may have an economic value that arises through their support of economic production and human welfare, or through protection of valuable assets and property. Moreover, given the direct dependence of many production systems and economic livelihoods in developing countries on natural resources and systems, valuing the environment as input is considered widely applicable to many important economic development and investment decisions in those countries (Aylward and Barbier 1992; Barbier 1994; Mäler 1991).

The general production function approach consists of a two-step procedure. First, the physical effects of changes in a biological resource or ecological function on an economic activity are determined. Second, the impact of these environmental changes is valued in terms of the corresponding change in the marketed output of the relevant activity. In other words, the biological resource or ecological function is treated as an 'input' into the economic activity, and like any other input, its value can be equated with its impact on the productivity of any marketed output.

More formally, if Q is the marketed output of an economic activity, then Q can be considered to be a function of a range of inputs:

$$Q = F(X_i...X_k, S), \qquad (4.3)$$

For example, suppose that the ecological function of particular interest is the role of mangroves in supporting offshore fisheries through serving both as a spawning ground and a nursery for fry. The area of mangroves in a coastal region, S, may therefore have a direct influence on the catch of mangrove-dependent species, Q, which is independent from the standard inputs of a commercial fishery, $X_i...X_k$. Including mangrove area as a determinant of fish catch may therefore 'capture' some element of the economic contribution of this important ecological support function. That is, if the impacts of the change in the mangrove area 'input' can be estimated, it may be possible to indicate how these impacts influence the marginal costs of production. As shown in Figure 4.1, for example, an increase in wetland area increases the abundance of crabs and thus lowers the cost of the catch. The value of the wetlands' support for the fishery – which in this case is equivalent to the value of increments to the wetland area – can then be imputed from the resulting changes in consumer and producer surplus.

In order for the production function approach to be applied effectively, it is important that the underlying ecological and economic relationships are well understood. As noted above, when production, Q, is measurable and either there is a market price for this output or one can be imputed, then determining the marginal value of the resource is relatively straightforward (Mäler 1991). If Q cannot be measured directly, then either a marketed substitute has to be found, or possible complementarity or substitutability between S and one or more of the other (marketed) inputs, $X_i...X_k$, has to be specified explicitly. Although all these applications require detailed knowledge of the physical effects on production of changes in the resource, S, and its environmental functions, applications that assume complementarity or substitutability between the resource and other inputs are stringent requirements for the information on physical relationships in production. Clearly, cooperation is required between economists, ecologists and other researchers to determine the precise nature of these relationships.

In addition, as pointed out by Freeman (1991), market conditions and regulatory policies for the marketed output will influence the values imputed to the environmental input. For example, in the previous example of mangroves supporting an offshore fishery, the fishery may be subject to open access

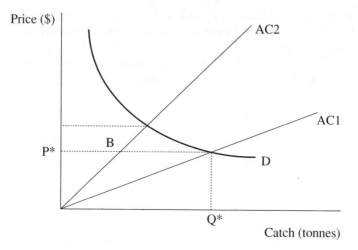

Note: The welfare impact of a change in wetland area on an open access fishery is the change in consumer surplus (area B).

Figure 4.1a   Welfare impact on open access fishery

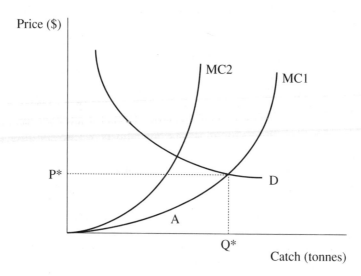

Note: The welfare impact of a change in wetland area on an optimally managed fishery is the change in consumer and producer surplus (area A).

Figure 4.1b   Welfare impact on optimally managed fishery

conditions. Under these conditions, rents in the fishery would be dissipated, and price would be equated to average and not marginal costs. As a consequence, producer surplus is zero and only consumer surplus determines the value of increased wetland area (see Figure 4.1).

Applications of the production function approach may be most straightforward in the case of single use systems; in other words, resource systems in which the predominant economic value is a single regulatory function, or a group of ecological functions providing support or protection for an economic activity in concert. In the case of multiple use systems – resource systems in which a regulatory function may support or protect many different economic activities, or which may have more than one regulatory ecological function of important economic value – application of the production function approach may be slightly more problematic. In particular, assumptions concerning the ecological relationships among these various multiple uses must be carefully constructed to avoid problems of double counting and trade offs between the different values (Aylward and Barbier 1992).

Finally, for some valuation problems, choosing whether to incorporate intertemporal aspects of environmental change can be important. For example, there are two ways in which the production function approach has been implemented to estimate the value of estuarine wetlands and mangroves in supporting offshore fisheries (Barbier 1997; Freeman 1993). The first is essentially a static approach, which either ignores the intertemporal fish harvesting process (that is, assumes single-period or static production) or assumes that fish stocks are always constant (that is, harvesting always offsets any natural growth in the fish population). Either assumption can be used to derive a market equilibrium for fish harvest, and thus to estimate changes in consumer and producer surplus arising from the impacts of a change in mangrove area on this static equilibrium. The second is essentially a dynamic approach, which attempts to model the effects of a change in mangrove area on the growth function of the intertemporal fishing problem. By solving for the long-run equilibrium of the fishery, the comparative static effects and resulting welfare impacts of a change in mangrove area on the equilibrium levels of stock, effort and harvest can be determined.

The rest of the chapter uses case studies from developing countries to illustrate the application of the production function approach to valuing the environment as an input into economic activitiy. Three case studies are chosen: the allocation of agricultural land between gum arabic systems versus competing annual crops in Sudan; diversion of water from downstream floodplains for upstream water developments in the Hadejia-Jama'are floodplain, northern Nigeria; and evaluating mangrove–fishery linkages in Campeche, Mexico.

4.4   ALLOCATING LAND AMONG COMPETING USES

The following case study (Barbier 1992) is a straightforward application of decision rule (2) through use of the above production function approach. In this case, a particular tree species, *Acacia senegal*, is the key environmental input, which in turn yields an important marketed output, gum arabic resin. However, the *Acacia senegal* tree also produces many additional environmental benefits, and a full analysis of the economic value of farming systems incorporating this tree needs to take into account these wider benefits as well. As this case study indicates, although it is reasonably easy to compare the marketed returns of gum arabic systems to the returns of competing agricultural systems, the wider environmental benefits of gum arabic systems need also to be assessed.

4.4.1   Case Study: Gum Arabic versus Annual Crops, Sudan

The gum arabic tree (*Acacia senegal*) is a naturally occurring species in the Sudano-Sahel region that serves a variety of valuable economic and ecological functions. The gum produced by the tree – the 'gum arabic' – is widely sought after in importing countries for use as an emulsifier in confectionery and beverages, photography, pharmaceuticals and other manufacturing industries. In addition, the *Acacia senegal* tree provides fodder for livestock, firewood and shade. There are also numerous indirect benefits associated with this tree; for example, its extensive lateral root system reduces soil erosion and runoff, as a leguminous tree it fixes nitrogen which encourages grassy growth for livestock grazing, it serves as a windbreak and is important in dune fixation. For these reasons, the tree is the preferred species in bush-fallow rotation and intercropping farming systems prevalent in the arid west of Sudan. On a larger scale, across the Sudano-Sahelian region, the gum arabic belt acts as a buffer against desertification.

The choice by farmers in Sudan to incorporate gum arabic trees in their farming systems will depend on whether the above benefits from a gum arabic-based system exceed those of alternative systems. The potentially high financial rate of return to a gum arabic based farming system coupled with its important environmental benefits would seem to imply that such a system would be ideal for combating desert encroachment and rehabilitating the gum belt of Sudan. However, in recent decades, distortionary government policies have meant that the real producer price of gum arabic in Sudan has fluctuated considerably, as has the relative price of gum to its competitor cash crops (sesame and groundnuts) and even food crops (sorghum and millet). Farmers' share of the export value of gum also remains low, which has been one reason for the recent increase in smuggling of gum to neighboring countries.

An economic analysis was conducted of six representative cropping systems containing gum arabic cultivation in Sudan (Barbier 1992). The results are indicated in Table 4.1. Although the analysis shows that all six systems are economically profitable, the relative profitability of gum compared to other crops in each system is generally lower than that of other crops; except in the Tendelti system of the White Nile where field crop damage occurs frequently. In most systems there are initial losses due to the need to establish gum gardens before they begin producing. This would suggest that maintaining the real producer price of gum by removing distortions in the market, as was assumed in the analysis, is a necessary economic incentive to encourage gum cultivation.

Table 4.1   Economic analysis of six cropping systems, Sudan

| | (1989–90 sudanese pounds per feddan, 10% Discount Rate) | | | | | |
	Acacia Senegal[1]	Sorghum	Millet	Groundnuts	Sesame	All crops
BN	2 989.57	4 606.83	2 931.58	–	–	**10 527.98**
WN	3 923.82	–432.99	486.30	5 330.92	8 605.12	**17 913.17**
NK	1 471.36	–	2 091.77	–	6 020.94	**9 584.07**
SK	882.99	1 644.44	–	13 109.44	13 776.95	**29 413.82**
ND	1 240.87	–	2 363.89	9 687.69	–	**13 292.45**
SD	1 884.02	3 830.80	3 775.60	9 715.61	–	**19 206.03**
All	**2 065.44**	**2 412.27**	**2 392.83**	**9 460.92**	**9 467.67**	**16 656.25**

Notes:
BN = Blue Nile Province, clay soils, largeholder
WN = White Nile Province, sandy soils, smallholder
NK = North Kordofan Province, sandy soils, smallholder
SK = South Kordofan Province, clay soils, largeholder
ND = North Darfur Province, sandy soils, smallholder
SD = South Darfur Province, sandy soils, smallholder
ALL = Average of all six systems

[1] Total NPV from gum, fuelwood and fodder, except for Blue Nile and South Kordofan (gum only)

Source: Barbier (1992)

The analysis in Table 4.1 suggests that it may be more economically profitable to replace the gum arabic component in each of the six systems with annual crops. However, despite the lower relative returns to cultivating gum arabic, there are several reasons why converting land under *Acacia senegal* to cultivating annual crops may not be desirable:

- Some land under *Acacia senegal* may not be suitable for growing annual crops, resulting ins very low and fluctuating yields.
- Fallowing land may be important to maintain its fertility; gum arabic is the ideal cash crop for this purpose.
- The environmental benefits of gum arabic trees (such as control of erosion/runoff, wind breaks, dune stabilization, nitrogen fixation) were not included in the analysis, and these may be significant in maintaining the yields of field crops within the farming systems.
- The role of the gum belt in controlling desertification certainly is significant in supporting and protecting farming systems in the region, and although this collective benefit cannot be captured in an analysis of individual systems, traditional farming communities in the gum belt region are very much aware of it.
- Risk-averse farmers may desire some of their land being held under gum cultivation, because the returns from gum – although lower than the maximum expected returns from the cash crops – may be less variable under stressful environmental and climatic conditions.
- Gum cultivation provides cash income to farmers outside the growing season for cash crops.

Thus, a fuller economic assessment of the wider environmental benefits of gum arabic systems, and not just the returns from marketed gum, would perhaps reveal the true economic value of these systems compared to annual crops.

4.5   UPSTREAM WATER DIVERSION

As discussed above, the type of ecological and economic externalities associated with upstream water diversion are fairly straightforward, 'unidirectional' problems. Water that is diverted upstream means less water downstream, and the result is that upstream activities benefit at the expense of downstream activities. Determining the optimal level of water diversion between upstream and downstream uses is therefore a critical issue. As Barbier (1998) has shown, by extending Equation 4.2 into a simple production function model of the river basin, it is possible to illustrate the key conditions underlying this important allocation decision. A case study of the impacts of upstream water project developments on the downstream floodplain in the Hadejia-Jama'are River Basin in northern Nigeria also illustrates the valuation and incentive issues associated with this particular type of externality.

The basic river basin model developed by Barbier (1998) considers two competing uses for water flowing through the basin: water diverted upstream for irrigated agriculture and water flowing downstream for natural floodplain agriculture. Thus floodplain agricultural production is entirely dependent on the stock of water available downstream and 'stored' in the naturally occurring floodplain. This downstream water supply, W, is freely available to the agricultural system, which uses a fixed proportion of it, kW.[3] Output per hectare in the agroecosystem, h_1, is therefore a function of the available water stock, W, and a vector of other inputs, z_1 (labor, purchased inputs, and so on). Assuming that the agricultural system produces for a market in response to a given market price, p^h, and faces a vector of given input prices, c, the discounted economic returns of present and future production in the agroecosystem can be represented as:

$$V^1 = V^1\left(z_1, W, t;\ p^h, c, \delta\right) = \int_0^T \left(p^h h_1 - c z_1\right) e^{-\delta t} dt$$

$$h_1 = h_1\left(z_1, W\right), h_{1i} > 0, h_{1ii} < 0, i = z_1, W, \tag{4.4}$$

where δ is the rate of discount and T is the time period over which the downstream agroecosystem is in operation.

However, the continuous diversion of water for upstream projects, such as irrigation or water supply, reduces the flow of water through the watershed and drainage basin, directly affecting the supply of water available downstream for the floodplain. This diversion can be represented by:

$$W(t) - W(0) = -\int_0^t d\ dt$$

$$\text{or } \dot{W} = -d \tag{4.5}$$

Thus d represents the amount of water diverted each period by upstream projects, and hence the amount of water no longer available for the stock of downstream supply, W. If it is assumed that water in a river basin is being continuously diverted upstream for an irrigated agricultural system, then the discounted returns per hectare for this system, V^2, may take the following form:

$$V^2 = V^2\left(z_2, d, t;\ p^h, c, \delta\right) = \int_0^T \left(p^h h_2 - c z_2\right) e^{-\delta t} dt$$

$$h_2 = h_2\left(z_2, d, \textstyle\int d\ dt\right) = h_2\left(z_2, d, W(0) - W(t)\right), h_{2i} > 0, h_{2ii} < 0, i = z_2, d, W(0) - W(t)$$

$$\tag{4.6}$$

where agricultural yield, h_2, is presumed to be an increasing function of both current water diversion, d, cumulative diversion into the upstream irrigation network, $\int d\,dt$, and variable inputs, z_2. Output is sold at the given market price for irrigated crops, p^h, and cost of inputs is c. In this simple example, it is assumed that there is no user charge imposed on the agricultural system for the irrigation water supplied through the upstream water project.[4]

In this case, the economic externality problem arises because the farmer benefiting from the diverted irrigation from the upstream water project is unconcerned about any resulting impacts on downstream water availability. For example, it is clear from Equation 4.6 that the economic agent would maximize discounted returns by choosing a rate of water diversion, d^i, in each period t, that would satisfy the following condition:

$$\frac{\partial V^2}{\partial d} = p^h h_{2d}\left(d^i\right) = 0, \quad \forall t \tag{4.7}$$

that is, from the standpoint of the upstream irrigation farmer, optimal diversion of water to the upstream irrigated agricultural system in every time period should occur until there are no more gains to be had from using additional water inputs.

In contrast, if there was a single river basin planning authority, this agency would be concerned with maximizing not only the returns to upstream irrigated agriculture (Equation 4.6) but also the returns to the downstream agroecosystem as well (Equations 4.4 and 4.5). Denoting λ as the costate variable, or 'shadow price', of the downstream water supply, the current value Hamiltonian, H, and relevant first order conditions of concern to the river basin authority might be:

$$H = \left(p^h h_1 - cz_1\right) + \left(p^h h_2 - cz_2\right) - \lambda d$$

$$\frac{\partial H}{\partial d} = p^h h_{2d}(d^*) - \lambda = 0$$

$$-\frac{\partial H}{\partial W} = \dot{\lambda} - \delta\lambda = p^h h_{2W(0)-W(t)} - p^h h_{1W} \text{ or } \frac{\dot{\lambda}}{\lambda} + \frac{h_{1W}}{h_{2d}} - \frac{h_{2W(0)-W(t)}}{h_{2d}} = \delta. \quad \forall t \tag{4.8}$$

In comparison with Equation 4.7 the first order conditions in Equation 4.8 show that the optimal rate of water diversion for the entire river basin occurs where the marginal benefit to upstream irrigated agriculture of diversion equals the shadow price, or value, of water supply to the downstream agroecosystem. By definition, $\lambda(t)$ is 'shadow price', or imputed value, of the downstream water stock, W, in terms of the net returns to the agroecosystem in the lower catchment.

As this shadow value is positive, and is likely to be increasing over time as W is depleted, then the optimal rate of diversion, d^*, for the entire watershed and drainage basin will be less than the rate, d^i, that an upstream farmer would decide on his or her own.[5]

Consequently, the valuation problem facing the river basin planner is to determine the contribution of the available downstream water to the returns to the lower catchment agricultural system, and how these returns might change over time as more water is diverted to the upstream project. Again, a basic production function approach to estimate downstream floodplain benefits, as indicated by Equation 4.3, is critical. As the following example indicates, overcoming this incentive problem and ensuring an optimal rate of diversion in a river basin system is particularly difficult if plans and development for upstream water diversion are already well advanced.

4.5.1 Case Study: Hadejia-Jama'are River Basin, Northern Nigeria[6]

In northeast Nigeria, an extensive floodplain has been created where the Hadejia and Jama'are Rivers converge to form the Komadugu Yobe River which drains into Lake Chad. Although referred to as wetlands, much of the Hadejia-Jama'are floodplain is dry for some or all of the year. Nevertheless, the floodplain provides essential income and nutrition benefits in the form of agriculture, grazing resources, non-timber forest products, fuelwood and fishing for local populations. The wetlands also serve wider regional economic purposes, such as providing dry-season grazing for semi-nomadic pastoralists, agricultural surpluses for Kano and Borno states, groundwater recharge of the Chad Formation aquifer and 'insurance' resources in times of drought. In addition, the wetlands are a unique migratory habitat for many wildfowl and wader species from Palearctic regions, and contain a number of forestry reserves.

However, in recent decades the Hadejia-Jama'are floodplain has come under increasing pressure from drought and upstream water developments. The maximum extent of flooding has declined from between 250 000 to 300 000 ha in the 1960s and 1970s to around 70 000 to 100 000 ha more recently. Drought is a persistent, stochastic environmental problem facing all sub-Saharan arid and semi-arid zones, and the main cause of unexpected reductions in flooding in drought years. The main long-term threat to the floodplain is water diversion through large-scale water projects on the Hadejia and Jama'are rivers. Upstream developments are affecting incoming water, either through dams altering the timing and size of flood flows or through the diversion of surface or groundwater for irrigation. These developments have been taking place without consideration of their impacts on the Hadejia-Jama'are floodplain or any subsequent loss of economic benefits that are currently provided by use of the floodplain.

The largest upstream irrigation scheme at present is the Kano River Irrigation Project (KRIP). Water supplies for the project are provided by Tiga Dam, the biggest dam in the basin, which was completed in 1974. Water is also released from this dam to supply Kano City. The second major irrigation scheme within the river basin, the Hadejia Valley Project (HVP), is under construction. The HVP will be supplied by Challawa Gorge Dam on the Challawa River, upstream of Kano, which was finished in 1992. Challawa Gorge may also provide water for the Kano City water supply. A number of small dams and associated irrigation schemes have also been constructed or are planned for minor tributaries of the Hadejia River. In comparison, the Jama'are River is relatively uncontrolled with only one small dam across one of its tributaries. However, plans for a major dam on the Jama'are at Kafin Zaki have been in existence for many years, and the dam would provide water for an irrigated area totalling 84 000 ha. Work on the Kafin Zaki Dam has been started and then stopped a number of times, most recently in 1994, and its future is at present unclear.

A combined economic and hydrological analysis was recently conducted to simulate the impacts of these upstream projects on the flood extent that determines the downstream floodplain area (Barbier and Thompson 1998). The economic gains of the upstream water projects were then compared to the resulting economic losses to downstream agricultural, fuelwood and fishing benefits.

Table 4.2 indicates the scenarios that comprise the simulation. Since Scenarios 1 and 1a reflect the conditions without any of the large-scale water resource schemes in place within the river basin, they are employed as baseline conditions against which Scenarios 2–6 are compared. Scenario 2 investigates the impacts of extending the KRIP-I to its planned full extent of 22 000 ha without any downstream releases. In contrast, Scenario 3 simulates the impacts of limiting irrigation on this project to the existing 14 000 ha to allow a regulated flood from the Tiga Dam in August to sustain inundation within the downstream Hadejia-Jama'are floodplain. Challawa Gorge is added in Scenario 4 and the simulated operating regime involves the year-round release of water for the downstream HVP, but not for sustaining the Hadejia-Jama'are floodplain. Scenario 5 simulates the full development of the four water resource schemes without any releases for the downstream floodplain. In direct comparison, Scenario 6 shows full upstream development, but less upstream irrigation occurs in order to allow regulated water releases from the dams to sustain inundation of the downstream floodplain.

In Table 4.3a, the impacts of Scenarios 2–6 upon peak flood extent downstream are evaluated as the difference between maximum inundation predicted under each of these scenarios and the peak flood extents of the two baseline scenarios. The gains in upstream irrigated area are also indicated for each scenario in Table 4.3a. The estimated floodplain losses are indicated in

Table 4.2   Scenario for upstream projects in the Hadejia-Jama'are River basin, northern Nigeria

Scenario (time period)	Dams	Regulated releases (10^6 m^3)	Irrigation schemes
1 (1974–85)	Tiga	Naturalized Wudil flow (1974–85)	No KRIP-I
1a (1974–90)	Tiga	Naturalized Wudil flow (1974–1990)	No KRIP-I
2 (1964–85)	Tiga	None	KRIP-I at 27 000 ha
3 (1964–85)	Tiga	400 in August for sustaining floodplain	KRIP-I at 14 000 ha
4 (1964–85)	Tiga	None	KRIP-I at 27 000 ha
	Challawa Gorge	348 yr^{-1} for HVP	
	Small dams on Hadejia tributaries		
5 (1964–85)	Tiga	None	KRIP-I at 27 000 ha
	Challawa Gorge	348 yr^{-1} for HVP	
	Small dams on Hadejia tributaries		
	Kafin Zaki	None	84 000 ha
	HVP	None	12 500 ha
6 (1964–85)	Tiga	350 in August	KRIP-I 14 000 ha
	Challawa Gorge	248 yr^{-1} and 100 in July	
	Small dams on Hadejia tributaries		
	Kafin Zaki	100 per month: Oct–Mar and 550 in August	None
	HVP	Barrage open in August	8 000 ha

Notes:
KRIP-I = Kano River Irrigation Project Phase I
HVP = Hadejia Valley Project

Source: Barbier and Thompson (1998)

Table 4.3b for each scenario compared to the baseline Scenarios 1 and 1a. Given the high productivity of the floodplain, the losses in economic benefits due to changes in flood extent for all scenarios are large, ranging from US$2.6–4.2 million to US$23.4–24.0 million.[7] As expected, there is a direct trade-off between increasing irrigation upstream and impacts on the wetlands downstream. Scenario 3, which yields the lowest upstream irrigation gains, also has the least impact in terms of floodplain losses, whereas Scenario 5 has both the highest irrigation gains and floodplain losses. The results confirm that in all the scenarios simulated the additional value of production from large-scale irrigation schemes does not replace the lost production attributed to the wetlands downstream. Gains in irrigation values account for at most around 17 per cent of the losses in floodplain benefits.

Table 4.3a   Impact of scenarios on mean peak flood extent and gains in total irrigated area

	Scenario 1	Scenario 1a	Gains in irrigated area (km^2)
Scenario 2	−150.62	−211.20	270
Scenario 3	−95.25	−55.83	140
Scenario 4	−265.02	−325.60	270
Scenario 5	−870.49	−931.07	1 235
Scenario 6	−574.67	−635.25	220

This combined hydrological-economic analysis would suggest that no new upstream developments should take place in addition to the Tiga Dam. Moreover, a comparison of Scenario 3 to Scenario 2 in the analysis shows that it is economically worthwhile to reduce floodplain losses through releasing a substantial volume of water during the wet season, even though this would not allow the Tiga Dam to supply the originally planned 27 000 ha on KRIP-I.

Although Scenario 3 is the preferred scenario, it is clearly unrealistic. As indicated above, Challawa Gorge was completed in 1992, and in recent years several small dams have been built on the Hadejia's tributaries while others are planned. Thus Scenario 4 most closely represents the current situation, and Scenario 5 is on the way to being implemented; although when the construction of the Kafin Zaki Dam might occur is presently uncertain. As indicated in Table 4.3b, full implementation of all the upstream dams and large-scale irrigation schemes would produce the greatest overall net losses, around US$20.2–20.9 million.

Table 4.3b   Impact of scenarios in terms of losses in floodplain benefits versus gains in irrigated production, net present value (US$ 1989/90 prices)

	Scenario 1 Irrigation value [1][a]	Scenario 1a Floodplain loss [2][b]	Net loss [2] − [1]	[1] as % of [2]	Floodplain loss [3][b]	Net loss [3] − [1]	[1] as % of [3]
Scenario 2	682 983	−4 045 024	−3 362 041	16.88	−5 671 973	−4 988 990	12.04
Scenario 3	354 139	−2 558 051	−2 203 912	13.84	−4 184 999	−3 830 860	8.46
Scenario 4	682 963	−7 117 291	−6 434 328	9.60	−8 744 240	−8 061 277	7.81
Scenario 5	3 124 015	−23 377 302	−20 253 287	13.36	−24 004 251	−20 880 236	13.01
Scenario 6	556,505	−15 432 952	−14 876 447	3.61	−17 059 901	−16 503 396	3.26

Notes:
a. Based on the mean of the net present values of per hectare production benefits for the Kano River Irrigation Project Phase I (see Barbier and Thompson 1998), and applied to the gains in total irrigation area shown in Table 4.3a.
b. Based on the mean of the net present values of total benefits for the Hadejia-Jama'are floodplain (see Barbier and Thompson 1998), averaged over the actual peak flood extent for the wetlands of 112 817 ha in 1989/90 and applied to the differences in mean peak flood extent shown in Table 3a.

These results suggest that the expansion of the existing irrigation schemes within the river basin is effectively 'uneconomic'. The construction of the Kafin Zaki Dam and extensive large-scale formal irrigation schemes within the Jama'are Valley do not represent the most appropriate developments for this part of the basin. If the Kafin Zaki Dam were to be constructed and formal irrigation within the basin limited to its current extent, the introduction of a regulated flooding regime (Scenario 6) would reduce the scale of this negative balance substantially, to around US$15.4–16.5 million. The overall combined value of production from irrigation and the floodplain would, however, still fall well below the levels experienced if the additional upstream schemes were not constructed.[8]

Such a regulated flooding regime could also produce additional economic benefits that are not captured in our analysis. Greater certainty over the timing and magnitude of the floods may enable farmers to adjust to the resulting reduction in the risks normally associated with floodplain farming. Enhanced dry season flows provided by the releases from the Challawa Gorge and Kafin Zaki dams in Scenario 6 would also benefit farmers along the Hadejia and Jama'are Rivers, while the floodplain's fisheries may also experience beneficial impacts from the greater extent of inundation remaining throughout the dry season. The introduction of a regulated flooding regime for the existing schemes within the basin may be the only realistic hope of minimizing floodplain losses. Proposed large-scale schemes, such as Kafin Zaki, should ideally be avoided if further floodplain losses are to be prevented. If this is not possible the designs for water resource schemes should enable the release of regulated floods in order to, at least partly, mitigate the loss of floodplain benefits which would inevitably result.

Currently, as a result of such economic and hydrological analyses of the downstream impacts of upstream water developments in the Hadejia Jama'are floodplain, both the states in northern Nigeria and the Federal Government have become interested in developing regulated flooding regimes for the upstream dams, and have been reconsidering the construction of the Kafin Zaki Dam.

4.6   DYNAMIC MODELS OF ECOLOGICAL SERVICES SUPPORTING ECONOMIC ACTIVITY

The production function approach can also be incorporated into intertemporal models of renewable resource harvesting in cases where the ecological function affects the growth rate of a stock over time. In such cases, the production function link is a dynamic one, as the ecological function affects the rate at which a renewable resource increases over time, which in turn affects the amount of off-take, or harvest, of the resource. The basic approach to valuation of an environmental input to renewable resource production in a dynamic context is outlined by Barbier and Strand (1998), Ellis and Fisher (1987), Freeman (1993), Hammack and Brown (1974), Kahn and Kemp (1985), McConnell and Strand (1989), and Swallow (1990) and (1994).

As shown by Barbier and Strand (1998), adapting bioeconomic fishery models to account for the role of a mangrove system in terms of supporting the fishery as a breeding ground and nursery habitat is fairly straightforward, if it is assumed in the fishery model that the effect of changes in mangrove area is on the carrying capacity of the stock and thus indirectly on production.[9] Defining X_t as the stock of fish measured in biomass units, any net change in growth of this stock over time can be represented as:

$$X_{t+1} - X_t = F(X_t, M_t) - h(X_t, E_t), F_X > 0, F_M > 0 \qquad (4.9)$$

Thus net expansion in the fish stock occurs as a result of biological growth in the current period, $F(X_t, M_t)$, net of any harvesting, $h(X_t, E_t)$. Note that the standard fish harvesting function is employed; that is, harvesting is a function of the stock as well as fishing effort, E_t. Instead, it is the biological growth function of the fishery that is modified to allow for the influence of mangrove area, M_t, as a breeding ground and nursery. It is reasonable to assume that this influence on growth is positive, that is, $\partial F / \partial M_t = F_m > 0$, as an increase in mangrove area will mean more carrying capacity for the fishery and thus greater biological growth.

Equation 4.9 can now be employed in a standard intertemporal harvesting model of the fishery, where depending on the management regime, harvesting over time can either be depicted to occur under open access conditions (effort in the fishery adjusts over time to the availability of profits) or under optimal management conditions (the discounted net returns from harvesting the fishery are maximized over time). The effect of a change in mangrove area can therefore be valued in terms of changes in the optimal path of harvesting over the period of analysis and in terms of the changes in the long run equilibrium of the fishery.

Figure 4.2 shows the fairly straightforward case analyzed by Barbier and Strand (1998), where the effects of a change in mangrove area is depicted in terms of influencing the long-run equilibrium of an open access fishery. In the figure, the long-run equilibrium of the fishery is depicted in terms of steady values for effort, E, and fish stocks, X. As discussed above, the carrying capacity of the fishery is assumed to be an increasing function of mangrove area, that is, $K = K(M)$, $K_M > 0$. Trajectory 1 shows an optimal path to a stable long-run equilibrium for the fishery. In this case, a decrease in mangrove area causes the long-run level of fishing effort to fall. As harvesting levels are generally

positively related to effort levels, the consequence of mangrove deforestation
is also a decrease in equilibrium fish harvest.

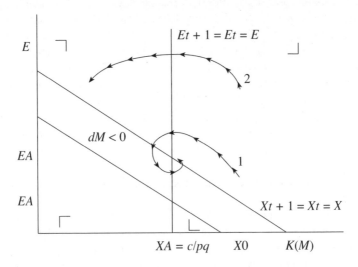

Note: The effect of a fall in mangrove area, *M*, on the long run equilibrium of an open access
fishery is to reduce the steady state level of effort, E^A. Since harvesting is an increasing function
of effort, long run harvesting output in the fishery will also fall.

Source: Barbier and Strand (1998).

*Figure 4.2   Mangrove loss and the long-run equilibrium of an open access
          fishery*

4.6.1   Case Study: Mangrove–Fishery Linkages, Campeche, Mexico[10]

Mexico's Gulf Coast states account for over half of the country's shrimp catch,
and the state of Campeche is responsible for one sixth of Mexico's total output
of shrimp. Campeche's shrimp fishery employs about 13 per cent of the state's
economically active population. In recent years the total number of boats in the
fishery have increased substantially, but the composition of the fleet has also
changed significantly. There has been a substantial decline in the number of
commercial vessels, whereas the artisanal fleet has expanded rapidly. From
1980 to 1987, production in the shrimp fishery fluctuated steadily from 7–8
thousand metric tonnes (KMT) but by 1990 output had fallen to 4.6 KMT.

The mangroves in the Laguna de Terminos are considered by ecologists to
be the main breeding ground and nursery habitat for the shrimp fry of the
Campeche fishery (Yañez-Arancibia and Day 1988). The mangrove area was
estimated to be around 860 km² in 1980, declining to about 835 km² in 1991,

a loss of around 2 km² per annum. The primary reason for the loss was the encroachment of population from Carmen, the large city adjacent to Laguna de Terminos. Future threats are expected to come from expansion of shrimp aquaculture through conversion of coastal mangroves, and possibly pollution.

Barbier and Strand model the effects of mangrove deforestation in Laguna de Terminos by use of comparative static analysis of the long-run equilibrium, as depicted in Figure 4.2. In their model of the Campeche shrimp fishery, they assume that the basic growth function of the fishery is logistic and that shrimp harvesting follows the conventional Schaefer production process, $h_t = qE_tX_t$. Thus Equation 4.9 becomes

$$X_{t+1} - X_t = [r(K(M_t) - X_t) - qE_t] X_t,$$ (4.10)

where r is the intrinsic growth of shrimp each period, K is the environmental carrying capacity of the system and mangrove area, M_t, has a positive impact on carrying capacity, that is, $K_M > 0$.

To estimate the comparative static effects of a change in mangrove area on long-run shrimp harvesting, Barbier and Strand assume a proportional relationship between mangrove area and carrying capacity; $K(M) = \alpha M$, $\alpha > 0$. As the shrimp stock is constant in the long-run equilibrium, $X_t = X_{t+1} = X$, then using this condition in Equation 4.10 and the Schaefer production function to substitute for X, the following relationship between shrimp production, mangrove area and effort is derived:

$$h = qEK(M) - \frac{q^2}{r} E^2 = q\alpha EM - \frac{q^2}{r} E^2.$$ (4.11)

The authors estimate Equation 4.11 by employing 1980–90 time series data on shrimp harvests, effort and mangrove area for Campeche, Mexico to derive the parameters $b_1 = aq$ and $b_2 = -q^2/r$.

A second condition of the long-run equilibrium of an open access fishery is that profits will be zero, that is, $ph = cE$, where p is the price of shrimp catch and c is the cost of fishing effort. In order to simulate the comparative static effects of a change in mangrove area, Barbier and Strand assume that this 'zero profit' condition holds for the Campeche shrimp fishery. Using actual price data on shrimp catches over this period, they calculate the costs of effort, c^A, necessary for the zero profit condition to hold for the Campeche fishery over 1980–90. Using the estimated parameters of Equation 4.11 with the price and cost data, the authors simulate the effects of a change of mangrove area on equilibrium harvesting and gross revenues in the Campeche shrimp fishery over 1980–90.

The results are depicted in Table 4.4. On average over the 1980–90 period, a marginal decline (in km^2) in mangrove area produces a loss of about 14.4 metric tonnes of shrimp harvest and nearly US$140 000 in revenues from the Campeche fishery each year. However, given the relatively small rate of annual mangrove deforestation in the region over the 1980–90 period – around 2 km^2 per year – the resulting loss in shrimp harvest and revenues does not appear to be substantial; only around 0.4 percent per year.

Table 4.4   Simulation results for the effects of mangrove loss on the open access equilibrium of the Campeche shrimp fishery, 1980–90

| | Simulation Estimates of a Marginal Change in Mangrove Area (dM) | | | | |
Year	Price (p) US$/kg[a]	Cost (c^A) US$/vessel[b]	Change in equilibrium harvest (dh^A) Metric tonnes	Change in equilibrium revenues (pdh^A) US$	Change %
1980	7.10	13 984	20.40	144 808	0.23
1981	9.68	15 628	16.72	161 826	0.20
1982	10.57	13 816	13.53	143 060	0.18
1983	9.80	13 636	14.41	141 197	0.18
1984	9.83	14 096	14.85	145 963	0.19
1985	9.80	16 687	17.63	172 798	0.20
1986	10.00	15 013	15.55	155 460	0.19
1987	10.22	14 363	14.55	148 731	0.20
1988	10.56	14 132	13.86	146 334	0.20
1989	10.21	10 000	10.14	103 547	0.17
1990	10.40	6 677	6.65	69 143	0.14
Mean	9.83	13 457	14.39	139 352	0.19

Parameter estimates $b_1 = 4.4491, b_2 = -0.4297$

Notes:
a. US$/kg, in real (1982) prices
b. c^A is the 'equilibrium' (real) cost per unit effort, defined as the cost level necessary to attain zero profit in the fishery, that is $c^A = ph^A/E^A$

Source: Barbier and Strand (1998)

The simulation in Table 4.4 also demonstrates how the economic losses associated with mangrove deforestation are affected by long-run management of the open access fishery. As noted above, the early years of the period of analysis (for example, 1980–81) were characterized by much lower levels of fishing effort and higher harvests (on average around 4 800 combined vessels extracting about 8.5 KMT annually). Table 4.4 shows that, if this earlier period represented the open access equilibrium of the fishery, the economic impacts of a marginal decline (km^2) in mangrove area would be a reduction in annual shrimp harvests of around 18.6 tonnes, or a loss of about US$153 300 per year. In contrast, the last two years of the analysis (1989–90) saw much higher levels of effort and lower harvests in the fishery (around 6 700 combined vessels extracting 5.3 KMT annually). As a consequence, if this latter period represents the open access equilibrium, then a marginal decline in mangrove area would result in annual losses in shrimp harvests of 8.4 tonnes, or US$86 345 each year.

Thus, the value of the Laguna de Terminos mangrove habitat in supporting the Campeche shrimp fishery appears to be affected by the level of exploitation. This suggests that, if an open access fishery is more heavily exploited in the long run, the subsequent welfare losses associated with the destruction of natural habitat supporting this fishery are likely to be lower. Intuitively, this makes sense. The economic value of an over-exploited fishery will be lower than if it were less heavily depleted in the long run. The share of this value that is attributable to the ecological support function of natural habitat will therefore also be smaller.

The management implications are clear: As long as effort levels continue to rise, harvests will fall, even if mangrove areas are fully protected. Moreover, any increase in harvest and revenues from an expansion in mangrove area is likely to be short-lived, as it would simply draw more effort into the fishery. Better management of the Campeche shrimp fishery to control over-exploitation may be the only short-term policy to bring production back to respectable levels, as well as realizing the more long-term economic benefits of protecting mangrove habitat.

4.7   CONCLUSION

Incorporating environmental values in investment decisions in developing countries will continue to be an important issue. As many environmental resources and services in these countries either directly or indirectly contribute to economic activity, the production function approach to valuing this contribution will continue to be an essential methodology.

In recent years there have been several developments in the use of this approach. This chapter has reviewed three key applications to resource management problems in developing countries. The case study of gum arabic in Sudan shows that it is important to consider the wider environmental benefits of a production system rather than just its marketed output. The case study of water diversion in northern Nigeria illustrates the need to model and analyse the downstream hydrological impacts of water diverted upstream. Finally, the case study of mangrove–fishery linkages in Campeche, Mexico indicates how the production function approach can be extended to a dynamic analysis of the impacts of mangrove deforestation on an offshore shrimp fishery.

There are of course many more applications of the production function approach to environmental valuation in developing countries. As this approach is developed and applied more frequently to a wide range of problems, its usefulness as a project appraisal and policy analysis tool should hopefully increase.

NOTES

1. It is assumed that all costs and benefits are discounted at some positive rate into present value terms.
2. The production function approach discussed here is related to the *household production function* approach, which is a more appropriate term for those surrogate market valuation techniques based on the derived demand by households for environmental quality. That is, by explicitly incorporating nonmarketed environmental functions in the modeling of individuals' preferences, household expenditures on private goods can be related to the derived demand for environmental functions (Bockstael and McConnell 1981; Freeman 1993; Smith 1991). Some well-known techniques in applied environmental economics – such as travel cost, recreation demand, hedonic pricing and averting behavior models – are based on the household production function approach. The *dose-response technique* is also related to the production function and household production function approaches; however, dose-response models are generally used to relate environmental damage (such as pollution; off-site impacts of soil erosion) to loss of either consumer welfare (such as through health impacts) or property and productivity (such as through damage to buildings or impacts on production).
3. The assumption that there is no cost of using the supply of water available to the agricultural system is certainly realistic for a floodplain system dependent on the natural recession of flood water as a source of irrigation. In the case of irrigation provided by a human-made reservoir and channel network, the assumption of a freely available supply suggests that the fixed costs of the water reservoir and network were absorbed by an external agency (for example, central or regional government), and there is no recurrent charge to the irrigated agricultural system for using water as an input. Obviously, this raises issues over the efficiency of water input use, and the possibility over time of excessive use relative to the supply of available water. Although an extremely important issue, particularly with regard to the supply of irrigated water (see Repetto 1986 for a discussion and examples), this problem is not an explicit focus of this chapter. The problem could easily be incorporated into the model by examining how the amount of water abstracted for irrigation in each time period, $k(t)$, influences the rate of depletion of the total downstream water stock available to irrigation, $dW/dt = - k(t)W(t)$, and assuming a cost of abstraction $c_w \geq 0$.
4. In what follows, for simplicity, the fixed costs of establishing the upstream water project and irrigation will also be ignored. See also the previous note on how water abstraction costs could be included.
5. Although it is possible that the optimal rate of diversion, d^*, may lead to complete depletion of the stock of water available downstream, W, over the planning horizon $(0,T)$. It is also possible that d^* may also be zero as $t \to T$. The inclusion of cumulative diversion into the upstream irrigation network, $\int d\,dt = W(0) - W(t)$, as an argument in h_2 suggests that output from the upstream agricultural project does not necessarily have to fall to zero if $d^* = 0$. It is fairly easy to work out the conditions determining the optimal path of $d(t)$ as well as the rate of change, dd^*/dt, from the first order conditions. See Barbier (1994) and Dasgupta and Heal (1979) for further discussion.

6. The references for this case study are Barbier and Thompson (1998). See also Barbier et al. (1993).
7. Note that one reason for these high losses in floodplain benefits is that the total production area dependent on the wetlands is around 6.5 times greater than the actual area flooded. This critical feature of a semi-arid floodplain, its ability to 'sustain' a production area much greater than the area flooded, is often underestimated and ignored. This in turn means that changes in flood extent have a greater multiplier impact in terms of losses in economic benefits in production areas within and adjacent to the floodplain, because of the high dependence of these areas on regular annual flooding. See Barbier and Thompson (1998) for more details.
8. Some of the upstream water developments are being used or have the potential to supply water to Kano City. Although these releases are included in the hydrological simulations, the economic analysis was unable to calculate the benefits to Kano City of these water supplies. However, the hydrological analysis shows that the proposed regulated water release from Tiga Dam to reduce downstream floodplain losses would not affect the ability of Tiga Dam to supply water to Kano. Although the potential exists for Challawa Gorge to supply additional water to Kano, it is unclear how much water could be used for this purpose. The resulting economic benefits are unlikely to be large enough to compensate for the substantial floodplain losses incurred by the Gorge and the additional upstream developments in the Hadejia Valley. Currently, there are no plans for Kafin Zaki Dam to be used to supply water to Kano. In addition, the economic analysis was unable to calculate other important floodplain benefits, such as the role of the wetlands in supporting pastoral grazing and in recharging groundwater both within the floodplain and in surrounding areas. Groundwater recharge by the floodplain may provide potable water supplies to populations within the middle and lower parts of the river basin, and supply tubewell irrigation for dry season farming downstream (Barbier et al. 1993).
9. For analytical convenience, a discrete time model of the fishery is employed here.
10. This case study draws on Barbier and Strand (1998).

REFERENCES

Aylward, B.A. and E.B. Barbier (1992), 'Valuing environmental functions in developing countries', *Biodiversity and Conservation*, **1**, 34–50.

Barbier, E.B. (1992), 'Rehabilitating gum arabic systems in Sudan: economic and environmental implications', *Environmental and Resource Economics*, **2**, 341–58.

Barbier, E.B. (1994), 'Valuing environmental functions: tropical wetlands', *Land Economics*, **70**(2), 155–73.

Barbier, E.B. (1997), 'Valuing the environment as input: applications to mangrove–fishery linkages', paper prepared for the 4th Workshop of the Global Wetlands Economics Network (GWEN), 'Wetlands: Landscape and Institutional Perspectives', Beijer International Institute of Ecological Economics, The Royal Swedish Academy of Sciences, Stockholm, Sweden, 16–17 November.

Barbier, E.B. (1998), 'The value of water and watersheds: reconciling ecological and economic externalities', paper prepared for the Conference on Managing Human-dominated Ecosystems, Missouri Botanical Gardens, St Louis, MO, 26–8 March.

Barbier, E.B. and I. Strand (1998), 'Valuing mangrove–fishery linkages: a case study of Campeche, Mexico', *Environmental and Resource Economics*, **12**, 151–66.

Barbier, E.B. and J.R. Thompson (1998), 'The value of water: floodplain versus large-scale irrigation benefits in northern Nigeria', *Ambio*, **27**(6), 434–40.

Barbier, E.B., M. Acreman and D. Knowler (1997), *Economic Valuation of Wetlands: A Guide for Policymakers*, Geneva: Ramsar Convention Bureau.

Barbier, E.B., W.M. Adams and K. Kimmage (1993), 'An economic valuation of wetland benefits', in G.E. Hollis, W.M. Adams and M. Aminu-Kano (eds), *The Hadejia-Nguru Wetlands: Environment, Economy and Sustainable Development of a Sahelian Floodplain Wetland*, Geneva: IUCN.

Bockstael, N.E. and K.E. McConnell (1981), 'Theory and estimation of the household production function for wildlife recreation', *Journal of Environmental Economics and Mangement*, **8**, 199–214.

Dasgupta, Partha S. and Geoffrey R. Heal (1979), *Economic Theory and Exhaustible Resources*, Cambridge: Cambridge University Press.

Dixon, John A., Richard A. Carpenter, Louise A. Fallon, Paul B. Sherman and Supachit Manopimoke (1988), *Economic Analysis of the Environmental Impacts of Development Project*, London: Earthscan Publications in association with the Asian Development Bank.

Ellis, Gregory M. and Anthony C. Fisher (1987), 'Valuing the environment as input', *Journal of Evnvironmental Management*, **25**, 149–56.

Freeman, A.M. (1991), 'Valuing environmental resources under alternative management regimes', *Ecological Economics*, **3**, 247–56.

Freeman, A.M. (1993), *The Measurement of Environmental and Resource Values: Theory and Methods*, Washington DC: Resources for the Future.

Hammack, J. and G.M. Brown Jr (1974), *Waterfowl and Wetlands: Towards Bioeconomic Analysis*, Washington DC: Resources for the Future.

Kahn, J.R. and W.M. Kemp (1985), 'Economic losses associated with the degradation of an ecosystem: the case of submerged aquatic vegetation in Chesapeake Bay', *Journal of Environmental Economics and Management*, **12**, 246–63.

Mäler, K-G. (1991), 'The production function approach', in J.R. Vincent, E.W. Crawford and J.P. Hoehn (eds), 'Valuing environmental benefits in developing countries', special report 29, East Lansing: Michigan State University.

McConnell, K.E. and I.E. Strand (1989), 'Benefits from commercial fisheries when demand and supply depend on water quality', *Journal of Environmental Economics and Management*, **17**, 284–92.

Repetto, R. (1986), 'Skimming the water: rent-seeking and the performance of public irrigation systems', research report no. 4, Washington DC: World Resources Institute.

Smith, V.K. (1991), 'Household production functions and environmental benefit estimation', in J.B. Braden and C.D. Kolstad (eds), *Measuring the Demand for Environmental Quality*, Amsterdam: North-Holland.

Swallow, S.K. (1990), 'Depletion of the environmental basis for renewable resources: the economics of interdependent renewable and nonrenewable resources', *Journal of Environmental Economics and Management*, **19**, 281–96.

Swallow, S.K. (1994), 'Renewable and nonrenewable resource theory applied to coastal agriculture, forest, wetland and fishery linkages', *Marine Resource Economics*, **9**, 291–310.

Yañez-Arancibia, A. and J.W. Day Jr (eds) (1988), *Ecology of Coastal Ecosystems in the Southern Gulf of Mexico: The Terminos Lagoon Region*, Mexico: UNAM Press.

PART III

Applications

5. Environmental outcomes assessment: using sustainability indicators for Central Europe to measure the effects of transition on the environment

Sandra Archibald and Zbigniew Bochniarz

5.1 INTRODUCTION

The growing interest in promoting economic and environmental policies that lead to sustainable development paths has increased the demand for information to assess environmental and economic outcomes. For economies in transition, such as those in Central and Eastern Europe, assessing the environmental effects of structural change in the economy, rising personal consumption, rapid transition to market-oriented economies and increased openness in trade and investment is critical. Equally important is assessing the outcomes of environmental and other policies designed to promote environmentally sound restructuring. Determining at what point rising incomes will lead to an increased demand for environmental protection remains an important empirical question. Environmental outcomes assessment depends critically on information on changes in environment quality which has not been available for Central and Eastern Europe.

This chapter draws on a set of sustainability indicators developed by the University of Minnesota (Center for Nations in Transition, 1997).[1] Current data, developed by international economic agencies and augmented with extensive primary data gathered from industry and government officials within the Central Eastern European Countries (CEEC), were used to develop a consistent historical series of economic, social, demographic and environmental indicators for the CEEC.[2] Data cover the period 1985–97.

Focusing on the six central European countries of Bulgaria, the Czech Republic, Hungary, Poland, Romania and the Slovak Republic, this chapter examines reported changes in environmental quality, as measured by key environmental pressure indicators, that have occurred following the major economic and political restructuring of the past decade. An econometric analysis is employed to sort out the degree to which observed changes in pressure indicators can be explained by the movement of critical economic and institutional variables of significance to the environment The critical factors examined include patterns of consumption, the composition of industry, the degree of privatization in the economy, environmental regulation, and openness with respect to trade and foreign direct investment. Some effects cannot be determined a priori (for example, the effects of trade or privatization) yet knowledge of these effects is critical for policy research and design and to build a comparative perspective for the region. This information is also crucial to assess the effectiveness of CEEC policies to achieve environmentally sound restructuring.

An assessment is also made regarding the impact that both model specification and definition of environmental indicators has on the direction and magnitude of the measured effects on the environment. Suggestions are offered regarding the usefulness of existing indices as practical guides to assess and design policy.

5.2   TRENDS IN SUSTAINABILITY INDICATORS

This section examines the initial environmental and economic conditions in the region at the beginning of the transition period that began in the late 1980s. Following this assessment, trends in selected critical factors are analyzed for the period 1989–95, utilizing the CNT Sustainability Indicators for the CEEC. The third section analyzes trends in key environmental pressure indicators for air quality in the region.[3]

5.2.1   The Initial Conditions in the Region

It is now well known that four decades under centralized economies have left Central and Eastern Europe with severe environmental degradation. Pollution has affected the quality of the environment and the natural resource base with implications for both human health and the economic well being of the region. At the beginning of the 1990s, pollution in the region was alarmingly high (Bochniarz, 1992). In comparison to the European Union, $1000 of GNP production in the region yielded air particulates approximately 60 times higher. Emissions of SO_2 and NO_x were, respectively, 30 and 8 times higher. Water quality in the region had also deteriorated over the past 30 years with some rivers in the region incapable of supporting most human uses. About 35 percent of the arable lands in the region could be classified as seriously degraded with half the forests exhibiting declines in productive yields from acid rain damage (Bochniarz and Toft, 1995). Compared with the West, the CEEC have significantly higher infant mortality rates, higher rates of cancer and respiratory illness, and lower average life expectancies.

The CEEC inherited poor economic conditions at the beginning of their transitional period. These economies were dominated by outdated energy-intensive 'heavy' industries and relatively undeveloped service sectors. All lagged in their participation in world trade and foreign direct investment relative to their share of total world output. The average share in world trade was about 50 per cent less than their share in the global gross product. In addition, at the end of the 1980s countries in the region were experiencing stagnation, or even negative growth, characterized by shortages. These conditions were often disguised in official statistics. Hungary and Poland, for example, experienced hidden as well as open inflation. Bulgaria, Hungary and Poland had serious problems servicing foreign debt. The large state-owned enterprises were inefficient and lacked organizational and management structures. Furthermore, basic market institutions such as property rights, a judicial system with necessary codes of commerce and capital market institutions were lacking.

The generally peaceful revolutions (with the exception of Romania) in the fall of 1989 changed the fundamental structure of the existing political systems and set a foundation for establishing market economies. The poor environmental and economic conditions at the beginning of the transition imposed a heavy burden upon leaders and policy makers to resolve both the economic and environmental problems simultaneously. Environmentally sound restructuring was needed. Economic stability and growth were also needed to improve quality of life and assure political stability.

A basic question is how the recent economic reforms and transition policies have and will affect environmental quality. There are two basic hypotheses evidenced in public opinion polls and likewise held among economists and environmentalists worldwide. The first, an optimistic one, posits that the transition to a market economy and democratic society will significantly improve the quality of the environment. The second, a more pessimistic one, is shared by a relatively large group of environmentalists and other groups within these countries opposing the major directions of the transition. This position suggests that market forces and an increasing desire to consume material goods will generate higher levels of pollution and induce an exploitation of natural resources, resulting in the sacrifice of environmental quality for economic gains.

5.2.2   Critical Factors Affecting the Environment Following Transition

The critical economic factors of environmental significance that have emerged since the transition began in the late 1980s are shown in Table 5.1. Indicators were selected to provide information on the changes in critical factors. Table 5.1 provides the expected effects on the environment, a definition of the critical

Table 5.1 Factors of environmental significance following transition

Factor	Effect on the environment	Definition	Indicator
Consumption patterns	Rising incomes expected to have a negative effect (increase pressure)	Per capita income; income growth rate	GDP per capita; Δ GDP in 1987 $US
Structure of the economy	Market reforms expected to have a positive effect (reduce pressure) due to efficiency gains	Contribution of private sector to the economy	Ratio of value added from private sector to total GDP
	Manufacturing is expected to have a negative effect (increase pressure)	Contribution of manufacturing sector to the economy	Ratio of value added from manufacturing sector to total GDP
Regulatory structure	Institutions to regulate the environment expected to have a positive effect (reduce pressure)	Extent of environmental regulation	Total dollars spent on environmental regulation
Openness	Enhanced openness of the economy is expected to have a positive effect (reduce pressure) due to efficiency gains	Contribution of trade to the economy	Ratio of exports and imports to GDP
	There are no a priori expectations about the effects of foreign direct investment	Contribution of foreign direct investment to the economy	Ratio of foreign direct investment to GDP
Country-specific effects	Larger countries are expected to have a negative effect (increase pressure)	Country size	Population in millions
	No a priori expectations about specific countries	Individual CEEC	Country-specific dummy variable
General efficiency gains	Efficiency gains are expected to have positive effects (reduce pressure)	Change over time in output per unit input	Time trend

factor and the indicator. Increased consumption that results from rising incomes is generally expected to increase environmental pressures, ceteris paribus. Changes in the structure of the economy include the development of a private sector and the decline in the manufacturing sector. These are critical factors predicted to both reduce and increase environmental pressures. Environmental regulation should reduce pressure on the environment. Increased openness of these economies in terms of traded goods and services is also predicted to impact the environment in a positive way, although some argue the opposite effect is possible.

5.2.3   Trends in Factors Affecting the Environment, 1989–95

Figures 5.1–5.6 plot the trends in the critical factors using the selected indicators over the period 1989–95. Average income per capita in the region (Figure 5.1) for this period was approximately $2400 in constant US dollars. There is significant variation among the CEEC as Figure 5.1 indicates.[4] There is also significant variation within the region regarding the change in per capita incomes over this period. On average, per capita income in the region declined by approximately 14 per cent. Bulgaria and the Slovak Republic evidenced income declines per capita of approximately 20 percent. For the Czech Republic and Romania, average declines were slightly less at 14 and 11 per cent respectively. Hungary and Poland's average per capita income declines over this period were reported to be significantly less at 5.6 and 4 percent. While per capita income declined overall, both the regional average and that for individual countries has shown an upward trend since 1993. However, by the end of 1995 none reported figures equivalent to levels achieved prior to reforms.

The degree to which individual countries have succeeded in establishing market economies is measured by the extent to which total GDP (Figure 5.2) is generated in the private sector. The reported average contribution of the private sector to total GDP for all countries in the region is 65 percent in 1995 and varies surprisingly little within the six countries. All but Bulgaria (32 percent) and Romania (45 percent) report between 60 and 69 percent privatization. Thus, a significant and dramatic increase in market economies is evidenced by these data.

Manufacturing value added as a percentage of GDP (Figure 5.3) averaged 43 percent over the period for the region as a whole. There was relatively small variation among countries. With the exception of Hungary (35 percent of GDP generated in the manufacturing sector), each of the six countries reports between 44 and 46 percent of GDP generated in the manufacturing sector. These data reflect output declines as well as the changing composition of the economy with the shift from heavy industry to services more generally. The percentage change in percentage of GDP generated by manufacturing over the period

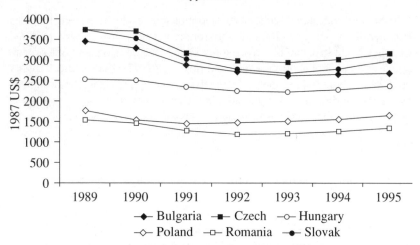

Figure 5.1   GDP per capita by country and region, 1989–95

varied, with Hungary reporting the least change (a decline of 19 percent). The Czech Republic, Poland and Romania reported declines of 24, 25 and 29 percent respectively; and Bulgaria and the Slovak Republic reported declines of 43 percent each.

The trend in foreign direct investment (FDI), measured as a percentage of GDP (Figure 5.4), was much more variable within the region. Average increases by country over the period are significant, but the beginning base was quite small.

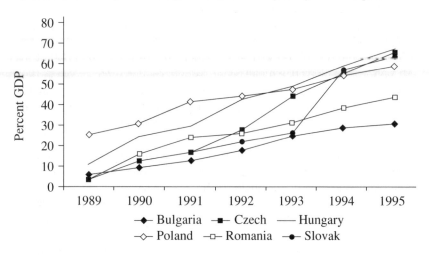

Figure 5.2   Share of GDP generated in private sector

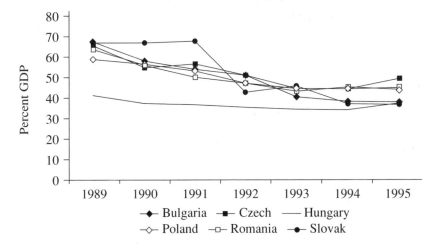

Figure 5.3   Manufacturing value added as percentage of GDP

With the exception of Hungary and Poland, net inflows of foreign investment were nearly non-existent at the beginning of the period. Hungary reports by far the largest share of FDI in the region with 42 percent of the reported US$28 billion in foreign direct investments made in the region over the period. Poland is second with 30 percent of the total and the Czech Republic third at 21 percent. Ninety-three percent of FDI in the region over the period has been in these three countries. In one sense, this indicator is a proxy for perceived political

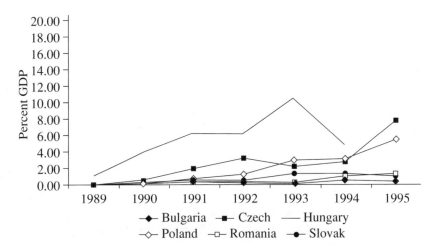

Figure 5.4   Foreign direct investment as percentage of GDP, 1989–95

and economic stability. On that basis, Hungary, the Czech Republic and Poland were perceived to be the most stable during this period.

The contribution of exports of goods and services to total GDP serves as a measure of the openness of these economies following transition (Figure 5.5).[5] Using this indicator, in 1995 Poland, Romania and Hungary report about one-third of GDP attributable to trade. Bulgaria reports approximately 50 percent

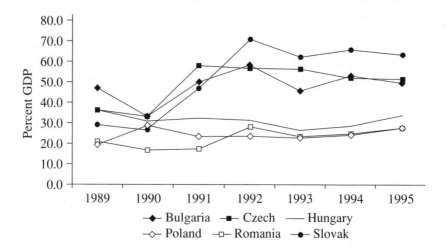

Figure 5.5   Exports of goods and services as percentage of GDP, 1989–95

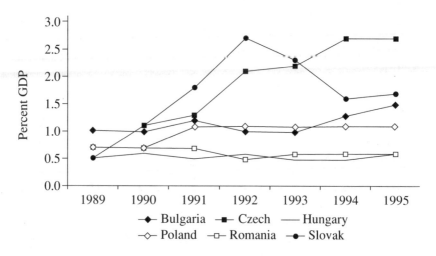

Figure 5.6   Environmental expenditures as percentage of GDP, 1989–95

of total GDP from trade. The figures for the Czech and Slovak Republics are higher at 52 and 63 percent of GDP in 1995 attributable to trade in goods and services.[6]

Environmental policy (either investments or regulation) as measured by the ratio of total environmental expenditures to GDP (Figure 5.6) indicates an average intensity of slightly over 1 percent of GDP for the region over the period. There is some variation across countries with Hungary and Romania on the low side (0.5 and 0.6 percent respectively) and the Czech and Slovak Republics on the high end with 1.8 and 1.7 percent. Bulgaria and Poland are in the middle with intensities of 1.1 and 1.0 percent respectively. The specific regulatory structures vary widely across the region but each country has established a significant set of regulatory policies and institutions since the transition.[7]

5.2.4 Trends in Key Environmental Quality Indicators Following Transition

The initial empirical analysis of the effects of economic growth and transition on the environment focuses on assessing trends in air quality in the region. While it is preferable to rely on indicators of environmental quality that measure the state of the environment, such data are not consistently available for these countries. Typically, pressure indicators are relied upon in these cases with changes in pressure indicators implying changes in environmental quality. Table 5.2 shows the six key pressure indicators related to air quality that were analyzed for the CEEC countries.

Indicators that were used in the empirical analysis follow the EUROSTAT (1997) framework which specifies key pollutants, defines the pressure and state indicators, provides alternative measures (for example, per capita) and identifies the likely scope of the effect (for instance, local or regional). Both total and per capita trends in key pollutants were examined; only trends in totals are reported here.

Figures 5.7–5.12 show trends in these selected air quality pressure indicators for the region and the six countries. Regional reductions in CO_2 emissions (Figure 5.7) were approximately 27 percent over this period. The largest absolute reduction was reported for Poland, which comprised nearly 32 percent of total regional reductions. The Czech Republic and Romania together comprised an additional 44 percent of the regional decline in CO_2 emissions. Poland's CO_2 emissions were reduced by 20 percent; the Czech Republic's by 22 percent. The largest percentage reductions were reported by Bulgaria (37 percent) and Romania (39 percent).

Trends in CO emissions (Figure 5.8) declined in the region by about 15 percent. Romania reported the largest initial levels and achieved the largest absolute reduction. Poland reduced CO emissions by about 25 percent. Romania

Table 5.2   Key air quality pressure indicators

Pollutant	Indicator definition and unit of measurement	State indicator	Alternative indicator definition	Scope of effect
Emissions of carbon dioxide (CO_2)	Total (or net) Emissions of CO_2 in kt per year	CO_2 concentrations, global temperature	None	Global climate change
Emissions of carbon monoxide (CO)	Total emissions of CO in kt per year	Concentrations of CO	Emissions of CO per unit of area; emissions per capita	Global, regional climate change
Emissions of sulfur dioxide (SO_2)	Total emissions of SO_2 in kt per year	Concentration of sulfates (SO_2), global temperature	An aggregated indicator for aerosol particles	Global, regional and local climate change Acidification
Emissions of nitrogen oxides (NO_2)	Total anthropogenic emissions of NO_2 in kt per year	Atmospheric nitrous oxide concentrations, global temperature	Emissions of NO_2 per unit of area; aggregate indicator for CO_2, CH4, and NO_2 emissions based on global warming potential	Global and regional climate change Ozone depletion
Emissions of particles (PM)	Total annual amount of suspended PM in kt per year	Concentration levels of (aerosol) particles in the atmosphere	Emissions of PM per capita	Regional, local air pollution
Emissions of volatile organic compounds (VOC)	Total emissions of VOC in kt per year	Atmospheric concentration levels of photochemical oxidants; tropospheric ozone concentrations, global temperature	Emissions of VOC per capital in kg	Global and regional climate change Acidification Ozone depletion

Source: Eurostat's Methodology Sheets, 1998

and Poland comprised about two-thirds of total CO emissions in 1989. Their combined share by the end of the period was reduced to 60 percent. The CO emissions in the remaining CEEC countries (with the exception of Hungary, which reported a slight decline) remained stable or increased slightly.

Regional reductions in SO_2 emissions (Figure 5.9) were slightly over 35 percent. Poland reported the largest absolute reduction in SO_2 emissions, but maintained its share of the total. The Slovak and Czech Republics reported the largest percentage reductions in SO_2 emissions averaging 58 and 45 percent. Hungary, Poland and Romania report emission reductions of approximately 33, 36 and 38 percent respectively, with Bulgaria slightly lower.

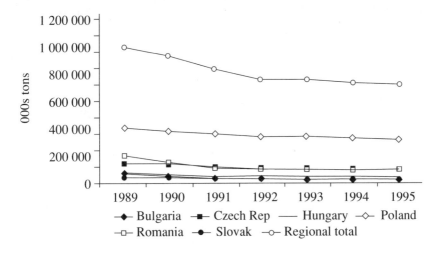

Figure 5.7   Regional CO$_2$ emissions, 1989–95

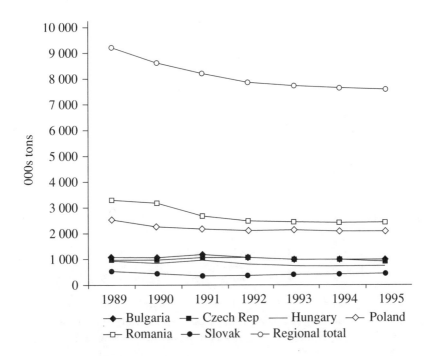

Figure 5.8   Regional CO emissions, 1989–95

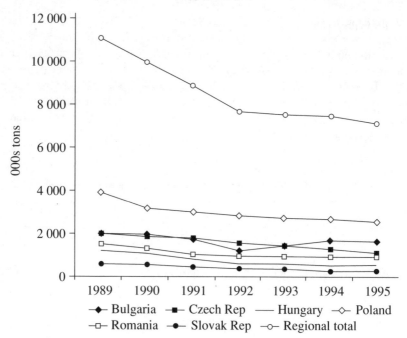

Figure 5.9   Regional SO$_2$ emissions, 1989–95

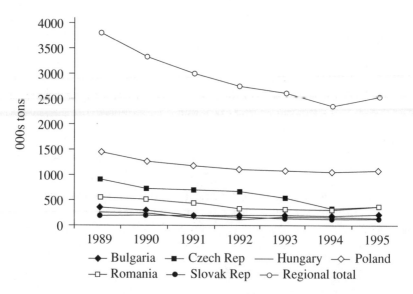

Figure 5.10   Regional NO$_2$ emissions, 1989–95

Emissions of NO_2 (Figure 5.10) were reduced by 32 percent for the region. At the high end, the Czech Republic reduced emissions by 55 percent with the Slovak Republic reporting the least reduction of 17 percent. The other four countries averaged reductions of about 26 percent over the same time period. The NO_2 pollution levels were at their lowest between 1992 and 1994 and increased in 1995 for all six countries with the exception of Hungary. This trend may be explained by the rapid growth in car fleets that occurred in most of the CEEC during the mid-1990s.

Volatile organic compounds (VOC) (Figure 5.11) decreased regionally about 25 percent with the largest percentage reductions in the Slovak and Czech Republics (67 and 49 percent). Other countries reduced VOC emissions by between 16 and 30 percent. Poland reported the largest absolute reduction but its share of the total remained unchanged. Romania's share of the region's total VOC emissions increased from 29 to 32 percent.

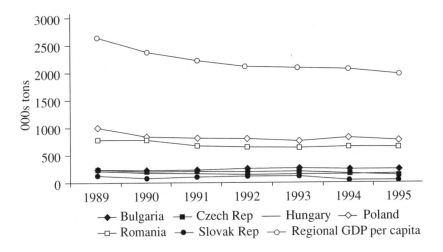

Figure 5.11   Regional VOC emissions, 1989–95

The most dramatic improvements have been reductions in particulate matter or PM (Figure 5.12). Region-wide, data indicate that PM emissions declined 46 percent over the period. For the Slovak Republic and Czech Republic, data indicate that particulates decreased by approximately 70 percent. Hungary and Poland reported reductions of approximately 42 percent and Bulgaria and Romania reduced emissions by 26 percent during the time period.

Total abatement of emissions – that is the reduction in emissions from the initial levels – can be used to indicate air quality improvements (Heal, 1996).

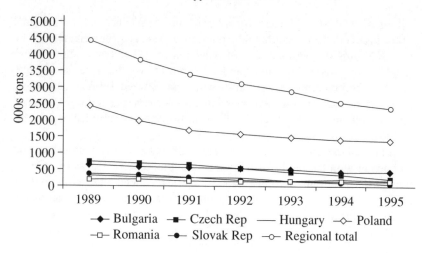

Figure 5.12   Regional particulate matter emissions, 1989–95

Table 5.3 provides summary estimates of total abatement of key air pollution emissions for the region.

Table 5.3   Total abatement of key air pollutants, 1989–95

Key air pollutant	Regional abatement (%)
CO_2	–27
CO	–17
SO_2	–26
NO_2	–32
PM	–46
VOC	–25

Given the evidence from the analysis of emissions of these key air quality pressure indicators it appears that pressure on the environment has been decreased significantly over the period within the region. These facts indicate that improvements in the state of the environment should begin to occur. However, ecological processes are much slower than economic processes and consequently positive changes in environmental quality are not immediately noticeable. There are some evident improvements in air pollution in the major cities, although the major cities still belong among the largest hot spots in Europe.

5.3   MEASURING THE EFFECTS OF CRITICAL FACTORS ON KEY AIR POLLUTION PRESSURE INDICATORS

Given the observed downward trends in pressure indicators presented above, can one conclude that the CEEC countries have been successful in reducing regional pollution emissions since the transition to market economies occurred? Not without further analysis. These countries endured a severe recession during the transition and that alone could account for the majority of the observed declines in pollutant emissions. As discussed above, the level of pollutant emissions depends upon a number of critical factors in addition to the decline in output evidenced during the transition, whose contribution to observed declines needs to be identified.

5.3.1   Identifying the Sources of Change

The trends in the critical factors affecting the environment put forth in Table 5.1 are key sources of the observed changes in air quality pressure indicators. The changing industrial structure of Eastern Europe, particularly the reduction in inefficient heavy industry, could explain some portion of the observed downward pressure on air quality indicators. Privatization, or the degree to which market reforms have been achieved, is also expected to have a signifi-cant effect on pollutant levels although there is debate about the observed direction of its effect. Some argue that privatization and industrial restructur-ing have been promoted with little awareness of the potentially negative environmental impacts (Pearce and Warford, 1993). Others believe that priva-tization has a positive effect through gains in efficiency of resource use if nothing else. Where environmental regulation has been effective, reductions in pollutant emissions should be observed over this period.

It is expected that declining incomes have contributed to a reduction in envi-ronmental pressures and that as incomes begin to rise again with economic recovery the result will be an increase in pollutant emissions. This increase is expected to continue well into the middle of the next century, although debate continues as to whether and at what point rising incomes might result in a slowing of pollution increases.

The increased openness of the economy with respect to trade is hypothesized by some economists to increase resource efficiency and should thus result in lower pollution levels while others argue that trade increases environmental pressures.

The effects of each of these factors on pollution emissions must be sorted out in order to determine the contribution of each to the observed reductions in environmental pressure identified above. Using statistical methods, we can analyze how each of the critical factors contributes to observed changes in pollution emissions and make some preliminary determination of the significance and level of these separate effects.

5.3.2 Previous Empirical Results

There is a small but growing body of literature whose objective has been to test empirically the effects of critical economic and structural factors on environmental quality. The existing literature focuses largely on estimating the relationship between economic growth and pollution pressure but has more recently addressed that between increased economic openness and pollution pressure (Lucas, 1996). Few studies examine the effects of privatization on environmental policy. Even fewer studies examine these effects for the CEEC specifically.

With respect to the relationship between income and pollution pressure, recent empirical analyses have concentrated on testing Kuznet's hypothesis that there exists an inverted U-shaped relationship between income growth and pollution levels (Shafik, 1994; Selden and Song, 1994; Grossman and Krueger, 1993 and 1995; Holtz-Eakin and Selden, 1995). The hypothesis is that pollution levels initially rise as income rises but beyond some income level the relationship reverses. Beyond that point as incomes grow so does the demand for environmental quality. Studies show mixed results but some evidence supporting Kuznet's hypothesis is emerging.

Grossman and Krueger (1993) use cross-country panel data on urban air pollution levels covering a large number of countries to estimate turning points at which atmospheric concentrations of suspended particulate matter (PM) and sulfur dioxide (SO_2) become decreasing functions of income. They estimate that turning points for these pollutants occur at levels of per capita GDP income of under $5000 (in 1985 US dollars). In a more recent study (1995), they re-affirm the relationships between income growth and pollution levels. In most cases, turning points are reached before a country reaches a per capita income of US$8000. They found no inverted U-curve relationship between heavy particulates and economic growth but did so for other pollutants, providing more evidence that turning points vary by pollutant type.

Turning points have also been found to be sensitive to population density. Seldon and Song (1994) found that turning points derived from models that did not control for population density were significantly higher than when population density was included. While empirical studies support the hypothesis regarding the relationship between income growth and increasing pressure on the environment, it is clear that estimates of the turning points vary: (1) among studies; (2) among key pollutants; and (3) with model specification.

There is less agreement in the literature regarding the relationship between the structure of the economy, particularly the role of trade, in generating higher or lower pollution levels. Lucas et al. (1992) found that a negative relationship could be established between openness and pollution. A subsequent analysis (Lucas, 1996) of 112 countries over the period 1970–89 identified a downward trend in emissions over time whose rate varied by pollutant type. Only a weak statistical relationship between openness and declines in CO_2 emissions was demonstrated. Lucas did find that more rapid growth in GDP per capita is not bought at a cost of higher CO_2 of emissions, given income levels. Furthermore, he supports previous research in identifying peak emissions points for only selected pollutants. For example, for CO_2 the estimated turning point was US\$24 586 in 1987; for VOC, US\$20 000. Emissions of NO_2 at first decline with income and then rise with a turning point beyond the range of observed data. The results with respect to the role of trade on specific of pollutants are mixed; some key pollutants decreased as exports increased while others increased. Less harm to the environment as exports increased was found among smaller countries.

Relying on data covering 20 years and 33 countries, Suri and Chapman (1998) obtain feasible generalized least squares estimates (FGLS) and demonstrate the inverted U. There has been little empirical analysis of the effects of privatization, changes in industry structure, increased openness, regulatory intensity and foreign direct investments on pollutant emissions for the CEEC specifically. Environmental quality changes for the CEEC that occurred in the early years of economic transition were reported in an unpublished paper (Vukina et al., 1995). Although the time series was short and the reliability of the data is questionable, the analysis indicates a strong relationship between environmental improvement and openness, and between environmental degradation and privatization. The authors argued that the decline in manufacturing output was largely responsible for observed reductions in pollution levels.

5.4   MODELING THE EFFECTS OF CRITICAL FACTORS ON AIR QUALITY PRESSURE INDICATORS

5.4.1   Objectives

The objective of this analysis is to examine empirically for the CEEC the relationship between the critical factors affecting the environment on the air quality pressure indicators. A regional analysis is critical given that these key air pollutants have global as well as local impacts. Furthermore, the indicators developed for the Pressure-State-Response (PSR) system are most appropriate to regional analysis (Eurostat, 1997).

A key objective is to examine consumption patterns, as measured by the level of income per capita, to determine the extent to which rising per capita incomes can be expected to contribute to increasing pollutant emissions and to test the inverse U-shaped relationship. The measure of income adopted is gross domestic product (GDP) measured at constant prices in local currency units and expressed in US dollars using the World Bank 1987 conversion factor (Bochniarz, 1995). It was necessary to use World Bank GDP data to obtain a sufficient time series for all six countries. To test for inverse U-shaped patterns, income per capita is included in quadratic form. In some models, growth in income per capita is included as well.

We also test the consequences of openness or outward orientation toward trade. Many environmentalists oppose trade liberalization on the grounds that it is detrimental to the environment. There is little empirical analysis of this hypothesis. Openness is measured as the ratio of exports and imports of goods and services to GDP. Lucas (1996) points out that because it is often the case that this ratio tends to be larger for small countries due solely to their size, an interaction term between the measure of economic openness and population should be included. This is done for selected models.

Because we are testing the hypotheses that economic reforms have not had a deleterious impact on the economy, measures of structural change are included. The measure of the extent of privatization (PRV) is the ratio of goods and services provided by the private sector to total GDP. Also important in the transition process in these countries is the role of Foreign Direct Investment (FDI). Here it is initially measured as net inflows of foreign direct investment as a percentage of GDP. There are no a priori expectations about the direction of the effects of FDI on emissions levels, although for sustainable development it is hoped that investments would be made to reduce pressure on the environment. Manufacturing value added (percentage of GDP) is used to capture the changes in the structure of the economy (MFD) resulting from transition.

The forces of economic transformation alone are not likely to reduce environmental pollution. Regulatory structures and investments are also needed to account for externalities and provide more environmentally friendly technologies. With appropriate regulatory institutions, it is possible that economic growth can continue without undue harm to the environment. Environmental expenditures (percentage of GDP) is used as a proxy for regulatory intensity. It captures investments in environmental improvement as well. Population and time are included to account for size effects as well as changes not related to those captured by the critical factors.

5.4.2   Model Specification

An econometric analysis is conducted using a pooled-time series data set for the six countries covering the period 1989–95. Earlier data are not reliable. Table 5.4 indicates the alternative models analyzed. Several alternative models are tested to determine the effects of various definitions of key pressure indicators as well as alternative hypotheses regarding the effects of time, population and the form of the relationship between income and pollutant emissions. Models 1 and 2 define the air pressure indicators alternatively as total emissions and per capita emissions. Both include a correction for population. Model 3 omits the population correction. Models 4 and 5 follow the specification in Lucas (1996) in order to compare the effects of including the key critical economic and institutional factors. All models are fixed effects models using country-specific dummy variables estimated by Feasible Generalized Least Squares methods.

Table 5.4   Alternative model specifications

Pressure indicator: CO_2, CO, SO_2, NO_2, VOC, PM	Model 1: Total emissions and population	Model 2: Per capita emissions and population	Model 3: Per capita emissions	Model 4: Lucas model: total and population	Model 5: Lucas model: per capita and population
Country	x	x	x	x	x
Time	x	x	x	x	x
GDP					
GDP2	x	x	x	x	x
PRV	x	x	x		
FDI	x	x	x		
MFD	x	x	x		
TRD	x	x	x	x	x
ENV	x	x	x		
TRD	x	x	x	x	x
POP	x	x		x	x
POP*TRD				x	x
ΔGDP				x	x

The general model used takes the reduced form following Kuznets' hypothesis that the relationship between income and environmental pressure follows an inverted-U curve. Given the above alternate specifications, we have the following general linear fixed effects regression model for the full model (Model 1) with appropriate changes for the various specifications defined in Table 5.4.

$$AP_{it} = \alpha_1 + \gamma_\tau + \beta_1 (GDP_{it}) + \beta_2 (GDP_{it})^2 + \beta_3 (PRV_{it}) + \beta_4 (FDI_{it})$$
$$+ \beta_5 (MFD)_{it} + \beta_6 (TRD_{it}) + \beta_7 (POP_{it}) + \beta_8 (ENV_{it}) + \varepsilon_{\iota\tau}$$
$$\text{with} \quad E(\varepsilon_{it}) = 0,\ Var(\varepsilon_{it}) = \omega_{\iota\tau}^2 \tag{5.1}$$

Where i denotes country and t represents time; AP is the vector of air pollution indicators outlined in Table 5.2 measured in 1000 metric tonnes or kilograms in the case of per capita specifications. The parameter α_i reflects specific country effects and γ_t the time effect. The six dependent variables measuring pollution pressures are defined in Table 5.2. Critical factors are as defined in Table 5.1: GDP is Gross Domestic Product per Capita (1987 constant US dollars); PRV is the measure of privatization or the private sector's contribution to GDP (per cent); FDI is net inflows of foreign direct investment as a percentage of GDP, and the indicator of openness is TRD (the sum of exports and imports of goods and services as a percentage of GDP); MFD is manufacturing value added (per cent of GDP), to reflect the structure of economy; ENV is environmental expenditures (per cent of GDP), to reflect regulatory intensity; POP is population in millions and ε is an error term.

In our analysis, the period effect γ_t is assumed to take the following form of time trend, $\gamma_t = \beta_t^* t$ where β_t, the coefficient of time trend, measures the annual increase in air pollution (if $\beta_t > 0$) or annual decrease (if $\beta_t < 0$). α_i, β_t, and β_i ($i = 1, \ldots, 7$) are coefficients to be estimated. The reduced form assumes that environmental outcomes are related to predetermined endowments and economic measures. Clearly some interdependence in environmental indicators is probable.

5.4.3   Discussion of Econometric Results by Pollutant Type for the Region

As stated above, alternative models were estimated to test for the appropriate specification of the indicators for key pollutants, the inclusion of time effects, the non-linear relationship between income and emissions, and the correction for population. The results for all are available from the authors. Table 5.4 shows the specification for Models 1–5. The econometric results for selected models are presented in Appendix A. Econometric results are quite good. The exceptions are Models 4 and 5 following the specification of Lucas (1996). Neither overall explanatory power, direction of effects or levels of statistical significance are as good as those obtained with Models 1–3. Therefore, they are not used in further analysis, but conclusions that might be drawn from them are compared to the preferred models. Generally, signs were consistent with expectations, with some exceptions that are related to model specification. R^2s are quite high for the preferred models and estimated coefficients exhibit the expected signs and a high degree of significance. As with some previous research, results were sensitive to a population variable. Moreover, coefficients are affected by the inclusion of population effects. Without this correction, coefficients do not take the expected sign and exhibit less statistical significance.

There appears to be little difference resulting from alternative definitions of pressure indicators, although when per capita emissions definitions are coupled with models excluding population effects, results are less valid statistically and signs are more often inconsistent with expectations. Overall, Models 1 and 2 with population effects included gave the most consistent and robust estimates.

Table 5.5 summarizes the effects from Models 1–3 from Appendix A. Column 1 indicates the critical factor. Key pollution indicators are listed across the top row. In each cell, the direction of effect derived from the econometric analysis is indicated. Unless noted, the direction of effect indicated (for example, increasing or decreasing) is based upon statistically significant parameter estimates in the several models with 'weakly' implying a consistency in signs across models but weak statistical significance. Where signs are not consistent across models, effects are denoted as indeterminate.

Time effects indicated a decreasing and significant relationship for Models 1 and 2 with population effects included (for Model 3 effects on SO_2, NO_2, VOC and PM were positive but not significant). The inverted-U curve hypothesis was supported for Models 1 and 2 (for Model 3, coefficients on SO_2, NO_2 and PM were statistically insignificant and positive). The effects of transformation to market economies (PRV) has a positive effect (decreases pressure) on the environment for all pressure indicators with the exception of SO_2 which was indeterminate. Foreign direct investment (FDI) is shown to increase pressure on the environment for this sample and time period. As manufacturing declines as a percentage of GDP, environmental pressures should lessen based on these estimates.

Increased openness generally has a positive effect on the environment (decreasing pressures) although for CO_2, SO_2 and NO_2 results were statistically weak. As regulatory intensity increases CEEC can expect environmental pressures to decrease. These results were uniformly strong with relatively weaker confirmation for SO_2 and VOC. The population variable indicates that more heavily populated countries are reducing pressures on the environment to a greater extent. This is true for all but NO_2, which is indeterminate.

Overall, these results confirm our expectations that factors other than the general decline in economic activity during these early years of transition to market economies have had a significant effect on reducing pressure on key environmental indicators. Table 5.6 provides some estimates of the regional average annual change in emission levels for each key pressure indicator as measured by the coefficient on the time trend from Model 1. These changes exclude effects of other critical factors and are probably attributable to efficiency gains realized over the period as well as to declines in production. Total emissions for all sources in the region exhibit a strong downward trend.

Table 5.7 provides estimates of income levels at which emissions reach peak levels for key pollutants from the five alternative models estimated. It is evident that these estimates vary significantly. Under some specifications, there were no peak emissions points. Clearly, those models that exclude critical explanatory variables related to economic structure (FDI, PRV, MFD) and regulation

Table 5.5 Summary of effects of critical factors affecting the environment on pressure indicators

Critical factors and expected effects		Key air pollutant indicators				
	CO_2	SO_2	NO_2	CO	VOC	PM
Time	Decreasing	Decreasing	Decreasing	Decreasing	Decreasing	Decreasing
GDP	Increasing	Increasing	Increasing	Increasing	Increasing	Increasing
GDP2	Decreasing	Decreasing	Decreasing	Decreasing	Decreasing	Decreasing
PRV	Weakly decreasing	Weakly increasing	Decreasing	Weakly increasing	Decreasing	Weakly decreasing
FDI	Increasing	Indeterminate	Weakly increasing	Increasing	Weakly increasing	Weakly increasing
MFD	Increasing	Indeterminate	Increasing	Increasing	Increasing	Increasing
TRD	Weakly decreasing	Weakly decreasing	Weakly increasing	Decreasing	Decreasing	Weakly decreasing
ENV	Decreasing	Weakly decreasing	Decreasing	Decreasing	Weakly decreasing	Decreasing
POP	Decreasing	Decreasing	Weakly increasing	Weakly increasing	Decreasing	Decreasing

Source: Appendix A, Results of Econometric Estimates

(ENV) appear to more consistently result in models with no peak emissions levels. This is consistent with Lucas' (1996) results (he did not include these critical variables). Perhaps the wide variation in empirical estimates of the income levels at which peak emissions are projected to occur reported in the literature can be explained in part by model specification. More analysis is needed to identify the source of variation among previous empirical results.

Table 5.6   Average annual regional rate of change for key pollutants for CEEC

Key air quality pressure indicator	Average annual percentage change
CO_2	−10.34
SO_2	−9.55
NO_2	−7.13
CO	−9.50
PM	−15.94
VOC	−6.19

Source: Appendix A, Model 1

Table 5.7   Regional turning points under alternative model specifications

Model	Income level at peak emissions by pollution indicator (Per capita income in US$ 1987)					
	CO_2	SO_2	NO_2	CO	PM	VOC
Model 1	3 302	3 506	3 283	2 858	3 264	3 107
Model 2	4 511	13 379	4 352	2 972	3 108	3 236
Model 3	5 251	No peak	4 221	2 880	No peak	3 185
Model 4	10 514	No peak	No peak	No peak	No peak	1 619
Model 5	No peak	No peak	No peak	2 657	No peak	1 713

Source: Appendix A

Table 5.8 uses the results from Model 1 to demonstrate how the econometric results can be decomposed to identify the separate effects of changes in critical factors on levels of key pollutant emissions. The numbers in Table 5.8 represent the effects of each of the critical factors on total emissions levels (measured in 1000 metric tonnes) from a 1 percent change in their contribution to GDP. For example, using the coefficient estimate on PRV from Model 1 every 1 per cent change in the share of GDP resulting from the private sector increases CO_2

emission levels by approximately 275 000 metric tonnes. However, the effect of increasing the share of GDP generated from the manufacturing sector has a significantly larger impact on total increases in CO_2. It is also clear that environmental regulation can have a significant effect in reducing levels of all key pollutants. In fact, for these estimates reductions associated with regulation far outweigh the small positive effects of privatization predicted by Model 1 on total emissions. Rising incomes are expected to contribute further to pollution levels, largely as a result of energy intensive consumption patterns.

Table 5.8   Decomposing reductions in regional pollution emissions from model 1 (1000 metric tonnes)

Indicator	GDP	GDP2	PRV	MFD	TRD	ENV	POP
CO_2	281 582	–42 634	275.26	1 866.60	–251.34	–7 467.34	–33 948.00
SO_2	2 580	–368	1.10	11.20	–0.66	–90.94	–659.53
NO_2	1 090	–166	1.59	6.00	0.97	–102.08	–150.51
CO	3 019	–528	3.39	15.20	–5.58	–77.06	37.03
PM	1 171	–179	1.95	4.48	0.48	–56.17	–660.19
VOC	819	–132	–0.84	4.30	– 0.91	–16.30	–125.74

Source: Model 1, Appendix A

5.5   CONCLUSIONS

This initial analysis using newly available data for the CEEC provides some important information regarding the relationships between key pollutant emission indicators and critical factors related to the economy and institutional reforms that have occurred in the CEEC over the past decade. Measurement issues aside, analysis indicates that economic and policy reforms have had a positive effect on the environment and can explain a significant share of the observed declines in emissions over the period. This analysis clearly points to the need for continued progress toward privatization, openness in trade and environmental regulatory infrastructure and investments. They are critical to future gains in environmental quality. Nonetheless, future increases in income in the absence of further policy initiatives to assure environmentally sound restructuring can be expected in the near term to increase pressure on the environment. This analysis also provides preliminary evidence that the demand for environmental quality is likely to occur for most pollutants at lower income levels than previously believed. This has important consequences for estimates made by policy makers about the growth of emissions in the future and the costs of achieving environmental gains.

Any conclusions must necessarily remain tentative given the simple econometric models employed in this analysis and the preliminary nature of the sustainability indicators. More work needs to be done in developing better measures of trade and foreign direct investments. While the results for air quality are encouraging, especially with respect to the strong contribution of environmental investments and regulation to reducing emissions over the period, there is some indication that a regional strategy for reducing air pollution is needed. A coordinated effort will be critical. Countries should also pay closer attention to foreign direct investments to assure they reduce environmental pressure. This is important given that foreign investments are expected to comprise a large share of total investment in the near future (Bochniarz, 1995).

The next steps in furthering the development of practical and reliable sustainability indicators to guide policy should include moving forward with the development of measures of environmental quality and improving the measures for critical economic and structural factors. For the CEEC specifically, microstudies at the firm level can be used to check the accuracy of reported data regarding income, production and investment levels. Methodologically, the likely interdependence of some of the independent variables in the analysis should be addressed with alternative modeling approaches. Overall, it appears that sustainability indicators will be useful in assessing policy effectiveness and in design of alternative policies to protect the environment.

APPENDIX 5A: ECONOMETRIC RESULTS

Pollutant: CO_2

Variable	Model 1 Total pollutants	Model 2 Per capita pollutants	Model 3 Per capita pollutants	Model 4 Total pollutants	Model 5 Per capita pollutants
Time	−14 479.04	−393.68	−311.52	−0.1541	0.005
	(5.20)	(3.39)	(2.50)	(1.88)	(0.03)
GDP	281 582.18	8328.71	5.34	26 687.96	2240.05
	(5.66)	(4.01)	(2.57)	(1.66)	(2.30)
GDP^2	−42 634.30	−923.13	−0.0005	−1269.14	191.62
	(5.31)	(2.76)	(1.48)	(0.23)	(0.58)
PRV	275.26	−17.09	−5.88	−	−
	(1.01)	(1.50)	(0.47)		
FDI	1 514.48	79.65	47.26	−	−
	(1.80)	(2.27)	(1.13)		

	Model 1	Model 2	Model 3	Model 4	Model 5
MFD	1 866.60	63.52	−11.86	−	−
	(3.17)	(2.58)	(0.48)		
TRD	−251.34	−14.20	3.95	0.47[a]	0.14[a]
	(0.82)	(1.11)	(0.49)	(0.10)	(0.67)
ENV	−7 467.34	−345.33	−533.37	−	−
	(1.27)	(1.40)	(2.01)		
POP	−33 948.01	−749.76	−	1.77	0.004
	(2.59)	(1.37)		(0.37)	(0.02)
TRD*POP	−	−	−	−0.0005[a]	0.009[a]
				(0.0066)	(0.06)
ΔGDP	−	−	−	−0.0069	−0.01
				(0.0837)	(0.06)
Adjusted R^2	0.99	0.97	0.97	0.43	0.43

Note: a Defined as exports by Lucas (1996)

Pollutant: CO

Variable	Model 1 Total pollutants	Model 2 Per capita pollutants	Model 3 Per capita pollutants	Model 4 Total pollutants	Model 5 Per capita pollutants
Time	−128.63	−5.27	−3.12	−0.0043	0.003
	(5.09)	(2.25)	(1.33)	(1.18)	(0.06)
GDP	3018.76	135.66	0.086	128.68	75.05
	(6.68)	(3.23)	(2.20)	(0.18)	(0.24)
GDP^2	−528.18	−22.82	−0.00001	62.62	−14.12
	(7.24)	(3.38)	(2.30)	(0.26)	(0.13)
PRV	3.39	0.06	0.07	−	−
	(1.36)	(0.25)	(0.29)		
FDI	15.19	0.38	0.1112	−	−
	(1.98)	(0.52)	(0.14)		
MFD	15.20	1.01	−0.3897	−	−
	(2.84)	(2.03)	(0.84)		
TRD	−5.58	−0.24	−0.10	0.31[a]	0.04[a]
	(2.01)	(0.93)	(0.67)	(1.46)	(0.58)
ENV	−77.06	−6.30	−4.31	−	−
	1.44	(1.27)	(0.86)		
POP	37.03	2.98	−	0.005	−0.0008
	(0.31)	(0.27)	−	(0.03)	(0.01)
TRD*POP	−	−	−	0.002 a/	0.002 a/
				(0.73)	(0.03)

ΔGDP	–	–	–	–0.003	–0.0015
				(0.87)	(0.03)
Adjusted R^2	0.98	0.87	0.86	0.28	0.85

Pollutant: SO_2

Variable	Model 1 Total pollutants	Model 2 Per capita pollutants	Model 3 Per capita pollutants	Model 4 Total pollutants	Model 5 Per capita pollutants
Time	–135.96	1.04	1.10	–0.003	–0.0004
	(3.24)	(0.29)	(0.32)	(1.08)	(0.006)
GDP	2579.87	48.66	0.0163	–29.85	–40.62
	(3.44)	(0.76)	(0.29)	(0.05)	(0.10)
GDP^2	–367.94	–1.82	0.000002	144.02	29.93
	(3.04)	(0.18)	(0.25)	(0.76)	(0.22)
PRV	1.10	–0.71	–0.69	–	–
	(0.26)	(2.03)	(2.00)		
FDI	9.20	–0.26	–0.2386	–	–
	(0.72)	(0.24)	(0.21)		
MFD	11.20	–0.07	0.20	–	–
	(1.26)	(0.09)	(0.30)		
TRD	–0.66	–0.14	–0.04	0.0014[a]	0.0013[a]
	(0.14)	(0.34)	(0.17)	(0.009)	(0.02)
ENV	–90.94	1.86	–1.54	–	–
	(1.02)	(0.24)	(0.21)		
POP	–659.53	–12.86	–	0.010	0.01
	(3.34)	(0.76)		(0.06)	(0.15)
TRD*POP	–	–	–	0.006[a]/	0.0009[a]
				(2.32)	(0.02)
ΔGDP	–	–	–	0.002	–0.0002
				(0.68)	(0.004)
Adjusted R^2	0.97	0.94	0.95	0.16	0.69

Pollutant: NO_2

Variable	Model 1 Total pollutants	Model 2 Per capita pollutants	Model 3 Per capita pollutants	Model 4 Total pollutants	Model 5 Per capita pollutants
Time	–34.95	–0.01	0.26	–0.13	–0.02
	(1.90)	(0.006)	(0.18)	(1.16)	(0.11)

GDP	1089.49	25.23	0.03	−7670.74	−54.66
	(3.31)	(0.91)	(1.04)	(0.35)	(0.05)
GDP^2	−165.95	−2.90	−0.000003	2551.02	7.48
	(3.13)	(0.65)	(0.74)	(0.34)	(0.02)
PRV	−1.59	−0.30	−0.28	−	−
	(0.88)	(1.97)	(1.92)		
FDI	6.88	0.42	0.29	−	−
	(1.24)	(0.89)	(0.61)		
MFD	6.00	0.19	−0.05	−	−
	(1.54)	(0.58)	(1.60)		
TRD	0.97	0.16	0.15	15.29[a]	2.98[a]
	(0.48)	(0.95)	(1.60)	(2.34)	(13.40)
ENV	−102.08	−6.95	−9.53	−	−
	(2.62)	(2.13)	(3.14)		
POP	−150.51	0.36	−	0.11	0.14
	(1.74)	(0.05)		(0.02)	(0.69)
TRD*POP	−	−	−	0.0009[a]	−0.010[a]
				(0.008)	(0.06)
ΔGDP	−	−	−	−0.10	0.007
				(0.93)	(0.04)
Adjusted R^2	0.96	0.88	0.86	0.10	0.84

Pollutant: Particulate Matter (PM)

Variable	Model 1 Total pollutants	Model 2 Per capita pollutants	Model 3 Per capita pollutants	Model 4 Total pollutants	Model 5 Per capita pollutants
Time	−85.60	0.63	1.08	−0.07	−0.02
	(4.11)	(0.59)	(0.82)	(0.58)	(0.13)
GDP	1171.16	8.61	−0.012	−5193.83	−78.89
	(3.15)	(0.44)	(0.57)	(0.22)	(0.08)
GDP^2	−179.38	−1.40	0.000001	1795.42	27.49
	(2.99)	(0.45)	(0.28)	(0.23)	(0.08)
PRV	1.95	−0.38	−0.38	−	−
	(0.95)	(3.57)	(2.84)		
FDI	7.89	0.40	0.12	−	−
	(1.25)	(1.22)	(0.26)		
MFD	4.48	−0.31	0.38	−	−
	(1.02)	(1.35)	(1.44)		
TRD	0.48	−0.16	−0.10	−1.77[a]	−0.04[a]
	(0.20)	(1.37)	(1.18)	(0.26)	(0.19)

ENV	−56.67	−6.74	−10.45	−	−
	(1.28)	(2.95)	(3.71)		
POP	−660.19	−17.38	−	19.14	3.34
	(6.74)	(3.42)		(2.76)	(17.40)
TRD*POP	−	−	−	−0.14[a]	0.010[a]
				(1.27)	(0.06)
ΔGDP	−	−	−	−0.09	0.002
				(0.77)	(0.01)
Adjusted R^2	0.98	0.96	0.86	0.25	0.89

Pollutant: VOC

Variable	Model 1 Total pollutants	Model 2 Per capita pollutants	Model 3 Per capita pollutants	Model 4 Total pollutants	Model 5 Per capita pollutants
Time	−22.82	0.63	0.84	−0.005	−0.02
	(3.08)	(0.90)	(1.29)	(1.56)	(0.28)
GDP	819.11	23.64	0.02	793.57	61.75
	(6.17)	(1.90)	(1.71)	(1.33)	(0.12)
GDP^2	−131.83	−3.65	−0.000003	−245.10	−18.02
	(6.16)	(1.82)	(1.62)	(1.21)	(0.10)
PRV	−0.83	−0.30	−0.32	−	−
	(1.14)	(4.37)	(4.88)		
FDI	2.06	0.16	0.27	−	−
	(0.92)	(0.78)	(1.23)		
MFD	4.30	0.19	−0.22	−	−
	(2.73)	(1.31)	(1.72)		
TRD	−0.91	−0.01	−0.005	0.33[a]	0.03[a]
	(1.11)	(0.17)	(0.11)	(1.87)	(0.29)
ENV	−16.30	0.16	−0.18	−	−
	(1.04)	(0.10)	(0.13)		
POP	−125.74	−4.41	−	0.33	0.04
	(3.60)	(1.34)		(1.83)	(0.37)
TRD*POP	−	−	−	−0.004[a]	−0.01[a]
				(1.26)	(0.13)
ΔGDP	−	−	−	−0.004	0.003
				(1.36)	(0.03)
Adjusted R^2	0.99	0.86	0.86	0.07	0.44

NOTES

1. The CNT *Sustainability Indicators* follow the *Pressure-State-Response* (PRS) framework developed by OECD which has been modified by the World Bank's *Environmental Performance Indicators*. The United Nations DP-CSD *Sustainability Indicator System* and the Wuppertal Institute's recent *Proactive Indicators* also influenced CNT's sustainability indicators. We would like to acknowledge the contributions of many who collaborated in the collection of this information: Alena Bradiakova, ETP Slovakia Foundation, Bratislava; Vilma Eri, Center for Environmental Studies, Budapest; Grazyna Lesniak-Lebkowska, Warsaw School of Economics, Warsaw; Krustina Mandova, ETP Foundation Bulgaria; Sofia Rodica Stefanescu, ETP Foundation Romania, Bucharest; Wojciech Stodulski, Institute for Sustainable Development, Warsaw; Viktor Trebnicky, Institute for Environmental Policy, Prague. We also want to acknowledge the important contributions of Research Assistants Ann Marie Schultz and Lan Xu.
2. The CNT *Sustainability Indicators* and a complete description of the framework is available from the Center for Nations in Transition, Humphrey Institute of Public Affairs, University of Minnesota. Much of it is available at http://www.hhh.umn edu/Centers/CNT.
3. A broader array of environmental indicators has been developed and is available from CNT.
4. It is important to note that there remains some question about the adequacy of the World Bank GDP data for these countries due to significant deficiencies in national accounting in the CEEC in the 1980s and the beginning of the 1990s.
5. Empirical research has shown that this measure is not adequate in many cases to measure the effects of openness in the economy. This is particularly true of small countries. Several alternative measures are explored in the empirical analysis that follows.
6. These data are misleading for the Czech and Slovak Republics. Trade within Czechoslovakia between these two regions became 'export' and 'import' trade after the creation of the separate republics.
7. A full discussion of these policies in contained in 'Measuring the effects of economic reforms and transition policies on environmental progress in Central and Eastern Europe', working paper, Center for Nations in Transition, Humphrey Institute of Public Affairs, University of Minnesota, May 1997.

BIBLIOGRAPHY

Bochniarz, Zbigniew (1992), *In Our Hands; United Nations Earth Summit '92: Capacities and Deficiencies for Implementing Sustainable Development*, Geneva-Minneapolis: UNDP.

Bochniarz, Zbigniew, Wladyslaw Jermakowicz and David Toft (1995), 'Strategic foreign investors and the environment in Central and Eastern Europe', in Erdener Kaynak and Tunc Erem (eds), *Innovation, Technology and Information Management for Global Development and Competitiveness*, Istanbul: IMDA.

Bochniarz, Zbigniew and David Toft (1995), 'Free trade and the environment in Central Europe', *European Environment*, **5**, 52–7.

Center for Nations in Transition (1997), *Sustainability Indicators for Central and Eastern Europe*, research report, Humphrey Institute of Public Affairs, University of Minnesota.

Economic Commission for Europe (1992), *Economic Bulletin for Europe*, New York: United Nations Publications.

Eurostat (1997), *Environmental Indicators*, European Commission.

Grossman, G.M. and A.B. Krueger (1995), 'Economic growth and the environment', *The Quarterly Journal of Economics*, May, 353–77.

Grossman, Gene and Alan B. Krueger (1995), 'Economic growth and the environment', *The Quarterly Journal of Economics*, **110**(2), 353–77.

Heal, Geoffrey (1996), 'International dimensions of environmental policy', in M. Bredahl, N. Ballenger, J. Dunmore and T. Roe (eds), *Agriculture, Trade and the Environment: Discovering and Measuring Critical Linkages*, Boulder, CO: Westview Press.

Holtz-Eakin, D. and T.M. Selden (1995), 'Stoking the fires? CO_2 emissions and economic growth', *Journal of Public Economics*, **57**, 85–101.

Lucas, R. (1996), 'International environmental indicators: trade income and endowments', in M. Bredahl, N. Ballenger, J. Dunmore and T. Roe (eds), *Agriculture, Trade and the Environment: Discovering and Measuring Critical Linkages*, Boulder, CO: Westview Press.

Lucas, R., D. Wheeler and H. Hettige (1992), 'Economic development, environmental regulation and the international migration of toxic industrial pollution: 1960–1988', World Development report, background paper no. 33, Washington, DC: World Bank.

Pearce, D.W. and J.J. Warford (1993*), World Without End: Economics, Environment and Sustainable Development*, New York: Oxford University Press.

Selden, Thomas and Daqing Song, (1994), 'Environmental quality and development: is there a Kuznets Curve for air pollution emissions?' *Journal of Environmental Economics and Management*, **27**, 147–62.

Shafik, N. (1994), 'Economic development and environmental quality: an econometric analysis', *Oxford Economic Papers*, **46**, 757–73.

Suri, V. and D. Chapman (1998), 'Economic growth, trade and the environment: an econometric evaluation of the environmental Kuznets Curve', *Ecological Economics*, **25**, 195–208.

UNEP (1995), *Environmental Policies and Practices of the Financial Sector*, United Nations Environment Programme Global Survey.

Vukina, T., J.C. Beghin and E.G. Solakoglu (1999), 'Transition to markets and the environment: effects of the change in the composition of manufacturing output', *Environment and Development Economics*, **3**, 582–98.

World Bank (1993), *Environmental Liability and Privatization in Central and Eastern Europe*, Washington, DC: World Bank.

6. Environmental impact assessment in Brazil

Dan Biller[1]

6.1 INTRODUCTION

Environmental Impact Assessment (EIA) has been an environmental policy trademark in several countries throughout Latin America. While not all sectors or projects are expected to undertake an EIA, this planning tool is present in many legal codes as a requirement for obtaining an environmental license. Projects cannot be legally undertaken without EIA studies if they are required. This ultimately transforms this planning tool into a policy instrument. Usually, EIAs are performed by accredited institutions, though governments do not always have regulations governing this type of service. Since the EIA is one of the first steps in the project cycle, the project proponent is faced with a choice of undertaking an informal assessment and risking being found in violation or complying with the requirement and paying an up-front cost associated with the EIA study.

As with many planning tools, there are several advantages to performing an EIA. On the regulator's side, it allows for preventive rather than corrective actions to be undertaken with ample time (Tlayie and Biller, 1994). It also provides a larger information set about the area where the project is to be implemented. Further, it often establishes a contract between the regulator and the project proponent through suggested mitigation measures. On the project side, it is an opportunity to gather additional information about issues that may generate costs at a later stage.

EIA can be traced back to the Second World War in the United States but became a formal requirement with the National Environmental Protection Act (NEPA) (Wiesner, 1995). In Brazil, EIA officially started as an environmental policy instrument in the early 1980s. As the popularity of this policy tool grew, the cumbersome aspects of its implementation also expanded. Currently, the effectiveness of EIA studies is often questioned, and study costs are substantial. This chapter analyses the EIA process in Brazil. Section 6.2 places the EIA study in the context of the Brazilian environmental regulatory framework.

Section 6.3 discusses the institutional side of the EIA process. Section 6.4 assesses the EIA in the project cycle in Brazil and briefly compares it with other examples. Section 6.5 takes a sectoral view and analyzes the EIA process in mining, which is one of the sectors with the greatest environmental scrutiny in the country. Section 6.6 presents concluding remarks, suggesting possible ways of improving the EIA process in the country.

6.2   BRAZIL'S REGULATORY FRAMEWORK

As in other federal systems, Brazil has a fairly decentralized system of power sharing. While decentralization is a way of addressing local concerns, it also generates significant costs if not carefully designed. In Brazil, these costs are often reflected in overlapping jurisdictions, which breeds conflicts among different agencies. In addition, conflicts among agencies at the same governmental level are not uncommon, generating contradictory information and cumbersome requirements.

The environmental institutional framework is not significantly different from other countries. Brazil has an environmental protection agency (best represented by IBAMA – Instituto Brasileiro de Meio Ambiente e Recursos Naturais Renováveis), yet it is placed within the Ministry of Environment and Water Resources. Particularly in the richer states, the composition of the state government may involve both an environmental secretary and environmental agency.[2] The system may be duplicated at a municipal level, though municipalities do not have environmental agencies. At times, the municipal environmental secretary acts as an agency itself.

Federal environmental regulations serve as a 'minimum standard' for the states, but some states have more stringent regulatory requirements. In general, richer states have stricter environmental standards and controls. Regardless of the environmental agencies, the judiciary may also get involved through public demands against polluters. Some states and municipalities have fairly independent environmental public district attorneys, who may open a lawsuit against anyone on environmental grounds without necessarily having a complaint from the local environmental agency. This frequently supports the efforts of environmental agencies, but also pressures them into action

The existence of cross-jurisdictions is to a certain extent inherent to the environmental field. Environmental problems seldom have clear-cut solutions, since they are usually cross-sectoral, involve multiple disciplines, and often affect sections of society in different ways. Moreover, they seldom stop at artificial human-made borders. In Brazil, the complexity of environmental problems is aggravated by at least two factors. Brazilian implementation capacity is still weak, and budgetary resources for environmental purposes are scarce and poorly used. The decentralization process has added further complications, since it raises fundamental constitutional issues and forces intense negotiations for resources and authority. Adapting the environmental regulatory framework to this reality may require amendments to the relatively new constitution (1988) and better inter-agency relations.

The current Brazilian constitution is quite detailed, specifying governmental activities and at times sectoral regulations. The constitution has a chapter devoted to the environment, though it doesn't clearly define the term. A clear definition is important, for legally it may be a pre-condition to the successful application of sanctions, fines and regulations in general. Further, it influences society's perceptions of issues, perhaps creating a bias towards a particular type of definition. In the case of the Brazilian constitution, the chapter tends to link environment to ecological services such as biodiversity potential in medical research and ecosystems such as the Amazon Forest and the Atlantic Rainforest, among others. Moreover, it specifically singles out the mining and nuclear sectors, but does not mention urban environmental issues. Opinion polls generally confirm the nexus between environmental concern and the so-called green issues as presented in the constitution.

The constitution clearly states the need for EIA prior to project implementation. The EIA is the only environmental policy instrument mentioned in the chapter. Yet, the chapter does not specify what constitutes an environmental impact, which is the actual target of the instrument. In addition, the constitution relies on legal codes to transform its rulings into regulations subject to enforcement. There are at least two key regulations in the Brazilian environmental legal code. Both precede the constitution. Law #6.938 of 1981 establishes the national environmental policy, emphasizing zoning, EIA, and licensing as environmental policy instruments. It defines the environment as a set of conditions, laws, influences and interactions of physical, chemical, and biological nature that allows, hosts and regulates all forms of life. Further, it defines the degradation of environmental quality as adverse change in its characteristics, and pollution as the degradation of quality caused by human activities that directly or indirectly:

1. damage the population's health, security and welfare;
2. create adverse conditions for social and economic activities;
3. unfavorably affect the biota;
4. affect the aesthetic or sanitary conditions of the environment;
5. dispose of materials or energy in disagreement with the established environmental standards.

Decree #88.351 of 1983 establishes the licensing system and the EIA study and its executive summary – Relatório de Impacto Ambiental (RIMA) – as its prerequisite. Table 6.1 describes the system in detail as presented by the decree (Sampaio, 1998, and MMA and PNUD, 1997).

Table 6.1   Decree #88.351 of 1983 – licensing and EIA

- Initial License (Licença Previa): Targets planning, feasibility and basic project stages. Firm needs to present the EIA/RIMA (RIMA corresponds to the EIA's executive summary) and a municipality certificate that clears the project given its laws.
- License for Installation (Licença de Instalação): Targets the instalation of the activity. Firm needs to present an Environmental Control Plan (PCA – Plano de Controle Ambiental) implementing the EIA/RIMA recommendations. At this stage, the firm also needs to present a license for forest clearing (if requested).
- License for Operation: Firm needs to show that the systems projected in the PCA were implemented.

Currently, the legal environmental provisions are complemented through regulations promulgated by the National Council on the Environment (Conselho Nacional de Meio Ambiente – CONAMA). CONAMA was instituted by law #6.938, and is composed by representatives from federal and state agencies, foundations, non-governmental organizations (NGOs), the private sector and unions through their respective associations. It also serves as an appeal body for sanctions.

6.3   INSTITUTIONAL SIDE OF EIA

While law #6.938 and decree #88.351 clearly place the EIA/RIMA as an environmental policy tool, they fail to provide details on what constitutes an EIA/RIMA and which projects should be required to undertake it. CONAMA resolution #001 of 23 January 1986 (001/86) arises primarily from the above mentioned law and decree. Its function is to institutionalize the EIA study and executive summary, thus being a key regulation in the licensing process.

As described in the next section, resolution #001/86 is quite specific on the question it is designed to answer. Yet, it does not clearly link the EIA/RIMA to environmental licensing, and fails to determine clear jurisdictions regarding the enforcement of the EIA/RIMA requirement. Depending on the nature of the project, all levels of governments can require that the EIA study addresses additional questions, which in turn may generate a substantial amount of interactions between the project proponent and the different regulators.

On the regulator's side, resolution #001/86 requires that the state environmental agency, IBAMA, and when applicable the municipality, have a period starting from the date the RIMA is received to give their evaluations. The resolution, however, leaves the length of this period open. The RIMA is also made available for public scrutiny with a period for comments contemplated without any pre-determined length. In theory, the interactions between the project proponent and the different regulators may go on indefinitely.

The resolution also determines that the study be undertaken by a multidisciplinary team independent but hired by the project proponent. These teams are generally coordinated by consulting firms. While the project proponent bears all costs of the EIA study, it also becomes a client of the multidisciplinary team. This may generate a conflict of interest since there may be a disincentive for the EIA team to criticize the original project proposed by the contracting agency.[3] In addition, the proponent covers the environmental agency's costs for licensing. Since there is no fixed upper bound regarding timing these costs can be substantial.

Resolution #001/86 generates a thriving EIA/RIMA industry, but clearly translates into substantial transaction costs. The environmental licensing process is slow, and due to the lack of human capacity, environmental agencies often cannot cope with demand. A very recent CONAMA resolution attempts to improve this situation. Resolution #237 of 19 December 1997 (#237/97) establishes relatively clear rules on the jurisdictional responsibilities among different layers of government and agencies regarding licensing. These rules include expiration periods for the different licenses and the timing for issuing them. In effect, however, it eliminates the EIA/RIMA as a pre-condition for environmental licensing, linking the process to environmental studies to be determined by the responsible agency. As compared to resolution #001/86, resolution #237/97 broadens the sectors subject to environmental licensing (see Table 6.2), but eliminates the need for a multidisciplinary team to undertake the environmental studies. Table 6.3 summarizes the key elements of resolution #237/97 regarding licensing.

Although the requirement for a multidisciplinary team disappears with the new resolution, the project proponent and the team become legally responsible for the information provided in the environmental studies. This is done via law #9605 of 12 February 1998, which establishes stringent sanctions and fines for providing poor information. Further, the law includes the possibility of legally holding responsible an ineffective environmental agency. Yet, the law neither enacts a way of assessing the quality of the information provided by the project proponent, nor provides benchmarks to measure the effectiveness of the environmental agency.

Table 6.2   Activities subject to environmental licensing

Mineral extraction and processing

* Exploration
* Open pit mining including alluvial deposits
* Underground mining
* *Garimpos* (artisanal mining)
* Oil and natural gas exploitation
* Non-metallic mineral industry (e.g. cement, glass etc.)

Metal industry
Machinery industry
Electronic industry including communications
Transportation industry
Wood industry and processing
Paper industry and mills
Rubber industry
Tanneries and leather processing
Chemical industry
Plastics
Textile industry
Food and food processing
Tobacco industry
Miscellaneous industry
Public works
Public services
Specific transportation
Tourist related complexes
Biodiversity related activities (e.g. agriculture, agroforestry, renewable
resource use)

Table 6.3   Licensing according to resolution #237/97

Responsibilities
IBAMA
* Cross country projects, oceanic projects, special economic zones, Indian ter-
ritories, federal conservation units.
* Projects involving two or more states.
* Environmental impacts across state and country boundaries.

Table 6.3   continued

- Activities involving radioactive material.
- Military bases and projects.

Note: IBAMA retains the right to delegate environmental licensing to state agencies or to act as substitute to these agencies.

STATE ENVIRONMENTAL AGENCY
- Projects involving more than one municipality and state conservation units.
- Projects in forests obeying laws of all levels of government.
- Environmental impacts across municipal boundaries.
- Delegated from the federal government.

MUNICIPAL ENVIRONMENTAL AUTHORITY
- Local environmental impact and if delegated from the state environmental agency.

Note: Only one level of licensing needed.

Timing for resolution
- Up to six months after licensing request is received.
- Up to twelve months after licensing request is received if EIA/RIMA and/or public hearings required.
- Timing is suspended if additional information required by the agency.
- Timing negotiable if justified.
- Project proponent has up to four months to answer inquires (negotiable).

Expiration period for licenses
- Initial License (Licença Previa): Follow project schedule but not greater than five years.
- License for Instalation (Licença de Instalação): Follow project schedule but not greater than six years.
- License for Operation: Follow PCA, with minimum of four and maximum of ten years.

6.4   EIA AND THE PROJECT CYCLE

Figure 6.1 describes the general scheme of the EIA. EIA concerns should start as early as the project proposal itself. As a planning tool, at least in theory, the process provides ample opportunity to apply its information in the adjustment of the original project proposal. Figure 6.2 overlaps the general EIA scheme with a typical project cycle of the World Bank. This approach is standard for other development banks as well. Both flow diagrams are similar to the initial Brazilian licensing process, which used EIA/RIMA as the basis.

Whether the project is based as a loan or not, environmental screening is the first step. In general, development banks screen projects according to operational directives and determine whether a full EIA study, a simplified environmental analysis, or no environmental analysis is required as a condition

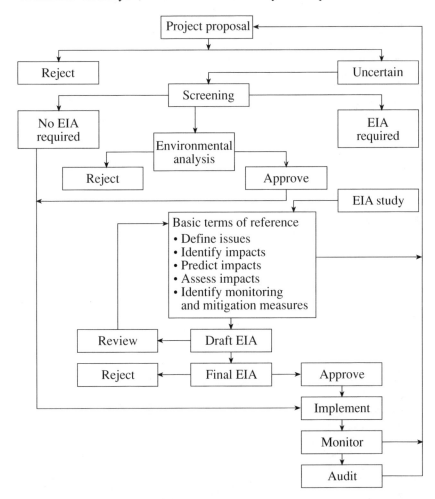

Source: The author, based on Wiesner (1995)

Figure 6.1   EIA general scheme

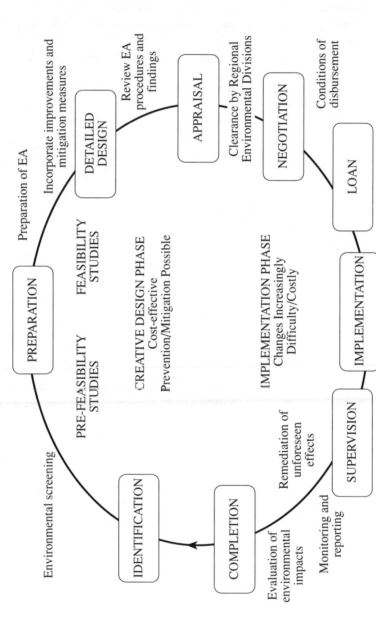

Environmental screening

PRE-FEASIBILITY
STUDIES

PREPARATION

Preparation of EA

FEASIBILITY
STUDIES

Incorporate improvements and
mitigation measures

DETAILED
DESIGN

Review EA
procedures and
findings

APPRAISAL

Clearance by Regional
Environmental Divisions

NEGOTIATION

Conditions of
disbursement

LOAN

CREATIVE DESIGN PHASE
Cost-effective
Prevention/Mitigation Possible

IMPLEMENTATION PHASE
Changes Increasingly
Difficulty/Costly

IMPLEMENTATION

IDENTIFICATION

COMPLETION

Remediation of unforeseen
effects

SUPERVISION

Evaluation of
environmental
impacts

Monitoring and
reporting

Source: The World Bank (1991)

Figure 6.2 Environmental assessment and the project

for loan analysis. In Brazil, there are two screening mechanisms in place. As discussed, resolution #237/97 requires that an extensive list of sectors undertake environmental studies. Alternatively, resolution #001/86 determines that 16 types of project are required to submit a full EIA/RIMA to the state environmental agency and IBAMA. These are listed in Table 6.4. Confusion may arise from the fact that some projects – such as mining – are mentioned in the list for both Tables 6.3 and 6.4.

Table 6.4   Projects requiring full EIA

- Roads of at least two lanes
- Railroads
- Port facilities
- Airports
- Large pipelines such as oil and ocean sewage outfalls
- Transmission lines over 230 KV
- Dams
- Hydrocarbon extraction
- Mining extraction
- Sanitary landfill and hazardous waste disposals
- Power plants over 10 MW
- Industrial and agro-industrial complexes
- Industrial zones
- Wood and firewood exploitation of over 100 hectares or large in percentile terms or in areas of environmental importance
- Urban projects over 100 hectares or in areas considered of environmental importance by the state or municipality
- Activities using 10 tons or more of charcoal per day.

Resolution #001/86 also establishes some broad guidelines and provides draft terms of reference for the EIA study and the RIMA. For example, the EIA study is required to contemplate all technologies and possible places for the project to be undertaken, and compare it with the hypothesis of not undertaking the project at all. The draft terms of reference include a diagnosis examining the physical, biological, and socioeconomic aspects, the identification of direct and indirect, positive and negative, short-, medium- and long-term impacts, including welfare related ones. Further, it includes the establishment of mitigation measures by requiring a menu of technical solutions. Finally, the EIA study should also include a monitoring program, indicating factors and parameters to be considered.

6.5   A SECTORAL VIEW: EIA IN MINING

While resolution #001/86 is specific to the EIA process, it does not discuss the licensing process itself. Until #237/97 was issued, the licensing process would be established through other resolutions in a sectoral manner. CONAMA resolutions #009/90 and #010/90 linked the EIA study to the licensing process for the mining sector. Mining is an interesting case, since it is specially singled out by the environmental chapter in the constitution. As described in Table 6.5, mining is also targeted in other constitutional chapters.

Table 6.5   Brazilian constitutional articles related to mining

---

- Article 20, IX defines underground mineral resources as the Federation's (União) property.
- Article 21, XXV defines as the Federation's responsibility to enable placer mining (*Garimpo*) through cooperatives, defining areas for the activity.
- Article 22, XII determines that only the Federation can legislate over mining resources.
- Article 23, XI determines that the Federation, its states and municipalities should register, follow, and inspect mining concessions under their jurisdictions. A complementary law should be designed to establish the rules of cooperation among the different government levels.
- Article 174, #3 establishes that the state will favor the association of placer miners (*Garimpeiros*) in cooperatives, taking into account environmental protection and their economic and social well-being. #4 states that those cooperatives will be given priority in terms of concessions in areas where they are active and in those established by article 21. Article 231 excludes indigenous areas from this article.
- Article 176 establishes the difference between mineral resources and land property, reminding that the former belongs to the Federation. The concession only recognizes the mining firm's property as mineral extraction. General guidelines for concessions are established in paragraphs 1 through 4, further establishing the landowner participation in the production results.
- Article 225 of the chapter on the environment determines that everybody has the right to a well-balanced environment. The state and society at large have the obligation to protect the environment for present and future generations. #1, IV determines that the State should require an environmental impact assessment (EIA) of any activity potentially damaging to the environment, and the EIA should be made public. #2 determines that those who exploit mineral resources are required to restore the degraded environment according to the technical solution stipulated by the state agency in charge under the law.

Source: MMA and PNUD (1997)

It is worth noting that the constitution displays a certain degree of openness for placer mining (*garimpo*), attempting to organize an informal activity. Nonetheless, regardless of the type of mining activity, the EIA requirement would be applicable to the sector as a whole. In theory, even with resolution #237/97 *garimpos* are still required to have an environmental license to be legally in operation. Table 6.6 links the licensing requirement to the the EIA requirement in the specific case of mining.

Table 6.6   Mining licensing and EIA

---

* Initial license (Licença Previa): as discussed in Table 6.1. For class II minerals (mainly used in construction and exploited in urban and peri-urban areas), simpler EIAs called Environmental Control Reports (RCA – Relatório de Controle Ambiental) are acceptable pending the decision of the agencies responsible.
* License for Instalation (Licença de Instalação): as discussed in Table 6.1. For certain minerals, a Bureau of Mines (Departamento Nacional Produção Mineral – DNPM) approved Economic Feasibility Plan (PAE – Plano de Aproveitamento Econômico) needs to be presented.
* License for operation: as discussed in Table 6.1.
* Recovery of degraded areas: decree #97.632 of April 10, 1989 requires that all mining activities present a Plan for the Recovery of Degraded Areas (PRAD – Plano de Recuperação de Áreas Degradadas) during the environmental licensing process. No performance bond is required.

The following CONAMA resolutions are also important:

* CONAMA resolution #001 (1986) regulates EIA/RIMA.
* CONAMA resolution #009 (1990) establishes procedures for licensing mineral research and extraction.
* CONAMA resolution #010 (1990) establishes the procedures for class II minerals.
* CONAMA resolution #237 (1997) regulates aspects of environmental licensing, the EIA/RIMA, and environmental studies.

Source: MMA and PNUD (1997) and CONAMA

Given the laws and regulations applicable to the mining sector, the sector is without doubt one of the main clients of environmental impact assessment services. In fact, even in states where mining is not traditionally a key sector, the number of mining EIAs may surpass EIAs from other sectors. For example, 57 percent of EIAs presented to the state environmental agency in São Paulo (the most industrialized state in Brazil) until 1994 came from the mining sector.

This may suggest that the mining sector is easier to regulate at least in the largely populated states (see MMA and PNUD, 1997).

6.5.1   The Institutional Side

The lack of jurisdictional clarity and the existence of inter-agency conflict adds significant costs to an already cumbersome environmental regulatory framework. Currently, it is not uncommon that a mining firm is required to present different projects and documents for a myriad of agencies involved in the regulatory process for the same venture. The lack of clarity spills over to the interpretation of codes, where some sectors, including mining, may be required to undertake environmental analysis of varying degrees of detail. Mining firms lose because they incur high transaction costs for producing documents that serve only to comply with bureaucratic requirements. Governments also lose since they do not have the capacity to analyze the materials received or enforce decisions, often being perceived as ineffective in the eyes of the general public. Finally, society loses since it is left to deal with serious environmental problems, which ought to have been addressed through the regulatory framework.[4]

Specifically regarding the mining sector, a firm often has to respond to pressure coming from a number of interested parties. Responsible agencies include the state environmental protection agencies, the federal DNPM, the IBAMA, and individual municipalities. The Federal Government is aware of this problem and has advanced the concept of *guiche único* or single window. Through this idea, mining firms would approach a single agency for delivery of project documentation and would receive all permits, regardless of the jurisdiction, through the same agency.

In certain regions, mining firms may also expect to face resistance by local communities, NGOs, and in some cases, *garimpeiros*. The degree of opposition to mining operations from the first two groups is an indicator of the level of environmental awareness in Brazil. *Garimpeiro* opposition to formal mining usually occurs where there are minerals with a high unit value and where economies of scale are not crucial for operations. It also serves to illustrate the lack of enforcement capacity in the country. Even with relatively easier special legislation as mentioned above, few *garimpos* have all the environmental requirements to operate. Nonetheless, if the price of the mineral is attractive they keep operating, even in areas where permits for mining companies are granted (see Biller 1994, and Biller 1997b).

6.6   CONCLUDING REMARKS

Brazil has had a longer legislative history in environmental issues than some other Latin American countries. This may be a blessing as well as a curse. The

Brazilian environmental process is hampered by an excessive reliance on legal codes that are often contradictory and difficult to enforce. The legislation commonly leads to competing claims of responsibility and overlapping jurisdiction. This adds substantial costs to firms without generating benefits to society at large.

While policymakers realize the problem, solutions often rely on the development of additional laws, decrees and resolutions. The result is a regulatory patchwork that generates legislative inconsistencies. In an attempt to consolidate the environmental legislation into a single law, the Brazilian congress recently established a working group to evaluate and propose solutions to this problem. Judging from the recent law and resolution, the working group has a difficult task ahead of it (see Andrada, 1997).

The EIA process as represented by the EIA/RIMA illustrates the legal confusion and lack of effective implementation. Since the early 1980s through law #6938, the EIA/RIMA exists as a policy instrument. The study was effectively regulated by CONAMA #001/86, and is the sole environmental policy instrument cited in the 1988 constitution. While CONAMA #001/86 is unclear regarding licensing procedures, jurisdictions and responsibilities (including possible penalties), it clearly states the basis of the EIA/RIMA study, who pays for it, how it should be undertaken, and how should it be used as a policy instrument. Over ten years have passed since #001/86, and a new resolution and law have been issued to solve the jurisdictional confusion. Even so, it solves some problems and generates others.

It is clear that law #9.605 and resolution #237/97 affect previous regulations, but it is unclear how they actually change them. This means that the consolidation of the legislation remains an issue. For example, considering the new regulation, EIA/RIMA is no longer a required policy instrument. Its use is determined by the responsible environmental agency rather than the established environmental code. EIA/RIMA is no longer required for specific projects and sectors unless specified by the environmental agency, but both resolution #001/86 and #237/97 coexist. To avoid a costly EIA/RIMA, some firms are likely to claim that through the new resolution a simpler environmental analysis should suffice.

More importantly, however, is the fact that the existing regulation is unable to address the issue of implementation. Unless closely regulated, the contractual arrangement does not promote quality environmental studies. Since the project proponent employs the EIA team, there is little incentive to indicate major environmental problems with the project. This is particularly true if the expectation is that the regulator cannot exercise a quality control function. Moreover, in an attempt to diminish costs the information provided may at times be incomplete. For example, data may be gathered in short time periods, failing to provide an accurate picture of the local environment being targeted.

While the quality of the EIA/RIMA is relevant, the enforcement of mitigation measures may be even more important. Since enforcement capacity is often weak, mitigation plans suggested in EIA/RIMA are seldom implemented. As with other countries, the penalties for degrading the environment are present in the legal code and are applied after the damage is done. A possible way of correcting this problem is to place instruments within the context of the EIA/RIMA process to ensure that mitigation measures are implemented.

Once again, mining may offer an interesting example. Mining firms are required to submit a restoration plan for degraded areas during the environmental licensing process, but no performance bond type scheme is in place. Only a post-licensing monitoring and enforcement plan can be established if the recuperation plan is being implemented as previously agreed. By using a performance bond, the regulator minimizes the risk of having a degraded mining site after mining is no longer undertaken. In the worst case scenario, the regulator would have funds from the bond to recuperate the site, avoiding the possibility that taxpayers assume the clean-up bill.

NOTES

1. This chapter was written while the author was at the Fundacao Getulio Vargas (Getulio Vargas Foundation – FGV/Brazil) and the Organisation for Economic Co-operation and Development (OECD/France). He is currently the Environment and Natural Resources Program Leader/ Senior Economist at the World Bank Institute (WBI). The opinions expressed here do not necessarily reflect the views of the above mentioned institutions.
2. An environmental agency is subordinated to the secretary. In theory, it is mainly responsible for undertaking monitoring and applying regulations, while the secretary focuses primarily on environmental planning.
3. The recent accounting scandals in the financial markets (for example ENRON) illustrate this type of conflict in another consulting industry.
4. A common example in Brazil is quarries near urban areas. Originally, they may have been legal but over time fail to renew licensing. For an example in the municipality of Rio de Janeiro, see Mussoi (1997).

BIBLIOGRAPHY

Andrada, Bonifacio de (3 September 1997), 'Consolidação da legislação ambiental Brasileira', Brasilia: House of the Brazilian Congress.
Biller, Dan (May 1994), 'Informal gold mining and mercury pollution in Brazil', policy research working paper no. 1304, Washington, DC: The World Bank.
Biller, Dan (February 1997a), 'Exhaustible resource management', European Union – Rio Group dialogue on sustainable development, organized by The Institute For European-Latin American Relations (IRELA), The Hague, Netherlands.
Biller, Dan (1997b), 'Mining under watchful green eyes', *Hemisfile*, Institute of The Americas, **8**(3), May/June.

Clemente, Ademir (ed.) (1997), *Projetos Empresariais e Públicos*, São Paulo, Brazil: Editora Atlas.

Comissão Estadual de Controle Ambiental (CECA), several regulations, Rio de Janeiro, Brazil.

Comissão Nacional do Meio Ambiente (CONAMA), several regulations, Brasilia.

Margulis, Sergio (1996), 'A regulamentação ambiental: instrumentos e implementação', texto para discussão No. 437, Instituto de Pesquisa Econômica Aplicada, October, Rio de Janeiro, Brazil.

Ministerio do Meio Ambiente, dos Recursos Hidricos e da Amazonia Legal and United Nations Development Programme (PNUD) (1997), *Diretrizes Ambientais Para o Setor Mineral*, Brasilia: MMA.

Ministerio do Meio Ambiente (1997), *A Caminho da Agenda 21 Brasileira: Principios e Ações 1992/97*, Brasilia: MMA.

Ministerio do Meio Ambiente (1998), *A Lei da Natureza: Lei de Crimes Ambientais*, Brasilia: MMA.

Mussoi, Paulo (1997), 'O campeão da poluição', *Jornal do Brasil*, Aug. 31

Oliveira, Antonio Inagê de Assis (1997), 'Observações sobre a resolução CONAMA No. 237/97, que dispõe sobre o licenciamento ambiental', mimeo, 12 January, Conselho Empresarial Brasileiro Para o Desenvolvimento Sustentável.

Sampaio, Francisco Jose Marques (1998), *Responsabilidade Civil e Reparação de Danos ao Meio Ambiente*, Rio de Janeiro: Lumen Juris.

The World Bank (1996), 'Brazil: managing environmental pollution in the state of Rio de Janeiro', *report no. 15488-BR*, August 22, Washington DC.

The World Bank (1991), 'Environmental assessment sourcebook', vols I–III, World Bank technical papers nos 139, 140 and 154, Washington DC.

Tlayie, Laura and Dan Biller (December 1994), 'Successful environmental institutions: lessons from Colombia and Curitiba, Brazil', LATEN dissemination note no. 12, Washington, DC: The World Bank.

Triana, Ernesto Sánchez and Eduardo Uribe Botero (eds) (1994), *Contaminación Industrial en Colombia*, Departamento Nacional de Planeación and Programa de Las Naciones Unidas Para el Desarrollo, Colombia.

Wiesner, Diane (1995), *EIA – The Environmental Impact Assessment Process: What it is and How to Do One*, Great Britain: Prism Press.

7. Setting goals, making decisions, and assessing outcomes in conservation programs administered by the US Department of Agriculture

Peter F. Smith

7.1   INTRODUCTION

This chapter focuses on the activities of the Natural Resources Conservation Service (NRCS), an agency of the US Department of Agriculture. NRCS has about 12 000 employees in some 2600 locations across the country. NRCS stresses partnerships with other units of government and the private sector as it helps land users conserve and enhance natural resources. Soil and Water Conservation Districts, which are locally led governmental institutions organized under state law, operate in nearly all the 3000 counties in the US. They provide another 8000 staff years of effort to further conservation and are key partners to NRCS.

NRCS provides assistance in natural resource enhancement to private landowners and units of government. It is primarily a technical agency, providing advice and conservation expertise in a wide range of disciplines including engineering, agronomy, wildlife biology and economics. It emphasizes an integrated natural resources planning approach based on ecosystems. In addition to its technical activities, NRCS administers financial assistance programs to provide incentives to farmers to adopt conservation systems. It also provides technical support for financial incentive programs administered by other federal and state and local governments.

About 75 percent of the land in the US, excluding Alaska, is owned privately or by state and local governments, and these owners have the responsibility for conservation on their land. The remainder is owned by the federal government. Non-federal land comprises about 570 million hectares. The largest land uses are rangeland, 158 million hectares; forestland, 154 million hectares; cropland 146 million hectares; and pastureland, 42 million hectares.

In order to have a clear understanding of outcomes assessment, it is necessary to start with a common understanding of some terms. 'Outcomes' are results, they are the 'ends' or the ultimate objectives of an activity. Improved recreational fishing is an outcome. 'Outputs' are 'means' to an end. Increased farmer adoption of nutrient management plans to reduce nutrient inputs to a body of water is an output. Outputs are steps toward obtaining outcomes. Historically, most US federal agencies have measured outputs, not outcomes.

Outcomes assessment is rapidly becoming a driving force in the formulation and implementation of natural resource and other policies, programs and budgets in the US. After funds are appropriated, outcomes assessment becomes a key determinant of resource allocation to address natural resource problems.

The objectives of this chapter are to describe some of the factors leading to increased emphasis on outcomes assessment; to present information on how environmental goals are set in the US; to show how goal setting and decision making are linked, with an emphasis on the Conservation Reserve Program; and to provide examples of how performance in meeting outcomes objectives can be measured.

7.1.1 The Government Performance and Results Act of 1994

Several factors are contributing to the increased emphasis on outcomes assessment. The major factor is the Government Performance and Results Act (GPRA) which was enacted in 1994. Briefly, this law requires federal agencies to specify the outcomes they will accomplish with programs and to link them to budget requests as budgets are formulated. Agencies are then held accountable for the outcomes they specified would be achieved in the budget request.

Agencies which fail to achieve the anticipated outcomes are required to explain why the outcomes were not achieved and what they will do differently in the future to achieve the outcome. It may be that the outcomes were unrealistic, and a new set will need to be developed. Ultimately, the program outcomes may be deemed impossible to achieve, or the program may be assigned to another agency to carry out.

GPRA requires federal agencies to develop a five-year strategic plan, and update it annually. The strategic plan contains the overall agency goals and objectives, outcomes which will result from achieving them, strategies for achieving the goals and objectives, and performance measures to measure progress.

7.1.2 Natural Resources Conservation Service's GPRA Goals

NRCS has two overall goals that reflect the partnership between people and the land (see the NRCS Strategic Plan). One goal deals with people and the other deals with natural resources. The two goals are intended to contribute to three broad national outcomes: sustainable, productive, and prosperous farms, ranches and communities; healthy people; and a healthy natural environment (land, water, air, wildlife, and so on).

The first goal is 'people' oriented and is intended to achieve a situation where individuals and their neighbors are working together as effective and willing stewards of the natural resources on their property and in their communities. Three objectives will support this goal:

a. Strong, effective grassroots conservation partnerships.
b. A diverse and well served customer base.
c. Science-based natural resource conservation information in the hands of private landowners and their communities.

The NRCS Strategic Plan establishes specific strategies for reaching all three of the objectives outlined above. For example, for the first objective (strong, effective grassroots conservation partnerships) the strategies include provisions to increase the training of field staff, broaden and strengthen conservation partnerships and to help achieve consensus in the locally led process through sound science, sensible economics, appropriate technology, and curent information.

Output based performance measures for these strategies include; the provision of two weeks of technical training every year to field staff who provide technical assistance; and the doubling by 2002 of financial and in-kind contributions by other federal, state, local and non-governmental organizations.

The second goal addresses natural resources: 'A healthy and productive land that sustains food and fiber production, sustains functioning watersheds and natural systems, enhances the environment, and improves urban and rural landscapes' (NCRS, 1997). The following objectives address this goal:

a. Healthy and productive cropland sustaining US agriculture and the envi ronment.
b. Healthy watersheds providing clean and abundant water supplies for people and the environment.
c. Healthy and productive grazing land sustaining US agriculture and the environment.
d. Healthy and productive wetlands sustaining watersheds and wildlife.

The NRCS Strategic Plan defines strategies to achieve all four of the objectives outlined above. For example, strategies to attain 'healthy and productive cropland' include the promotion of conservation planning and management approaches that improve soil quality, the intensification of conservation on cropland that is not highly erodible, the facilitation of a transition to sustainable systems on cropland that is highly erodible.

Outcome based performance measures for these strategies are based on improvements from 1992 levels by the year 2002. Objectives include reducing, by one-third, the acreage of non-highly erodible cropand that experiences erosion greater than T (the soil loss tolerance rate), a similar reduction for non-highly erodible land that is experiencing soil loss greater than 2T, and the incorporation of 50 percent of all US croplands into management plans that include conservation systems that enhance soil quality.

7.2   SETTING GOALS

7.2.1   Some Basics

In the US, environmental goals and policies are articulated in several ways at several levels of government. Legislation provides the most important and powerful means. Legislation originates in the legislative branch and requires approval by the executive branch. It is subject to judicial review and enforcement. Major natural resource issues such as air and water quality, pesticide safety, wetlands protection and endangered species are addressed through legislation at the national and state and sometimes the local level.

Presidential executive orders are policy statements of the Executive Branch which articulate goals for the behavior of federal agencies in the context of present legislation. They are used to direct federal agencies to emphasize certain priorities. For example, in the 1970s an executive order was issued to direct federal agencies to protect wetlands in carrying out federal programs. Similarly, an executive order directs federal agencies to purchase goods and services from firms which are in compliance with environmental laws and regulations. State governors issue executive orders setting policy to guide the behavior of state agencies.

7.2.2   Some Technical Aspects

In total, the NRCS strategic plan contains eight goals with supporting information similar to that provided for the 'healthy and productive cropland' example described above. Setting goals requires baseline data and information on resource conditions as well as the ability to measure or model resource conditions in the future to measure results of activities.

Several data sources serve as a foundation for setting conservation goals. A key data series is NRCS's own National Resources Inventory (NRI) which collects data on natural resource conditions every five years on a scientific sample of 800 000 points across the country. The first NRI was completed in 1982 and we are in the process of analyzing the 1997 data. Each of the points was visited during the 1982 NRI and a subsample is visited during successive inventories. Most data collection today is through the interpretation of aerial photographs and satellite images. The NRI is most useful in understanding land use changes, changes in plant and water cover and soil erosion. The NRI is especially powerful because of the other data layers that can be used in its interpretation, such as soil survey information. For example, we are able to determine: if the land most suitable for crops is being cropped; the potential to increase cropland; and marginal areas which may be suitable for conversion from cropland to other uses.

The NRI will also be the primary database used to measure our performance in reducing erosion as outlined above. Other key data sources are the US Census of Agriculture and of Population; and water and air quality information collected by the US Environmental Protection Agency (EPA), US Geological Survey (USGS) and state agencies.

7.2.3   Public Preferences at the Local Level

NRCS emphasizes a 'bottom-up' approach to setting conservation goals. NRCS staff facilitate and provide natural resource and program information to local people through a 'locally led process.' Soil and Water Conservation Districts lead the process and involve a broad range of local, state and federal agencies and the private sector, as well as the public. The process reveals local natural resource problems and sources of assistance to address them from all sources, not just the USDA. An example of a locally led goal could be improved water quality such that a local water body supports recreation. The process would then identify possible approaches to address the problem, which may include erosion control assistance from the NRCS or grants from EPA to improve riparian habitat.

In fact, the goals in the NRCS strategic plan were developed through a locally led process. The local goals were then assembled at the state and regional levels into a national strategic plan which includes local, state, regional and national goals.

7.2.4   Public Preferences at the National Level

Local goal setting takes place in a framework of national (and state) preferences as contained in national (and state) legislation. The focus here is on national legislation. Since NRCS is a federal agency, its policies and programs implement this legislation. Goals applying to agriculture and its performance in protecting natural resources arise in both agricultural and nonagricultural legislation.

Important goals for agriculture are also set in laws administered by the US Environmental Protection Agency (EPA) and the US Department of the Interior

(DOI). For example, EPA administers the Clean Water Act. This law has a goal of attaining water of sufficient quality to support fishing and swimming in all waters in the US. Tens of billions of dollars have been invested in controlling point sources of pollution since the 1960s and great progress has been made in cleaning up pollution from them. A remaining source of water pollution is from nonpoint sources and agriculture is a significant contributor to this problem. A major Clean Water Initiative was announced by the President in February 1998 to address nonpoint sources involving EPA, the USDA , other federal agencies and the states. Many agricultural natural resource conservation programs are important water quality improvement tools and are being focused toward addressing water quality problems. This approach is consistent with a key theme of the Clean Water Initiative, to make the programs operated by different agencies work together to attain water quality improvement outcomes.

Another example is the Endangered Species Act, which is administered by DOI. This law protects threatened and endangered species and their habitats. Some state laws also protect endangered species within a state. Since agriculture is the dominant land use in the US, the great majority of endangered species live at least part of their life cycle on or near farmland, including range land and woodland. Endangered species protection, a national goal, has become a desired outcome for locally led conservation efforts.

7.2.5   Conflict Resolution

Goals set at the local level through a 'bottom-up process' are not always consistent with 'top-down' national goals. Resolution occurs through a planning process in which many interests are brought to the table, usually by a local conservation district. All conflicts may not be resolved but participation and a better understanding of where differences exist often leads to compromise situations. NRCS plays a key role in facilitating a broad base of participation.

7.3   MAKING DECISIONS

Decision making in USDA conservation programs is aimed at meeting goals and achieving outcomes. With the desired outcomes in mind, criteria are established for choosing among alternative means to attain them. In many situations, decision making criteria are established to avoid damage to natural resources, such as endangered species or wetlands. Using natural resource values to place constraints on behavior has been a traditional approach.

Two fairly new conservation programs reverse this traditional approach. The Conservation Reserve Program (CRP) and the Environmental Quality Incentives Program (EQIP) are designed so that decisions are made to benefit important resources rather than to minimize damage to them. They are positive resource conservation programs. In fact, the criteria used in decision making are really used for *ex ante* performance evaluation. This section examines the CRP and how resource protection criteria in the CRP are used to reach desired outcomes.

7.3.1 The Conservation Reserve Program

The CRP is an environmentally based land retirement program which was authorized by the 1985 Food Security Act. Through the CRP, landowners enter into 10 year rental agreements with the federal government to convert cropland to a conserving use (15 years for land converted to trees). The annual cost of the CRP is about US$2 billion. Up to 15 million hectares of land can be taken out of production through the CRP. Presently, there are about 12.5 million hectares enrolled in the CRP. Over the 12 year life of the CRP, it has evolved from an erosion control and production adjustment program to an environmental outcome (performance) resources conservation program.

Landowners compete for CRP contracts in order to obtain the 10 year rental payments. The competition is based on the environmental benefits which will be produced by a contract and the rental rate the landowner is willing to accept for the contract. An Environmental Benefits Index (EBI) is used to determine environmental benefits. USDA has been directed by Congress to maximize environmental benefits per dollar spent and the EBI and the rental rate are used to make that determination.

USDA has established and follows an analytical process through which the EBI scores and rental rate offers from a specific sign up (or round of bidding which occurs during a specified period of time) are compared with each other and with EBI scores developed for all eligible land that, in the long run, would be likely to bid in to the CRP. The 'likely to bid' analysis finds the highest EBI scores that are possible within the 15 million hectare legal program limit. The combination of the competitive bidding process, the environmental scores of the offers submitted, and the long run likely to bid analysis are key factors which are used in CRP decision making to insure that environmental benefits per dollar spent are maximized.

The EBI embodies the key variables and their weights which form a basis for measuring the environmental performance of the CRP. The EBI is reviewed and modified if necessary on a continuing basis. The EBI used for the sixteenth signup, which took place in 1998, is discussed below.

The formula for the EBI involves summing point values for six environmental factors and a cost factor. The total number of points obtained is used to choose among contract offers. The variables in the formula and the points associated with them are the basis for performance and outcome measures for the CRP.

7.3.1 The Wildlife Factor (N1) Maximum Weight = 100 Points

This factor evaluates the expected wildlife benefits of the offer. It is composed of six subfactors which determine the quality of the wildlife habitat to be produced and the improvements expected over the existing situation for wildlife habitat on the land in question. The following formula is used to calculate the wildlife factor:

$$N1 = (N1a/50) \times (N1a+N1b+N1c+N1d+N1e+N1f) \qquad (7.1)$$

The subfactors are:

1. Wildlife cover benefits

(N1a): 0 to 50 points. This subfactor evaluates the cover existing or to be established on the offered land. It is the most critical factor impacting wildlife benefits. Planting mixtures are assigned points based on their wildlife conservation benefits with the better cover types being awarded the highest scores. For example, planting of one or two species of an introduced grass species is worth 10 points. Planting a mixed stand (minimum four species) of at least three native grasses and at least one shrub, forb, or legume best suited for wildlife in an area or any native prairie restoration mix of 5 or more species is worth 50 points.

2. Endangered species

(N1b): 0 to 15 points. This factor rewards landowners for furthering a desired outcome: endangered species protection. Zero points are awarded where no listed or candidate species is benefited and 15 where the cover provides habitat best suited to a listed or candidate species.

3. Proximity to water

(N1c): 0 to 15 points. Easy access to water increases the value of wildlife habitat. Fifteen points are assigned if the land is within 0.25 miles from a permanent water body and 0 points if it is more than a mile from such a water body.

4. Adjacent protected areas

(N1d): 0 to 15 points. Land in the CRP has greater wildlife habitat value if it is adjacent to areas managed by federal or state governments or other entities to benefit wildlife. Land within 0.25 miles of such an area receives 15 points and 0 if it is more than a mile from such an area.

5. Contract size

(N1e): 0, 2, or 5 points. In general, larger contiguous blocks of habitat provide greater benefits than smaller areas. Points are awarded based on how the offer relates to the average size of a contract within a state.

6.   Restored wetland to upland percentage
(N1f): 0, 1, 5, or 10 points. This factor rewards those offers which restore wetlands as well as uplands. Offers with the appropriate percentage of restored wetlands relative to uplands to provide optimum nesting habitat for waterfowl receive maximum points.

7.3.2   The Water Quality Factor (N2) – 0 to 100 Points

Improving water quality is a high priority national goal in the US. This factor evaluates the potential impacts that CRP may have on both surface and ground water quality. It includes four subfactors.

1.   Location points
(N2a). This subfactor incorporates state designations of water areas requiring water quality improvement. Offers with more than 51 per cent of the area in a designated water quality area receive 30 points.

2.   Ground water quality benefits
(N2b). This factor evaluates the leachability of soils for pesticides and nutrients. Point scores are based on the soils offered for enrollment into the program.

3.   Surface water quality benefits
(N2c). This factor evaluates the amount of sediment that may be delivered into streams or other water bodies and the population that may be impacted. Points are awarded on a site-specific basis and are determined by inherent water erosion, distance to the water resource, and the county in which the offer is located.

4.   Wetland benefits points
(N2d). This factor evaluates the water quality improvements associated with wetlands. If 10 percent or more of the offer is cropped wetlands, 10 points are added.

7.3.3   The Erosion Factor (N3) – 0 to 100 Points

Traditional erosion has been addressed by the CRP program. It is the only truly on-site factor considered in the EBI and is intended to help maintain the long-term productivity of the land for future generations. An original concept about the CRP was that it would be an option for farmers who farmed highly erodible land which could not be farmed and still meet conservation compliance requirements. The erosion factor is based on the inherent potential erodibility of the land using the Erodibility Index (EI). A weighted average EI is calculated for each offer.

7.3.4   The Enduring Benefits Factor (N4) – 0 to 50 Points

This factor awards points to offers where the conservation measures installed are likely to remain in place beyond the contract period. Applicants may increase their score by offering practices likely to remain in place after contract expiration. For example, new hardwood tree plantings are awarded 50 points while native grass seeding is awarded 10 points.

7.3.5   Air Quality Benefits from Reduced Wind Erosion (N5) – 0 to 35 Points

This factor also awards points for addressing off-site damages. It is composed of the sum of three subfactors:

1.   Wind erosion impacts
(N5a): 0–25 points. Points are assigned based on the potential wind erosion and the size of the human population impacted. Land with towns and cities downwind is assigned higher point values.

2.   Wind erosion soils list
(N5b): 0–5 points. Point values are assigned on the basis of a list of soils that are susceptible to wind erosion and contribute significantly to non-attainment of air quality standards. These soils have a dominant component of volcanic or organic material. If at least 51 percent of the soils in the offer are comprised of these soils the offer is awarded 5 points.

3.   Air quality zones
(N5c): 0–5 points. This factor awards 5 points to offers when at least 51 percent of the offer is located in an area contributing to non-attainment of air quality standards or impacting Class 1 air quality zones such as National Parks.

7.3.6   State or National Conservation Priority Areas (N6) – 0 to 25 Points

This factor awards points to offers which will improve resource condition in designated conservation priority areas. These include air and water quality and wildlife areas. It is a mechanism for incorporating the locally led conservation process. In order for points to be awarded, at least 51 per cent of the offer must be located in the priority area and the offer must be consistent with the goals of the priority area. The test for consistency is that at least 40 per cent of the possible points for the issue of concern in a priority area (water quality, for example) must be obtained for that issue as a rating factor.

7.3.7   Cost (N7) – Total Points are Determined after each Signup Ends

The cost factor consists of three elements. The first provides 10 points if no government cost share is requested to establish the conservation practice. The second provides one additional EBI point for every whole dollar below the maximum acceptable rental rate (MAR), not to exceed 15 points. (The MAR is a limit set on CRP rental rates in each county as determined by soil productivity.) This provides some score advantage to offerers with relatively low bids.

The third factor provides more points for eligible offers submitted for rental rates lower than the calculated maximum payment rate. The decision on how to weight this factor is made after the signup. This decision takes into account the number of acres offered and the funding available to use in the CRP as well as market and other information.

The EBI used in the CRP program provides a major example of how decisions are made to achieve conservation outcomes. It can be characterized as a 'top-down' driven program, based on overall, national resource conservation priorities (although these priorities were developed through a locally led process in the past and are generally reflected in federal legislation). In addition, CRP land is set aside from agricultural production, making the attainment of outcomes through *ex ante* decision making more certain.

7.3.8   Brief Assessment of the EBI

The EBI had many strong points. Advantages include relative ease of understanding, empirical basis, objectivity and operability at the local level. However, it also presents challenges. For example, while cost is a consideration, there is no direct inclusion of the demand for wildlife habitat for hunting at the local level. It is a process oriented system, aimed at selecting among CRP offers based on expected environmental performance. Actual outcome measures, such as reduced soil erosion and improved water quality, or simulations of them, are required to assess program effectiveness.

7.3.9   The Environmental Quality Incentives Program (EQIP)

EQIP is another major resource conservation program which differs in several respects from the CRP. It is a cost share program (about US$200 million is available annually) for the implementation of conservation practices on land that remains in production. In addition, specific resource concerns and priorities for addressing them are set at the local level within a state, regional and national context. It is more of a 'bottom-up' program since specific outcomes and weights to be assigned to them are determined at the local level. Federal funds allocated to EQIP projects are expended on the basis of maximum environmental benefits per dollar spent. Environmental benefits in EQIP are maximized through four essential elements:

1. Identification of priority areas within states in order to target assistance to areas of greatest need or benefit.
2. Identification of statewide conservation priorities such as specific systems that are needed across the state, both within and outside of priority areas.
3. Allocation of funds from the national level to the states, based on resource needs, coupled with incentives to states with high performance proposals.
4. Use of a competitive process involving an 'offer index' for individual farms or tracts seeking cost sharing or incentive assistance.

7.4   MEASURING PERFORMANCE

A key point to stress from the previous section is the importance of having a set of goals and making decisions to progress toward those goals. A number of practical performance measurement methods are used by NRCS to measure progress.

7.4.1   The Political Process

The political process is a highly effective means to measure performance. Feedback from the local level to members of Congress is a powerful mechanism for measuring customers' satisfaction with conservation programs. For the CRP for example, feedback takes several forms. First, there are landowners who are unsuccessful in bidding for contracts. They express concern about the variables used in the EBI and their weights when they fail to attain enough points to qualify for a contract. Where there is validity to their arguments, they have resulted in some modifications to the EBI to help refine and improve the EBI as a measure to judge performance.

Other feedback to the Congress comes from those who benefit from the conservation programs. These include environmental, fish and wildlife interests who generally support the programs and who provide information on improved fish and wildlife habitat and populations and their resulting success in bird watching, fishing and hunting.

Although this information is often very site specific and qualitative, it provides an important measure of performance since it can be a key factor in programmatic support in the Congress.

7.4.2   Progress Reporting System

NRCS operates a progress reporting system to help measure performance and outcomes. In the first section of this chapter, it was noted that NRCS has two overall goals in its strategic plan and they are the focus of the progress reporting system. The system is an automated record keeping system which tracks technical and financial assistance provided to landowners. For example, data on feet of terraces planned and any cost sharing arrangements are entered in the landowners' records. These data can be aggregated at different levels; local, state, regional and national.

There are many problems with this system. First, it measures outputs, not outcomes. Feet of terraces may be intended to improve water quality by keeping sediment out of water. However, measuring feet of terraces does not directly tie to water quality improvement. To move from outputs to outcomes, models which can simulate the effects of the outputs on outcomes are used.

This system does provide a basis for simulating physical and biological outcomes of the installation of conservation measures. Combined with models, knowledge of the number and location of conservation practices applied can be used to develop an understanding of their effects on factors such as soil erosion and water quality. NRCS is developing a performance measurement system to model the natural and human resource effects of conservation.

7.4.3   The National Resources Inventory (NRI)

The most effective means to measure outcomes is through monitoring of physical and biological conditions. The NRI, briefly described earlier in this chapter, is the main outcome measure used by NRCS. This nationwide monitoring program, carried out every five years, is statistically reliable at the state level and below the state level in most states. In addition, beginning in 1996, annual 'mini' NRIs were instituted to collect data with national level statistical reliability on key variables. For example, there was concern that the 1996 Farm Bill's Freedom to Farm provisions could result in farmers' abandoning some conservation practices and subsequent increases in soil erosion. The first 'mini' NRI found that this concern was not warranted.

7.4.4   Monitoring Conducted by Other Federal and State Agencies

NRCS relies on data collected by other agencies to help measure performance and outcome attainment. Other sources of data have become more important as the Congress has broadened NRCS's responsibilities to areas such as water and air quality. NRCS does not have adequate numbers of trained staff members or the technology needed to monitor outcomes in these areas.

The EPA, as the principal federal environmental regulatory agency, works with the states to monitor water quality. Every two years, states are required to report to the EPA, which in turn reports to the Congress, on the status, conditions and trends in water quality. These reports include data on the types of pollution present in waters and their sources. Because of the large geographical expanse of agricultural land use, agriculture has been identified as a key source of nonpoint source pollution. Agricultural nonpoint sources are viewed as one of the remaining significant challenges to attaining fishable and swimable waters in many areas of the US. A recent Presidential Clean Water Action Plan calls for closer cooperation among federal agencies in assessing and monitoring water quality and in taking steps to address nonpoint and point sources of pollution.

7.5. SUMMARY

This chapter has described how the GPRA of 1994, along with other forces, has driven NRCS to be more performance and outcomes oriented. Such an orientation requires that goals be set to serve as a basis of measurement. There is an emphasis on locally led conservation and locally set goals, but these must be generated in the context of regional and national requirements which may either constrain or support the locally led objectives. Goal conflicts must be resolved at the local level to attain local acceptance.

Outcome assessment requires decisions to be made that are in concert with the agreed upon goals. The EBI, used in the CRP program, is an effective framework for making and documenting decisions at the local level. The EBI includes natural resource values which the public has decided are important and provides a technically based and transparent means of evaluating them, permitting a comparison of one proposal to another.

7.6 LOOKING AHEAD TO THE FUTURE

Trends toward reduced federal budgets and taxpayer demands for value from government expenditures will continue. These trends will lead toward more emphasis on accountability and outcomes measurement. Goals will continue to be set at the local, regional and national levels with the emphasis on the local level.

NRCS is continuously reviewing and improving its tools for making decisions and assessing outcomes. We have major initiatives under way to improve the EBI and to develop a more generic 'Conservation Benefits Index' or CBI to use in applying economic logic to decision making at the farm level. The CBI will be applicable to all NRCS programs, and perhaps conservation programs carried out by other USDA agencies and other organizations. In addition to providing decision support, it will help NRCS staff to better account for the benefits of conservation work, and it will improve communications by making the information about benefits more concrete.

BIBLIOGRAPHY

The Government Performance and Results Act of 1993, Public Law 103–62, 103rd Congress of the United States, Washington, DC.

The Federal Agriculture Improvement and Reform Act of 1996, Public Law 104–127 (the 1996 Farm Bill), 104th Congress of the United States, Washington, DC.

US Department of Agriculture, Natural Resources Conservation Service (September 1997), *Strategic Plan*, http://www.nrcs.usda.gov/

US Department of Agriculture, Natural Resources Conservation Service, *National Resources Inventory, Fact Sheets*, http://www.nrcs.usda.gov/

US Department of Agriculture, Farm Service Agency, *Conservation Reserve Program Fact Sheets*, http://www.usda.gov/

8. Alternative criteria for judging the success of agro-environmental policy in the UK*

Nick Hanley and Martin Whitby

8.1 INTRODUCTION

This chapter reviews different means for assessing one particular section of UK land use policy, namely agri-environmental schemes. These schemes have become an increasingly important part of UK agricultural policy, although the spending associated with them is still dwarfed by spending on more conventional aspects of farm support. These policies have as their goal the production of environmental benefits, in return for opportunity-cost-based payments to participating farmers: an application of the 'provider gets' principle for public goods provision (Hanley et al., 1998a). We consider the evolution of these schemes, and the dominant model for their design. Alternative criteria for assessing the performance of these policies are then set out and results from appraisals noted. We concentrate in particular on the increasing use of cost-benefit analysis (CBA) in this respect. Finally, possible reforms of agri-environmental policy (AEP) are evaluated in the light of these criteria. Evaluations of AEP in other European contexts may be found elsewhere: see, for example, Dabbert et al. (1998).

8.2 TRENDS IN AGRO-ENVIRONMENTAL POLICY

In this chapter, we define as agro-environmental policy (AEP) any policy implemented by farm agencies or ministries, for which funding comes out of agricultural support budgets, and which is concerned mainly with encouraging or enforcing the production of environmental goods, as joint products with food and fibre outputs. There are now many examples of such policies within the Organisation for Economic Co-operation and Development (see OECD, 1995). In Britain, as in the European Union more widely, the late 1980s and 1990s have seen a modest and gradual reform of farm support policy under the Common

Agricultural Policy (CAP), as a shift away from output-related support, and towards area-based payments and payments for the supply of environmental goods (Billing, 1998). Area support payments now constitute the largest single component of CAP spending in the UK. Under the most recent CAP reform proposals, Agenda 2000, further incremental change is proposed, as reductions in price support for arable crops, beef and sheepmeat, with increasing use of area-based support. In the UK, this may have particularly important impacts in Less Favoured Areas (upland areas qualifying for special support measures), with movement away from headage payments discouraging excessively high stocking rates in fragile hill upland areas. Agenda 2000 also promises a 'prominent role' for environmental measures under the CAP. This change in policy direction was originally due to the budgetary pressures of surplus production and of increasing community demand for environmental quality, and more recently because of demands from the World Trade Organization (and the US government) for a reduction in trade-distorting measures.

In 1985, the EU's *Green Handbook* advocated combining environmental policies with agricultural market and income support policies to produce environmental benefits. Expression was given to these sentiments in the UK-proposed Article 19 of the 'Structures Regulation' in 1985 (797/85). Regulation 1760/87 then allowed member states to claim up to 25 percent of the compensation paid under such arrangements from the Guidance Section of FEOGA, allowing spending on environmental outputs from national agricultural budgets for the first time. In the UK, this major change was introduced by the 1986 Agriculture Act, followed swiftly by the introduction of the first major element of AEP, the Environmentally Sensitive Areas scheme, in 1987. In 1992, the EU 5th Action Programme on the Environment set as a priority 'the establishment of a sustainable and environmentally-friendly agriculture'. Also in 1992, the increasing budgetary costs of the CAP, pressure from the Uruguay round negotiations and the promise of even bigger budgetary pressures from EU enlargement, led to reductions (of up to 30 percent) in the level of price support, the introduction of area payments and the use of compulsory set-aside.

'Accompanying measures' to these reforms included the Agri-Environmental Regulation 2078/92, which encouraged the much wider use of AEP throughout the EU. The standard model put forward was one of a contractual agreement between farmers and the state in return for environmental service provision. Regulation 2078/92 leaves the details of actual policy design up to individual member states, under the subsidiarity principle. In Britain, this led to the introduction of a large number of schemes (detailed below), all based on largely the same design principle: that of voluntary co-operation in return for payments. Increases in spending on AEP in the UK can be seen by total spending or by spending on individual schemes. Total spending, which includes payments to farmers, operating costs and monitoring costs, has increased from £33 million in 1992–3 to £86 million in 1996–7 (Agriculture Committee, 1997). For the largest single scheme (Environmentally Sensitive Areas), spending in England has risen from £2.9m in 1987–8 to £33m in 1996–7 (see Figure 8.1), while in Scotland it has increased from £57 807 to £3.76m over the same period. Despite this, for the UK as a whole, spending on AEP is still a very small percentage of total spending on agricultural support: for example, in 1995–6 it accounted for only 2.5 percent of the total £2857 million CAP spending in the UK. In the EU as a whole, spending on AEP was 1.4 billion ECUs in 1996, which was about 3 percent of total CAP spending of 41.2 billion ECUs in the same year. Regulation 2078/92 allows for a 50 percent refund of AEP spending to member states, rising to 75 percent in Objective One areas. For the UK the Fontainebleau settlement of 1983 means that the EU contribution is less, at around 17 percent of the total costs of the schemes.

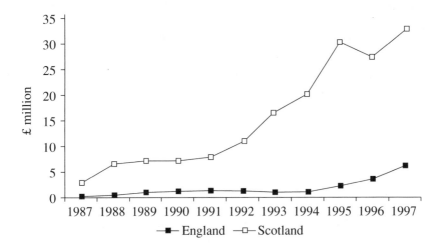

Figure 8.1   *Spending on ESAs*

8.3   AGRO-ENVIRONMENTAL POLICY IN THE UK

In the UK, the environmental goods which have been targeted by AEP are predominantly wildlife habitat and landscape quality (of course, these are jointly produced). There is much less emphasis on the control of non-point source pollution from farming than in the US, the Netherlands or Denmark. This may be due to the focus of public concerns regarding farming's impact on the countryside (for example over issues such as hedgerow loss and declines in farmland birds: see Figure 8.2); and to the fact that farm-sourced non-point pollution is not viewed as a particularly serious problem in most areas of the UK. All of the habitats covered by the AEP are semi-natural, in that some degree of human intervention/management is necessary to keep them in a 'most desired' condition. For example, heather moorland requires a particular grazing and heather management pattern to remain as such, and not revert to either scrub woodland or rough grazing. Again, this is rather different from the wilderness concept of nature in, say, the western US.

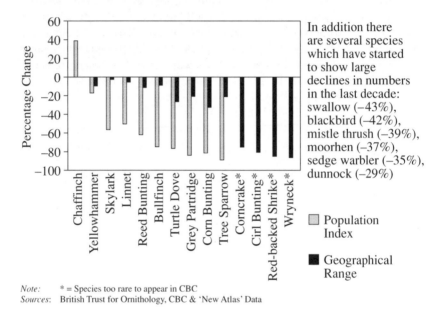

In addition there are several species which have started to show large declines in numbers in the last decade: swallow (−43%), blackbird (−42%), mistle thrush (−39%), moorhen (−37%), sedge warbler (−35%), dunnock (−29%)

Note: * = Species too rare to appear in CBC
Sources: British Trust for Ornithology, CBC & 'New Atlas' Data

*Figure 8.2   Changes in UK farmland bird population numbers, 1969–94,
                range 1968–91*

The schemes so far implemented in the UK include:

*   Environmentally Sensitive Areas;
*   Countryside Stewardship;
*   Nitrate Sensitive Areas and Nitrate Vulnerable Zones;
*   Organic Aid;
*   Habitats;
*   Countryside Access;
*   Moorland;
*   Arable Incentive; and
*   Scottish Countryside Premium (which supersedes Habitats, Heather Moorland and Set-Aside Access in Scotland).

We now outline the key features of four of the schemes listed above. For a more comprehensive review, see Hanley et al. (1999).

8.3.1   Environmentally Sensitive Areas Scheme

* Primary benefits: wildlife conservation; landscape effects
* Secondary benefits: water quality; recreation; archaeological benefits

Environmentally sensitive areas (ESAs) are designated in areas of national significance, where the conservation of wildlife and landscape depend on particular farm practices which are changing, or are likely to change, in a way which would damage this interest. There are now 43 ESAs in the UK, covering an area of 3 362 633 ha. The total area entered under contract in 1997 accounted for 1 152 554 ha (34 percent of the total)[1] and 14 843 farmers. ESAs cover a wide range of habitat/landscape types, including hay meadows, wet grasslands, lowland heath, chalk downland and heather moorland. Payment rates are aimed at two objectives: preventing a loss of conservation interest (Tier One); and enhancing and expanding conservation interest (Tier Two and above). The primary benefits generated by the scheme are wildlife and landscape conservation. These accrue to visitors, residents (both are use values) and the general public (non-use values). Secondary benefits comprise the protection/enhancement of certain lower-grade archaeological sites; and possible water quality improvements (for example, in river valley grassland management, due to less fertilizer/pesticide use and the creation of buffer strips). In addition, there may be benefits in terms of enhanced recreation opportunities and rural employment.

8.3.2   Countryside Stewardship Scheme

* Primary benefits: wildlife; landscape
* Secondary benefits: archaeological sites; recreation (access)

The Countryside Stewardship scheme (CS) has developed into the main agro-environmental policy instrument outside of ESAs, as it applies to the 'wider countryside'. Its objectives are to improve and protect wildlife habitat and landscape beauty, and to improve access. A large number of eligible habitat/landscape types are specified, for example, lowland heath and limestone grasslands. Restoration of old farm buildings using 'appropriate' methods and materials is also allowable. Standard per hectare payment rates are offered, which may be either ongoing (per annum) or one-off (capital items). The Ministry of Agriculture, Fisheries, and Food (MAFF) took over administration of the scheme in 1996, by which time 5312 agreements covering 96 913 ha of land and 3640 km of hedgerow restoration had been signed. The CS thus both safeguards existing environmental quality on eligible land, and allows for expansion and enhancement of safeguarded habitats/other sites. Primary benefits are in terms of wildlife protection and landscape quality; secondary benefits are in terms of archaeological site protection, and recreation. Applications to enrol in the CS scheme are currently assessed by a points scoring system within MAFF, since the scheme is over-subscribed.

### 8.3.3	Nitrate Sensitive Areas Scheme and Nitrate Vulnerable Zones

- Primary benefits: (human health effects); water quality improvements
- Secondary benefits: habitat protection, landscape protection

There are 32 Nitrate Sensitive Areas (NSAs) in the UK. By 1996, 24 000 ha were enrolled in the scheme, involving 410 farmers. The NSA and NVZ schemes are motivated by legal requirements under the EU directive (91/976) to prevent nitrate pollution in sensitive areas. The primary benefits of the schemes are thus to reduce nitrate levels in drinking water; and potentially, to reduce eutrophication damages where nitrate is the limiting nutrient. In general, nitrate-limited eutrophication is more likely in marine waters than in fresh waters, where phosphate is typically the limiting nutrient (for example, Loch Leven in Fife), although some examples of nitrate-related eutrophication exist in the UK (such as the River Ythan). The primary benefit of the NSA scheme is thus to reduce risks to human health. Secondary benefits relate to reduced eutrophication. It may be that there are non-use benefits from less nitrates being present in water courses; this was found in a study in Sweden by Silvander and Drake (1991). Furthermore, since run-off of organic fertilizers (manure) is an important source of biological oxygen demand, water quality benefits in terms of higher dissolved oxygen levels may be a by-product of the scheme. Another secondary benefit of the NSA scheme relates to some of the management requirements on farmers who join the scheme, which will generate landscape and conservation benefits. For example, farmers must agree to protect hedges and field trees. Some 68 Nitrogen Vulnerable Zones (NVZs) have been designated in England and Wales, covering 600 000 ha, and one NVZ in Scotland. The mandatory measures to be adopted in NVZs are still under discussion: NVZs constitute the only mandatory element of British AEP.

### 8.3.4	The Arable Stewardship Scheme

- Primary aim: wildlife enhancement
- Secondary aim: reduced chemicals run-off

This began operation in 1998, as a collaboration between the government, the Royal Society for the Protection of Birds, English Nature and the Game Conservancy. Farmers in two pilot areas (in Cambridgeshire and the West Midlands) are being offered payments of up to £620/ha. to reduce herbicide use, leave stubble over winter and leave land fallow, in order to encourage farmland birds.

8.4   THE DOMINANT MODEL

All the elements of AEP in the UK share a common framework, and this is the 'management agreement' model (Hodge, 1994). The implicit property rights assumption behind this is that farmers/rural land managers have the right to carry out the most profit-maximizing activity on their land, irrespective of the external costs (and benefits) of doing so. If farming in a more environmentally-sensitive manner imposes costs on farmers, then society must compensate them for these costs. Society has thus no prior property right (either legal or presumptive) to environmental outputs, but must subsidize farmers to produce them (Bromley and Hodge, 1990). This position is re-enforced by an absence of regulations to restrict/ impose environmental performance on farmers, except in a very few cases.[2]

This management agreement model has resulted in a set of policies whereby farmers are offered payments in return for environmental outputs. These payments may be uniform across the country (as with Countryside Stewardship); uniform or tiered within certain areas (as with the ESA scheme), but varying across these areas; or individually negotiated (as with management agreements under the Wildlife and Countryside Act). Required environmental outputs may be either uniform or variable, and may operate throughout the country (as in the Organic Aid scheme) or in designated areas only (as in the Nitrate Sensitive Areas scheme). Participation in such schemes is always voluntary, and is not required to qualify for other support payments (that is, no cross-compliance requirements are in place). Finally, management agreements may either be offered to prevent a deterioration of environmental quality below the current baseline (as in Tier One payments in ESAs), or to secure an improvement in quality or quantity terms over the current baseline.

As with any policy which arranges the transfer of property rights, these activities involve transactions costs which must either be borne by the state or by the individuals/agencies making the transfer. Obviously, heavy transaction costs of negotiating will, if imposed on landowners, serve as a substantial deterrent to entering schemes. This leaves policy makers with a choice, either they must compensate landowners for these costs or they must take steps to minimize them. In practice both expedients are found. In agreements made under Regulation 2078/92 the compensation paid to landowners and farmers is generally sufficient to cover their costs of making agreements, while under the Wildlife and Countryside Act arrangements in Sites of Special Scientific Interest and earlier arrangements, the state undertakes to reimburse contractees for these costs. If this is not done then either the rate of response to policies will be lower than desired or the provision of public goods in the countryside will become dependent on the altruism of landowners.

Two broad classes of criteria for assessment of policy that seem appropriate for AEP are (i) efficiency and (ii) effectiveness-based. Efficiency measures include cost-benefit analysis (CBA) and cost-effectiveness analysis (CEA). The use of CBA is discussed in detail in Section 8.6. CEA (that is, the calculation of the costs of meeting a pre-defined target) seems to have been little used, although the potential usefulness of CEA in a land-use context has been shown in a recent study of native pinewoods regeneration by MacMillan et al. (1998). We now consider different measures of effectiveness.

8.5   EFFECTIVENESS MEASURES

Policy effectiveness has been judged on two grounds: participation and ecological outcomes. Participation-based approaches have dominated appraisal of AEP in the UK. Measures include farmer sign up rates (percentage of qualifying farmers entering into the scheme), and area participation (percentage of eligible area entered into a scheme). Table 8.1 gives some details on these participation measures for selected AEPs. However, the fact that many habitats are affected by more than one scheme makes such scheme-related participation measures of limited usefulness, and suggests the need for habitat-based measures. These could relate the area of habitat safeguarded under all AEP schemes with the national area of that habitat. Some 28 percent of neutral grasslands are included within designated ESAs, for example, whilst only 1 percent (2973 ha) of the total area of moorland (510 000) is included (Stewart et al., 1997). Moorland is also protected under Countryside Stewardship (18 587 ha) and under the Moorlands Scheme (10 505 ha), but this still leaves the great majority of this habitat unprotected.

Participation approaches are rather indirect measures of the effectiveness of schemes, where the ultimate objective is improvement in environmental conditions, since they measure promised changes in management actions rather than the consequences of actual changes in actions. It is, after all, perfectly possible to explain high participation rates in terms of the generosity of payment rates alone. Moreover, given the uniform payment rates offered, those farmers with the lowest opportunity cost of entering could be expected to do so first. There is no control over whether these farmers provide below-average environmental benefits (indeed, they might well be farmers who can meet the conditions of the management agreement at no extra cost, implying they receive payments for doing nothing).

Table 8.1   Examples of participation rate measures of scheme success

Scheme	Area entered	Farmers entered	Total 'eligible' area	Area entered as proportion of total area (%)
ESAs: all English	446 330		1 149 902	48
West Penwith	6 312	199	6 914	91
Clun	40 397	950	50 500	80
Pennine Dales	15 728	801	24 000	65
Somerset levels	14 996	995	25 900	58
South Downs	11 264	245	51 700	22
Breckland	5 659	129	51 600	11
Countryside stewardship	92 585	5284	–	–
Habitats scheme	5 100	301	–	–
Moorland scheme (E)	9 026	15	510 000	1
Organic aid scheme	4 673	101	All farmed area	
Nitrate sensitive areas: all	19 611		35 089	56
N Lincs	5 836	45	8 568	68
Aswarby	1 777	29	2 169	82
Hopwas	15	3	174	9
Broughton	258	8	1 407	18

Ecological measures offer a more direct means of assessing policy effectiveness. Such measures are aimed at measuring the ecological performance of schemes, and comparing this with either expected change or baseline conditions. They thus relate to environmental outputs rather than management inputs. Expected changes can be predicted, for example, using vegetation succession models based on the NVC system to predict the number and type of plant communities observed. More direct measuring of changes in the ecological condition of land could also relate to changes in the pressures on environmental systems, such as where reductions in grazing levels are important, as in the case of the Heather Moorlands scheme.

Direct ecological measures of policy impact have been extensive. The largest programme of evaluation has been concerned with ESAs. In England, for example, ecological appraisals take place for each ESA every five years, as part of a formal review process. The 1996–7 round of evaluations found that:

- In the South Downs ESA, landscape quality has been enhanced due to reversion from arable land to grassland.
- Declines in meadow diversity have been halted, and in some cases reversed, in the Pennine Dales.
- Bird numbers have increased in the Somerset Levels and Moors ESA, compared with a situation of rapid decline prior to the policy being introduced.
- However, land outside the ESA boundary and on non-agreement land has experienced intensification in the Somerset levels and Pennine Dales.[3]

The process of identifying ecological improvements in this way is complicated by boundary revisions to ESA: for example, the Pennine Dales ESA trebled in size after redesignation. Consistent, long-term ecological time-series data may thus be unavailable, whilst improvements in some cases have been patchy. It is also the case that in some ESAs, the direction of change in landscape features has been the same for both participating and non-participating farms, implying that environmental change has not been caused by the ESA. In addition, it is possible to find reports of desirable environmental features declining in both participating and non-participating farms. Examples of both these phenomena are reported for the Somerset Levels and Moors ESA (MAFF, 1991; ADAS, 1996).

Monitoring of Nitrate Sensitive Areas has concentrated on measuring nitrate levels in drain waters of fields entered into the scheme, and comparing these with pre-scheme levels. Groundwater surveys have also been undertaken, although the long length of percolation times means effects are delayed here. In surveys over three winters following the introduction of the NSA scheme, the Agricultural Development and Advisory Service (ADAS) found that NO_3 concentrations had been significantly reduced by the planting of cover crops and by conversion from arable to grassland. Reductions in leaching under cereals were much lower. In the ten NSAs monitored, four areas now complied with the EU 50 mg/l limit, and two more were within 10 percent of compliance. Computer modelling of predicted changes in N in soil water is also undertaken, using survey results from participating and non-participating farms.

A monitoring exercise of the Countryside Stewardship scheme surveyed 120 farms prior to entry in 1991–2, and then re-surveyed them two years later. Ninety-one percent of these farms showed environmental improvements on at least one criterion over this period, with many improving on more than one criterion (for example, wildlife and access). Of the other 11 sites, three showed no change and eight showed damages. A biological monitoring strategy is in place for all three habitats covered by the Habitats scheme, comprising a baseline survey in 1995 (before any farms entered the scheme) and further surveys in 1997–8 and 1998–9. Similar monitoring work has been commissioned for the (Heather) Moorland scheme.

However, it is worthwhile noting that monitoring costs may well be higher for ecological measures in general, compared with participation measures. The overall monitoring costs of the ESA programme in 1992–3 were estimated at £3.6 m, or 16 percent of total scheme costs; this figure had fallen to 5 percent of total scheme costs of £39m in 1996–7 (Whitby et al., 1998). For all AEP schemes under regulation 2078/92, monitoring costs fell from 12.5 percent of the total costs in 1992–3 to 7.5 percent in 1995–6. Whitby et al. (1998) speculate that this fall (which was accompanied by a similar fall in running costs, but an increase in payments to farmers) is due to relatively high transaction costs in the early years of a new policy initiative, which decrease as agents get more familiar with the policy and as institutions (such as standard contracts and self-reporting) are established which reduce these transaction costs.

It should also be noted that not all environmental effects attributed to individual schemes may be additional, in the sense that they would not have resulted in the absence of the policy initiative. Ensuring that environmental outputs pass this additionality test is clearly important, since otherwise farmers are being paid for a zero environmental gain, but this does involve identifying what would have happened in the absence of the policy being appraised. This alternative state of the world may be quite different to the current situation, due to the dynamic nature of the system. Ecological measures may also fail as an indicator of long-term change, since the time period over which such data is available is very limited. Participation rates might fare better in this regard.

A further problem with cost-effectiveness measures is that there may very easily be long delays in the appearance of intended beneficial policy outcomes. Many ecological processes may require decades to reach a desired state and it is possible that policy contracts will never produce the desired result in some cases. Yet the contracts used in AEP are typically for ten years (in rare cases for 20 years) and there is virtually no constraint on the farmers' behaviour after the end of the contract. Once the contract has ended the farmer may freely revert to any set of agricultural practices even if they destroy all the accumulated benefit of several years of conformity with a contract to produce environmental goods. Most of these contracts will ensure the accumulation of natural capital at the taxpayers' expense. It is arguable that society may claim some rights over the disposal at the end of contracts, though this is not easy to provide without discouraging farmers from taking up contracts (Whitby et al., 1996).

It is also interesting to note that an opportunity lost in the individual farmer contract-based approach is that of influencing strategic land management over substantial areas. By emphasizing individual contracts we lose the possibility of managing whole blocks of land in an ecologically homogeneous way – for example, to produce wildlife corridors or improve catchment performance. This idea, which comes from MacFarlane and Smith (1997), has been proposed for the Lake District ESA, an ESA which virtually coincides with the National Park designation, where a landscape-scale approach has obvious advantages. Finally, we note that neither of the effectiveness measures address the issue of whether, from a society's point of view, the costs of AEP are justified by the benefits.

8.6   EFFICIENCY AS A CRITERION: COST-BENEFIT ANALYSIS OF AGRI-ENVIRONMENTAL SCHEMES

In the UK, the use of cost-benefit analysis (CBA) in the appraisal of policies which impact on the environment has become more widespread within government departments and agencies. A particular spur for this trend was the publication in 1991 of the Department of the Environment's *Policy Appraisal and the Environment* (DoE, 1991). Government departments principally responsible for AEP have made increasing use of the CBA approach, especially in terms of commissioning studies to estimate the monetary value of the environmental benefits, with particular focus on ESAs. These studies have all been carried out *ex post*, and may have been used to justify government action already undertaken for reasons other than producing a potential Pareto improvement. Nevertheless, results have been interesting.

8.6.1   Types of Benefit, and Applicable Benefit Measurement Methods

In summary, the AEP schemes discussed above are designed to deliver the following types of benefits:

* Protection and/or enhancement of wildlife habitats will generate both use and non-use values in terms of direct utility effects, but will also generate biodiversity protection benefits which are additional to these (for example, in terms of ecosystem resilience).
* Protection/enhancement of landscape quality again may be expected to generate use and non-use benefits in terms of direct utility impacts, although it could be assumed that non-use values will account for a smaller percentage of total economic value than use values for landscape relative to wildlife.
* Protection/enhancement of water quality due to lower pesticide use/run-off, and lower or better managed fertilizer and manure use could possibly generate both use and non-use values.
* Protection/enhancement of minor (unscheduled) archaeological and historical sites, may possibly generate both use and non-use values.

- Enhanced access possibilities is clearly a direct use, rather than non-use, value, although a positive option value may also exist for preserving the option of future access.

8.6.2   Evidence from Empirical Studies

Stewart et al. (1997) have summarized results from existing studies of environmental benefits for AEP. As mentioned above, ESA valuation has dominated, with very little work being done on other schemes. The Contingent Valuation Method (CVM) has been used in all the studies reported except one (Foster and Mourato, 1997). CVM is a survey-based method which directly elicits preferences for environmental goods from individuals (see Hanley and Spash, 1994) for a description of the method). Comparison of results across the studies is complicated by a diversity of survey designs (for example, between open-ended and dichotomous choice designs) and beneficiary categories (between, for example, residents, visitors and the general public). Table 8.2 summarizes these results; Table 8.3 shows more detail for a number of ESA studies.

As may be seen, per person values vary widely, but this is to be expected given the diverse nature of the schemes appraised. Where non-use values are included, aggregate benefit figures rapidly become very large. Aggregation is particularly difficult in the cases of the NSA and Organic Aid schemes, where benefit estimates come from studies not originally targeted at the AEP schemes themselves.[4] Table 8.2 also reports the exchequer costs for each scheme appraised, and as may be seen aggregate benefits outweigh these costs by a very large margin. Given that social costs are likely to be less than exchequer costs due to the presence of price support (see below), this conclusion would become even stronger.

Several problems may be noted in connection with the valuation results reported in Table 8.2:

1. The very large magnitude of non-use values[5] limits CBA's ability to discriminate between projects (since admitting non-use values means schemes are almost bound to pass the CBA test). This is a conundrum: we suspect non-use values exist, but including them may lead to our criterion losing its appeal.
2. No value estimates exist for a majority of schemes, including the second largest scheme, Countryside Stewardship.
3. Benefit figures are expressed as per household or per individual, whereas per hectare amounts might be more useful in many cases (for example, if consideration was being given to extending an ESA). Here the well known problem of average values being used to represent marginal values applies. Very few estimates of the marginal value of changes in AEP exist, two

Table 8.2   Cost-benefit analysis of agro-environmental schemes

Agri-environmental Scheme	Benefit estimate per person (£)	Aggregate benefits (£)	Scheme exchequer costs (£)	Net value (£)	Valuation method (£)
Mourne Mountains and Slieve Croob ESA Moss and Chilton (1997)	Not known	13 090 000	2 042 823	11 047 177	CVM
South Downs ESA Willis et al. (1993)	1.98 to 27.52	263 177 to 79 835 000	970 000	(–)707 000 to 78 865 000	CVM
Somerset Levels and Moors ESA Willis et al. (1993)	2.45 to 17.53	101 422 to 52 637 000	1 859 000	(–)1 757 000 to 50 778 000	CVM
Stewartry ESA Gourlay (1995)	3.00 to 22.56	371 840 to 1 825 268	430 000	(–)58 160 to 1 395 268	CVM
Loch Lomond ESA Gourlay (1995)	2.28 to 32.8	229 600 to 3 211 311	70 000	159 600 to 3 141 311	CVM
Breadalbane ESA Hanley et al. (1998b)	22.02 to 98	92 938 to 44 100 000	396 796	(–)206 796 to 43 703 204	CVM
Breadalbane ESA Hanley et al. (1998b)	107.55	636 050[1] to 4 841 363[2]	396 796	239 251 to 4 444 567	CE
Machair ESA Hanley et al. (1998b)	13.4 to 378	75 539 to 26 800 000	101 981	(–)26 442 to 13 298 019	CVM
Machair ESA Hanley et al. (1998b)	23.15	256 039[1] to 563 864[2]	101 981	154 058 to 461 883	CE
Norfolk Broads ESA Bateman et al. (1994)	142 to 150	Not known	1 821 300	Not known	CVM
NSA Hanley (1990)	16.17	13 506 311[3]	1 500 000	12 006 311	CVM
Organic Aid Foster and Mourato (1997)	17.59	17 060 000[4]	419 000	16 640 000	CR

CVM = contingent valuation; CE = choice experiment; CR = contingent ranking

Notes:
1. Residents only
2. Residents plus visitors
3. East Anglia only
4. Based on saving one bird species only; aggregated over RSPB members.

exceptions being the study by Moss and Chilton of the Mourne Mountains/Slieve Croob ESA in Northern Ireland; and in the case of the Farm Woodlands Scheme (Hutchison et al., 1996). Both these studies found evidence of marginal benefits diminishing in value as the area protected increased.

4. The production of environmental benefits following contractual agreement between the farmer and the government regarding promised changes in management actions is typically subject to both uncertainty and time lags. For example, the effect of reducing stocking levels on heather moorland recovery may be uncertain, and may take many years to occur at a significant level. As Hodge and McNally (1998) note, there is a problem for the researcher in knowing (i) whether land managers can meet the terms of ESA-type contracts; (ii) whether they will actually meet these terms after the contract is signed, given asymmetric information; and (iii) whether these management changes will produce the desired outcomes.

It is often not clear how CVM researchers put across these uncertainties and time lags to respondents, if at all. In the work by Hanley et al. (1998b) on Breadalbane ESA, respondents were shown photo montages of how the area would look 'at maturity' of the scheme, but no explicit mention was made in the survey materials about how long this would take, nor about how likely the changes shown were to occur.[6] This was also the case in the Garrod and Willis (1994) study of the Somerset Levels, where respondents were shown pictures of the landscape 'with' and 'without' the ESA, but

Table 8.3   Comparing contingent valuation method estimates for ESAs in the UK (WTP, £/hsld/yr)

ESA	Residents	Visitors	General public
Hanley et al., 1998b			
Breadalbane	31.43[1]	73.00[2]	22.02[1]
Machair	13.66[1]	–	13.37[1]
Willis et al., 1993			
South Downs	27.52[1]	19.47[1]	1.98[1]; 7.47[2]
Somerset levels	17.53[1]	11.84[1]	2.45[1]
Gourlay, 1996			
Loch Lomond	20.60[1]	1.98 per visit[1]	n/e
Stewartry	13.00[1]	2.53 per visit[1]	n/e
Bullock and Kay, 1997			
Southern Uplands	n/e	69.00[2]	83.00[2]

Note: 1 = open

were not told about the likelihood of the 'with' scenario actually coming about, nor about how long it would take. If benefits are actually uncertain, then households would be willing to pay less than if the outcome was certain: in this case, existing 'willingness to pay' estimates for ESAs are biased upwards.

As Hodge and McNally (1998) have pointed out, there is indeed a general problem with applying CBA to such policies, namely that of correctly identifying the counterfactual: what the landscape and wildlife interest of an area would be without the policy in place. In the Garrod and Willis (1994) study, the assumption was that without the ESA in place, agricultural intensification would continue, leading to a consistent decline in environmental quality. This is hard to predict, especially given current and likely future reforms in farm policy. However, CBA is not the only policy analysis tool to face this counterfactual problem.

5. As some areas of the country (and some habitats) are affected by more than one policy instrument, it can be difficult to disentangle the effects of, say, the ESA scheme itself distinct from management agreements on Sites of Special Scientific Interest (SSSIs). Colman et al. (1993) note that in Breckland ESA, conservation benefits may be due more to SSSI designation than to ESA designation. Hodge and McNally make a similar point for the Somerset Levels. The risk is thus that the CBA analyst ends up valuing a landscape/habitat, rather than a policy instrument, since the links between the policy instrument and the public good are complex (Bonnieux and Weaver, 1996).

6. Value estimates also appear to be scheme-specific: this is of interest with respect to benefits transfer. Whilst mixed academic support exists for the practice of benefits transfer[7] (see Bergland et al., 1995, or Downing and Ozuna, 1996), policy makers in practice must make use of benefits transfer in some form to allow environmental valuation to become part of routine policy appraisal (ENDS, 1998). The UK government had appeared to sanction a benefits transfer practice (based on adjusted mean values) for appraising the benefits of water quality improvements (FWR, 1996). However, recent legal rulings have cast doubt over the appropriate future direction of benefits transfer policy (ENDS, 1998).[8] It may be that valuation methods which more directly address the value of individual landscape/habitat attributes, such as choice experiments or Multi-Attribute Utility models, would perform better with regard to benefits transfer.

7. Finally, each of the value estimates reported in Table 8.2 were collected for each scheme in isolation. From what we know of nesting effects and part-whole bias in CVM, and more general path dependency problems in CBA, it would not be proper to add individual scheme aggregate values to produce a total 'all ESAs' or still less an 'all programme' estimate of benefits, since

willingness to pay (WTP) for all ESAs together will be less than the sum of WTPs estimated for individual ESAs.

Estimates of scheme costs are in principle more straightforward, as budgetary records are kept of payments to farmers, as well as some of the transactions costs of the scheme. In the former regard, Whitby et al. (1998) make the point that payments to farmers mis-state the opportunity costs of the schemes to society, since these costs are more correctly valued as the net value of output foregone, priced at shadow prices which exclude compensation (subsidy) amounts. These are net values since resources (such as fertilizer) are saved by not producing output, or by producing at a lower intensity, and since farmers may well switch to alternative crops. In terms of correcting for subsidy payments, Saunders (1996) shows that the social opportunity costs of lost wheat, barley, and sheepmeat outputs are 91 percent, 48 percent and 30 percent of their exchequer costs, whilst the social opportunity costs of suckler cow outputs is actually negative. Applying such figures to the whole ESA scheme in England, Whitby et al. find that the social opportunity costs of the scheme in 1994–5 (in terms of the net value of lost output) were also negative. With respect to transactions costs, Whitby et al. note that data is only available on the public sector costs of transacting AEP bargains, but that farmers will also face costs (for example, of drawing up farm plans, and negotiating entry to a scheme). From a CBA viewpoint, the value of resources used up in transacting and enforcing bargains are a relevant component of costs; Whitby et al.'s estimate of these transactions costs for UK ESAs was £8 million in 1994–5, and this is the only positive resource cost of the policy. On-going revisions to the Common Agricultural Policy are replacing price support with direct income supplements based on farm areas, and payments for agri-environmental outputs: this will move resource costs of reductions in farm output closer to farm-gate costs over time.

8.7 COMBINING MEASURES

It is perfectly feasible to combine CBA and environmental effectiveness measures to assess policy. Environmental effectiveness could be regarded as a type of sustainability measure, since it relates to physical measures of elements of the natural capital stock. CBA is an efficiency measure, and is neither a necessary nor sufficient condition for sustainability. But it does offer an (albeit imperfect) means of incorporating citizen preferences into decision-making, in a way which is generalizable (especially if the benefits transfer/adding up problems referred to above can be resolved). Citizen preferences should almost certainly contribute to decision making in many cases (Randall, 1997). In the final section of this paper, we indicate how this combined approach could be applied to three possible reforms of AEP.

8.8   ASSESSING POSSIBLE CHANGES TO AEP

In this section, we look at possible reforms to AEP (or the conditions under which it is applied), and speculate how each one would perform on both efficiency (CBA) and effectiveness criteria. We discuss CBA outcomes in terms of the likely impact on benefit/cost ratios; and refer to an ecologically-based measure of effectiveness, which picks up changes in the composition of the natural capital stock.

8.8.1   Reducing Conflicts with Production and Income Support Measures

One of the main features behind the low take-up rate in some AEP schemes is conflicts between the payments offered, and financial rewards under other aspects of the CAP. Many examples exist. Headage payments to sheep grazing, under the HLCA scheme, provide a direct counter-incentive to farmers in Moorland Scheme areas to reduce stocking rates, since each ewe taken off the hill means a loss in headage payments. Farmers might also lose quota entitlements for HLCAs by reducing stocking rates. For the Habitats scheme, Wildlife Trust figures show that a farmer entering land into the saltmarsh part of the scheme would suffer a £500 per hectare loss due to the Arable Areas payments scheme, whilst on water fringes the net loss would be around £175/ha. In the Countryside Premium scheme, the World Wildlife Fund in evidence to the Select Committee of Parliament showed that a farmer in a species rich neutral grassland area in a river valley would receive 10 times as much per ha for converting to potatoes compared with entering the scheme (Stewart et al., 1997). AEP payment rates are thus too low relative to production-related subsidies, the effect of which is to (i) depress sign-up rates and (ii) increase the apparent costs of conservation.[9]

A reduction in, for example, headage payments for ewes in upland areas would be potentially beneficial on both the criteria referred to above. If headage payments are cut, then, ceteris paribus, the minimum necessary payment for the Moorland scheme, to achieve a given reduction in stocking rate, could fall too (for empirical evidence, see Hanley et al., 1998a). If there is no change in stocking rate, environmental benefits are constant whilst scheme costs fall, implying an increase in the benefit/cost ratio. Balanced against this would be the net value, priced at shadow prices, of lost output, but as hinted at above, this amount could well be negative. Alternatively, payment rates could be maintained, which given the fall in opportunity costs would mean more farmers entering the scheme. Benefits should increase (although CVM might not be able to register this), increasing the benefit/cost ratio again. The ecological measure of effectiveness, if it is truly a measure of environmental outputs, traces impacts on the natural capital stock. In the first case, this would stay constant and in the second case increase. On both criteria, then, such a reduction in headage payments might be approved.

8.8.2   Redesigning the Transfer Mechanism

At present, farmers are offered fixed payment rates in return for a given environmental output. As many authors have noted, this over-compensates all farmers except for the marginal ones, assuming that the private costs of producing the environmental output vary across farms. A recent study by the National Audit Office (1997) concluded that there was a substantial element of over-compensation in ESA payments, although some farmers were under-compensated. An alternative design, which has been used in the US for soil conservation since 1986, and which has been recently put forward in the context of AEP by Latacz-Lohmann and Van der Hamsvoort (1997), is to auction conservation contracts. The government specifies a list of environmental outputs which it wishes to achieve. Farmers then bid for these contacts, with the lowest prices being accepted up to either the aggregate environmental target or the budget allocation.

Under a fixed-price arrangement, infra-marginal suppliers of the environmental good earn producers' surplus, or informational rents, due to the inability/unwillingness of the government to operate a perfectly differentiated payments system. Under the auction, farmers tender sealed bids stating their required minimum payments. Assume for the moment that all environmental outputs covered by the auction are homogeneous. Then, as Latacz-Lohman (1998) shows, bidding reveals the farmers' type (that is, their opportunity costs of participation), and reduces information rents. This means the cost to the government of securing a given level of environmental outputs also falls; or that, for a given budget, a greater level of environmental outputs can be bought. If environmental outputs are heterogeneous, then bids could be weighted by expected environmental benefits, but here the government would need far greater information to conclude the auction, increasing *ex ante* transactions costs.

In terms of our two criteria, then the effects depend on the budget allocation. For a fixed budget, more environmental outputs are produced at a constant exchequer cost. The value of increased environmental quality would then be compared with the net social value of any reductions in output and any net changes in transaction costs. Informational rent reductions constitute a transfer from the producer to the taxpayer. On ecological effectiveness grounds, the auction under a fixed budget delivers an increase in natural capital. If the level of environmental output is held constant, and the budget is reduced, then the effect on natural capital depends on whether the environmental output is homogeneous.

However, we should note here that problems of collusion in repeated auctions may reduce their cost-effectiveness; this seems to have been the experience in the US (Latacz-Lohmann, 1998). Moreover, there is no data on the transactions costs of auction systems.

8.8.3   Focussing on Environmental Features

Currently, many elements of AEP in the UK are focused on defined areas of the countryside, rather than defined habitats or wildlife populations. For example, the ESA scheme offers payments within a defined geographic area, within which there will be a diversity of farm types and a diversity of habitats, of variable conservation interest and variable quality. A national scheme (which would probably be an extension of the Countryside Stewardship scheme) which offered payments for target improvements in a range of specified habitats would be a more direct way of achieving environmental goals, and would permit the merging of several current schemes. It would also reduce environmental wastage in current schemes where payments may be made for increases/non-decreases in ecologically less interesting habitats (such as *Molinia-Nardus* rough grasslands). This would have the merit of assisting the UK in fulfilling its obligations under the Habitats Directive. Recent changes to the Countryside Stewardship scheme have followed in this direction, as additional habitats have been brought within its aegis. However, it would mean an end to the ESA scheme amongst others. Monitoring/reporting would then be carried out on a habitats/species basis, rather than an area uptake basis; results from monitoring could be integrated into the Countryside Information System data base, supplemented by NVC classifications as a measure of diversity/quality (Stewart et al., 1997).

In terms of our criteria, such a reform would produce uncertain effects on the value of environmental benefits, but the best guess would be that benefits would rise, since the scheme would be better targeted at what is valuable (habitats and species) rather than geographic areas. The implications for monitoring and other transaction costs are unknown, but could perhaps be inferred by comparing current data on transaction costs for Countryside Stewardship with that for ESAs.[10] It is possible that, should a uniform payment rate system be retained, then payment rates would have to rise, if for example including farms from outside ESAs increased the average opportunity cost of participation. Changes to the effectiveness measure would seem likely to be positive, since low-quality habitat (for example rough grassland within an ESA boundary) would be replaced by high-quality habitat (such as heather moorland just outside a boundary). Moving to a national scheme from the locally-based ESA scheme could increase information asymmetries, and also increase the spread of compliance costs. This might encourage a move away from standard rate payments and towards auctions or variable payment schemes.

8.9   CONCLUSIONS

Both economics and ecology have contributions to make to the assessment of AEP. Economics can address the efficiency of policy, in terms of evaluating its net social benefits through CBA, whilst ecologists can study the effectiveness of schemes in terms of environmental outputs. This can be related to measures of the natural capital stock, and thus to the concept of sustainability (defined here as a non-declining natural capital stock over time). However, there is no need to see the criteria as being mutually exclusive, but rather they are best viewed as complementary in policy assessment. This is important if both criteria are of relevance to policy-makers and to society at large.

Nevertheless, many significant problems exist with both approaches. For CBA, the issues of aggregation of non-use values, part-whole bias, benefits transfer and calibration complicate issues. The observation can also be made that if including non-use values for UK AEP benefits leads to benefits that always massively exceed costs, then this decreases both the credibility and the attractiveness of the CBA approach to decision-makers, who may perhaps prefer to use it more as a tool for ranking options (that is, only relative benefits are considered reliable). It may also be that CBA has a more useful decision-making role in terms of its ability to marshal arguments for and against a change, and if monetization of benefits and costs is avoided. Measurement of the social opportunity costs of AEP is also in its infancy, and much work remains to be done if measures of the full social costs of AEP, including transactions costs, are to be provided. Identifying the counter-factual in CBA analyses is also difficult, whilst uncertainty and time lags in the production of benefits need to be better handled. CBA is also of limited use in advising on the best design of AEP, and, as currently conducted, does not on the whole address itself to marginal changes in designation (for example, in increasing the size or changing the required management practices of an ESA).

Ecological measures of effectiveness suffer from aggregation problems, from uncertainty over outcomes (for instance, in predicting changes in floristic diversity due to changes in management practice), potentially high monitoring costs, and the difficulty of quality-weighting (that is, the comparison of areas of a given habitat type of different qualities, such as varying degrees of over-grazing in the case of heather moorland).

Proposals under Agenda 2000 will produce a further redirection of agricultural budget spending away from production and towards environmental payments and direct income support. The former will imply that AEP expands in scope and coverage in the UK and throughout the EU. We have shown how a combined assessment method which uses criteria based on both economic efficiency and strong sustainability can be used to assess proposed changes to this land use policy. However, we have also alluded to remaining problems in implementing this combined approach. Addressing these problems will become an increasingly important task for research.

NOTES

*   British usage and spelling retained where appropriate
1.   The lower figure of 2 655 515 ha is given for the 'eligible area', total sign-ups are 43 percent of this total.
2.   An example of such an exception is recent 'due care' requirements on the storage of farm wastes.
3.   In a sense, this is to be expected. Given that the costs of signing up to the ESA vary across farms, and that the payment rate is uniform, one would expect those farms not signing up to be more profitable enterprises.
4.   Although in the latter case, the study is concerned with the impact of pesticide reductions on wild birds: a recent MAFF review of the Organic Aid scheme concluded that 'the most important benefit [because it was not delivered by other farming systems] was the virtual absence of pesticides and the impact of that on biodiversity'.
5.   Non-use values are values to people who do not directly use the resource, for example by visiting it. Non-use values have proved to be a significant part of total value for many environmental resources, but are relatively problematic to estimate and interpret.
6.   For an example of a CVM study which explicitly incorporates uncertainty over environmental outcomes, see MacMillan et al., 1996.
7.   Benefits transfer refers to the practice of using estimates of environmental values gained in one context to predict environmental values in a similar, but different, context.
8.   Although in fact the objection made relates more to the size of the benefiting population for non-use values than the process of mean values adjustment.
9.   This 'inflation' of policy costs also affects forestry policy, in that planting grants have had to be raised in line with HLCA payments.
10.   In 1995–6, £2 million was spent on running costs under Countryside Stewardship, to maintain a total of 5284 agreements, implying a per-agreement cost of £378. The equivalent figures for the ESA programme were £7.463m on 7463 agreements, implying a per-agreement cost of £945 (Agriculture Committee, 1997).

REFERENCES

ADAS (1996), 'Environmental monitoring in the Somerset Levels and Moors ESA, 1987–1995', Report to MAFF, London.
Agriculture Committee (1997), *2nd Report: ESAs and Other Schemes Under the Agri-Environment Regulation*, London: HMSO.

Bateman I., K. Willis and G. Garrod (1994), 'Consistency between contingent valuation estimates: a comparison of two studies of UK national parks', *Regional Studies*, **28**(5), 457–74.

Bergland O., K. Magnussen and S. Navrud (1995), 'Benefits transfer: testing for accuracy and reliability', Discussion paper 95–03, Dept of Economics, Agricultural University of Norway.

Billing P. (1998), 'Towards sustainable agriculture: the perspectives of the Common Agricultural Policy in the EU', in S. Dabbert, A. Dubgaard, L. Slangen and M. Whitby (eds), *The Economics of Landscape and Wildlife Conservation*, Oxford: CAB International.

Bonnieux F. and R. Weaver (1996), 'Environmentally Sensitive Areas schemes: public economics and evidence', in M. Whitby (ed.), *The European Environment and CAP Reform*, Oxford: CAB International.

Bromley D. and Hodge I. (1990), 'Private property rights and presumptive policy entitlements', *European Review of Agricultural Economics*, **17**(2), 197–214.

Bullock C. and J. Kay (1997), 'Preservation and change in the upland landscape: the public benefits of grazing management', *Journal of Environmental Planning and Management*, 40, 315–44.

Colman D., J. Froud and L. O'Carroll (1993), 'The tiering of conservation policies', *Land Use Policy*, **10**(4), 281–92.

Dabbert S., A. Dubgaard, L. Slangen and M. Whitby (1998), *The Economics of Landscape and Wildlife Conservation*, Oxon: CAB International.

Department of the Environment (1991), *Policy Appraisal and the Environment*, London: HMSO.

Downing M. and T. Ozuna (1996), 'Testing the reliability of the benefit function transfer approach', *Journal of Environmental Economics and Management*, **30**, 316–22.

ENDS (1998), Environmental Data Services newsletter, March.

Foster V. and S. Mourato (1997), 'Behavioural consistency, statistical specification and validity in the contingent ranking method: evidence from a survey of the impacts of pesticide use in the UK', CSERGE working paper 97–09, University of London.

FWR (1996), *Assessing the Benefits of Surface Water Quality Improvements*, Marlow, UK: Foundation for Water Quality Research.

Garrod G. and K. Willis (1994), 'Valuing biodiversity and nature conservation at the local level', *Biodiversity and Conservation*, 3, 555–65.

Garrod G., K. Willis and C. Saunders (1994), 'The benefits and costs of the Somerset Levels and Moors ESA', *Journal of Rural Studies*, **10**(2), 131–45.

Gourlay D. (1996), 'Loch Lomond and Stewartry ESAs: a study of public perceptions of policy benefits', unpublished PhD thesis, University of Aberdeen.

Hanley N.D. (1990), 'The economics of nitrate pollution', *European Review of Agricultural Economics*, **17**, 129–51.

Hanley N. and C. Spash (1994), *Cost-Benefit Analysis and the Environment*, Cheltenham: Edward Elgar.

Hanley N., H. Kirkpatrick, D. Oglethorpe and I. Simpson (1998a), 'Principles for the provision of public goods from agriculture', *Land Economics*, **74**(1), 102–13.

Hanley N., D. MacMillan, R. Wright, C. Bullock, I. Simpson, D. Parsisson and R. Crabtree (1998b), 'Contingent valuation versus choice experiments: estimating the benefits of Environmentally Sensitive Areas in Scotland', *Journal of Agricultural Economics*, 1–15.

Hanley N., M. Whitby and I. Simpson (1999), 'Assessing the success of agri-environmental policy in the UK', *Land Use Policy*, **16**(2), 67–80.

Hodge I. (1994), 'Rural amenity: property rights and policy mechanisms,' in *The Contribution of Amenities to Rural Development*, Paris: OECD.

Hodge I. and S. McNally (1998), 'Evaluating the Environmentally Sensitive Areas: the value of rural environments and policy relevance', *Journal of Rural Studies*, **14**(3).

Hutchison, G., S. Chilton and J. Davis (1996), 'Integrating cognitive psychology into the contingent valuation method', in W. Adamowicz and W. Philips (eds), *Forestry, Economics and the Environment*, Oxford: CAB International.

Latacz-Lohmann U. and C. van der Hamsvoort (1997), 'Auctions as a means of creating a market for public goods from agriculture', *Journal of Agricultural Economics*, **49**(3), 334–45.

Latacz-Lohmann U. (1998), 'Mechanisms for the provision of public goods in the countryside', in S. Dabbert, A. Dubgaard, L. Slangen and M. Whitby (eds), *The Economics of Landscape and Wildlife Conservation*, Oxford: CAB International.

MacFarlane R. and S. Smith (1997), 'Implementing agri-environmental policy: a landscape ecology perspective', in A. Cooper and J. Power (eds), *Species Dispersal and Land-use Processes*, Coleraine: University of Ulster.

MacMillan D., N. Hanley and S. Buckland (1996), 'A contingent valuation study of uncertain environmental gains', *Scottish Journal of Political Economy*, **43**(5), 519–33.

Macmillan D.C., D. Harley and R. Morrison (1998), 'Cost-effectiveness of woodland ecosystem restoration', *Ecological Economics*, **27**(3), 313–24.

MAFF (1991), 'The Somerset Levels and Moors ESA', Draft report on monitoring. London: Ministry of Agriculture, Fisheries and Food.

Moss J. and S. Chilton (1997), 'A socio-economic evaluation of the Mourne Mountains and Slieve Croob ESAs', Belfast: Queens University, Centre for Rural Studies.

National Audit Office (1997), *Protecting Environmentally Sensitive Areas*, London: HMSO.

OECD (1995), *Amenities for Rural Development: Policy Examples*, Paris: OECD.

Randall A. (1997), 'Taking benefits and costs seriously', Paper to Landscape Valuation workshop, Agricultural University of Norway, Aas.

Saunders C. (1996), 'Financial, exchequer and social costs of changes in agricultural output', Working paper, Centre for Rural Economy, University of Newcastle-on-Tyne.

Silvander U. and L. Drake (1991), 'Nitrate pollution and fisheries protection in Sweden', in N. Hanley (ed.), *Farming and the Countryside: An Economic Analysis of External Costs and Benefits*, Oxford: CAB International.

Stewart L., N. Hanley and I. Simpson (1997), 'Economic valutation of the agri–environmental schemes in the United Kingdom', report to Ministry of Agriculture, Fisheries and Food and HM Treasury, September.

Whitby M.C., I.D. Hodge, P.D. Lowe and C.M. Saunders (1996), 'Conservation Options for CAP Reform', *ECOS*, vol. 17, no. 3/4, pp. 46–54.

Whitby M., C. Saunders and C. Ray (1998), 'The full cost of stewardship policies', in S. Dabbert, A. Dubgaard, L. Slangen and M. Whitby (eds), *The Economics of Landscape and Wildlife Conservation*, Oxford: CAB International.

Willis K., G. Garrod and C. Saunders (1993), 'Valuation of the South Downs and Somerset Levels ESAs', Centre for Rural Economy, University of Newcastle-on-Tyne.

9. The Danish pesticide programme: success or failure depending on indicator choice[*]

Alex Dubgaard

9.1 INTRODUCTION

In 1986 the Danish Government introduced a Pesticide Action Plan aiming at removing all pesticides identified as unacceptably hazardous and, in addition, reducing usage of the remaining pesticides by 50 percent. A decade later the programme seems a success: half the active ingredients previously approved for sale in Denmark are by now removed from the market, and the quantity of active ingredients applied has dropped by more than 40 percent. Nevertheless, within the large constituency of interested parties there are widely differing views regarding the extent to which the policy targets are appropriate. Pesticide manufacturers and the agricultural organizations maintain that the focus should be on removing or restricting the use of pesticides which pose documented risks to human health or the environment – and that this objective has been realized. On the other hand, environmental and consumers' organizations claim that even with the stricter registration standards, there is no guarantee that pesticide usage does not represent a serious risk to human health and the environment.

Unfortunately, existing risk assessment techniques are incapable of identifying an aggregate measure of potential environmental impacts from pesticide usage. Environmental hazards and observed impacts from pesticide usage are measured on different scales, and so far, a set of weights to combine these effects into a composite evaluation index has not been defined. There is a need, therefore, to develop an assessment system capable of integrating the multidimensional side-effects into a unique environmental impact indicator. This would facilitate an assessment of the efficacy of the pesticide programme in realizing the policy targets.

Efficacy does not guarantee that goals are achieved in a cost-efficient way. Economic theory suggests that financial instruments are generally more efficient than regulatory environmental policy measures. The Danish environmental policy arsenal consists of mainly regulatory measures, but it does include a pesticide tax. However, the tax is an *ad valorem* levy with little scope for targeting the incidence in accordance with the variation in environmental risk posed by different chemicals. A better targeting of the pesticide tax would (also) require a composite indicator to aggregate the environmental attributes of pesticides and place the individual compounds in different environmental risk categories.

The present chapter examines a selection of different approaches to the construction of pesticide impact indicators. The Danish pesticide programme is reviewed and its achievements are evaluated using different indicators. Finally, a suggestion is made as to how an integrated impact index could be constructed to improve the targeting of the Danish tax on pesticides.

9.2   RELEVANCE OF ENVIRONMENTAL POLICY INDICATORS

Environmental economics demonstrates how financial instruments like taxes and subsidies can be used to correct market failure and, at least in theory, achieve a socially optimal level of pollution. The 'indicators' required to identify the optimum are monetary measures of the marginal environmental costs associated with pollution and the marginal abatement costs. Nevertheless, most of the environmental indicators available are specified in incommensurate physical units, rather than money, and therefore not applicable for the determination a of socially optimal level of a polluting activity.[1]

9.2.1   Physical Environmental Indicators Versus Values

The use of physical indicators may be seen as a provisional solution: 'It is only because we are not now capable of making reliable estimates of these values [externalities] that we turn to indicators to proxy for the values' (Heimlich, 1995). Economic valuation theory has developed a range of techniques for measuring environmental costs and benefits in monetary terms, and pesticide valuation studies have been conducted in several countries.[2] However, economic valuation of all relevant pesticide externalities is an enormous empirical task, and so far there is probably no complete, empirically founded monetary estimate of the external costs from pesticide use (Pearce, 1998).

Economic valuation also involves unsettled theoretical and methodological issues. The concept 'a socially optimal pollution level' rests on the assumption that individuals/society are always willing to make trade-offs between environmental quality and other goods. Ultimately, the most critical barrier to the wider application of economic estimates may be an ethically based refusal (by political decision makers and citizens in general) to make trade-offs at the margin between market goods (money) and hazards to human and environmental health.[3] The reluctance to define economic trade-offs in pesticide policy matters may be explained by the existence of scientific uncertainties (for example unknown interactive effects of different chemicals) and possible irreversibility of effects from pesticide usage.[4]

Even without measures to identify a social optimum, economic analysis may help decision makers analyse the outcomes of alternative pesticide policies rationally. An obvious second-best approach would be to aim at realizing pre-specified environmental standards in a cost-efficient way; the so-called efficiency without optimality approach (Baumol and Oates, 1988). The role of pesticide indicators in this context would be to delineate policy targets and assess the achievements towards their realization. The Danish pesticide programme will be used to illustrate how an environmental policy has created a need for comprehensive performance assessment tools or indicators.

9.3   THE DANISH PESTICIDE PROGRAMME

The overall objective of the 1986 programme was to 'protect pesticide users and the general public, as well as the environment, from the hazards of pesticides' (Ministry of the Environment, 1986). The principal strategy is to reduce the inherent hazards[5] of pesticidal chemicals as well as the degree of exposure to pesticides. The hazard component is addressed through the implementation of stricter and more comprehensive human health, groundwater protection, and ecotoxicology criteria for pesticide registration/cancellation. Environmental fate data and measures of pesticide use intensity (volume or number of applications) serve as proxies for the exposure component.

9.3.1   Environmental Yardsticks

It is possible to distinguish the following environmental categories as the major areas of concern (Ministry of the Environment, 1986, and Environmental Protection Agency, 1997b):

- human health hazards;
- groundwater protection;
- ecotoxicology;
- indirect ecological effects; and
- uncertainty (unidentified risks).

The human health component of the pesticide programme focuses on food safety and pesticide applicators' safety. Indicators of human health hazards are acute lethality and chronic toxicity; the latter includes reproductive, teratogenic (deformities in unborn offspring), mutagenic, and carcinogenic effects.

The groundwater protection objective is not only to secure the supply of safe drinking water or avoid purification costs. Preserving all groundwater resources in an uncontaminated state is an endpoint of concern in its own right. Groundwater risk indicators include various environmental fate determinants such as solubility, mobility in soil and degradation time.

Ecotoxicology concerns the (direct) effects from the use of pesticides on non-target species. Risk indicators are acute and chronic toxicity to non-target species of mammals, birds, fish, earthworms, and so on and environmental fate factors.

The indirect ecological effects are adverse impacts on biodiversity which are not attributable to the toxic or physico-chemical properties of pesticides. The basic assumption is that a certain level of biological diversity in insects and wild plants (weeds) is necessary to maintain agricultural land's ecological function as a wildlife habitat. This leads to the 'radical' conclusion that the intensity of insect and weed control must be relaxed; with lower yields as a consequence.

Uncertainty may be said to exist when probabilities of different outcomes are unknowable; or at least currently unidentified. It is the underlying assumption of Danish pesticide policy that it is impossible to attach a probability distribution of the future state of nature to all the hazards associated with pesticide use. Following this line of reasoning, reduced pesticide usage, which is analogous to reducing environmental exposure to pesticides, is considered an objective in its own right.

9.3.2 Pesticide Registration

Pesticide registration/cancellation relies mainly on *ex ante* indicators of environmental hazards in the form of laboratory performance tests (for example lethality in exposed populations) and physico-chemical properties affecting the environmental fate of a pesticide (such as water solubility and degradation time).[6] Hazards are evaluated in relation to reference thresholds for the specified criteria. The Pesticide Action Plan also strengthened the role of *ex post* indicators in the form of observed pesticide impact data, for instance the incidence of pesticide detections in groundwater. The most important features are the implementation of an extensive groundwater surveillance programme in combination with legislation facilitating the prohibition of pesticides found in groundwater.[7]

9.3.3 Quantitative Reduction Targets

In addition to reductions in the specific hazard components the Pesticide Action Plan requires that pesticide usage in Denmark must be halved. This is construed as a 50 percent reduction in the volume (kilo) of active ingredients applied as well as a 50 percent reduction in the annual number of treatments per unit area (measured as the number of standard full-dose equivalents available per hectare). It may seem a contradiction to maintain quantitative reduction targets in addition to the hazard control measures. However, with risk assessments being based mainly on extrapolations of experimental data, long-term effects of pesticides may not be adequately captured through the testing procedure. Hence, the rationale behind this part of the policy is that even with stricter registration requirements, there is no guarantee that pesticide usage does not represent a risk to human health and the environment (Berson et al., 1997; Pesticide Committee, 1999). The usage reduction targets may be interpreted as an application of the precautionary principle.[8] In addition, pesticide usage has biodiversity effects which are independent of the intrinsic properties of the chemicals used. As mentioned above this is due to the fact that the intensity of pest control affects biodiversity by reducing food sources for wildlife in the farmed landscape.

9.3.4 The Need for Pesticide Policy Indicators

The effort to strengthen the Danish pesticide policy has resulted in a dramatic increase in the number of target criteria. This in turn creates a need for the development of adequate policy assessment tools. Construction of relevant pesticide policy indicators is considerably complicated by the fact that the adverse environmental impacts of pesticides are multi-dimensional. In general it is not possible to simultaneously minimize all of these dimensions when choosing among different pesticide policies. Existing Danish surveillance programmes and risk assessment techniques do not attempt to integrate the different environmental impact categories. There is a need, therefore, to identify assessment tools capable of giving a composite picture of the environmental impacts from pesticide usage and provide an overall measure of progress toward the realization of policy targets. The following review of indicator varieties seeks to identify relevant approaches to the construction of adequate pesticide policy indicators.

9.4 PESTICIDE INDICATORS

The Organisation for Economic Co-operation and Development (OECD) uses a Pressure-State-Response (PSR) framework to organize and link indicators (OECD, 1997). It is the assumption that human activity exerts pressure on the environment, which in turn affects the state of the environment, leading eventually to a policy response. Pressures from human activities on the environment may be measured in the form of emissions, use of raw materials, hazardous chemicals and so on. The state indicators of environmental conditions (for example ambient pollution levels) reflect the ultimate objectives of environmental policy-making. Response indicators measure to what extent society acts to prevent or reverse environmental damage.

In the present context pressure type of indicators are of primary relevance. This is due to the time lag between the application of pesticides and a measurable environmental impact. For example, a long percolation time means that a state indicator of pesticidal residues in groundwater would not adequately reflect the impact of current policy measures. Pressure-type pesticide indicators can be subdivided into measures that are either intended to support *ex ante* policy decisions or *ex post* assessments of pesticide policy performance. Indicators ranking pesticides according to their (potential) environmental impact are relevant as *ex ante* decision tools for the selection/exclusion of pesticides. Most of the ranking methods are versions of the Environmental Impact Quotient defined below. *Ex post* assessment of policy achievements calls for measures of changes in the environmental pressure from the volume of pesticides used during a given time period. Ecotoxicology Load Indicators are used for that purpose. Another type of *ex post* indicator is the use intensity index. These can range from simple measures of the total amount (kilograms) of active ingredient applied per hectare to somewhat more elaborate treatment frequency indicators providing technology-adjusted measures of pest control intensity.

Levitan (1997) distinguishes between the checklist and the composite index approach to the construction of pesticide indicators. The checklist approach is a multi-attribute system which does not attempt to integrate the scores of the environmental variables into a single composite index value. In contrast, the composite index value approach provides an overall rank order among different pesticides. The latter approach is of primary relevance to the pesticide policy assessments in this chapter. In a generalized form the composite index can be specified as $b_1x_1+b_2x_2+...+b_nx_n$ where each x is the (continuous numerical) score assigned to a physico-chemical property (such as solubility) or a categorical assessment of a hazard (for example high, moderate, low, or no impact). The b coefficients are weights reflecting the relative importance of the trait to the assessment system.

9.4.1 Environmental Impact Quotient

The Environmental Impact Quotient (EIQ) integrates different hazard categories into a composite index value for a given pesticidal ingredient or a formulated product (Kovach et al., 1992). The intended use of the EIQ is as a decision tool for farmers seeking to minimize the adverse effects from pesticide usage through the selection of the least damaging products. Kovach subdivides the environmental impact into a farmworker component, a consumer component and an ecological component. Within each component the environmental impact is specified as a function of the ingredient's toxicity and exposure properties. For example, a measure of risk to consumers from pesticide residues in food is modelled as a function of the ingredient's mammalian toxicity score and relevant exposure or persistence characteristics (half-life on plant surfaces and systemicity).

Of course, the basic concept behind the Environmental Impact Quotient does not depend on the categorization and sub-categorization of the individual risk factors. In the following, two versions of the Environmental Impact Quotient are specified in generic terms.

9.4.2   Ingredient Environmental Impact Quotient (IEIQ)

The *IEIQ* ranks single ingredients according to their aggregate environmental impact. In generic notation the *IEIQ* may be specified as follows:

$$IEIQ_i = \sum_{k=1}^{m} \alpha_k \bullet t_{ki} \qquad (9.1)$$

where:

$IEIQ_i$ = environmental impact quotient for ingredient i
α_k = importance weight of toxicity/exposure factor k
t_{ki} = type k toxicity/exposure factor score of ingredient i, for example acute dermal toxicity, plant surface half-life, and so on.

Scaling and weighting of pesticide attributes makes it possible to aggregate multidimensional information into a one-dimensional measure; the Environmental Impact Quotient. The 'cost side' of aggregation is a loss of details which could be important for the interpretation of alternatives. Dushoff et al. (1994) criticize the Environmental Impact Quotient approach for arbitrariness and the value judgements involved in the determination of the importance weights of various risk factors (effects on farmworkers, consumers, birds, fish and so on). Also, scaling of effects is complicated by the fact that dose-response relationships for pesticides may be nonlinear and interactions between different pesticides are complex and difficult to generalize.

9.4.3   Compound Environmental Impact Quotient (CEIQ)

An environmental impact quotient for a formulated product (*CEIQ*) may be obtained by multiplying (and summing) the quantities of active ingredients in a standard dose of the compound with the respective ingredients' *IEIQ*:

$$CEIQ_f = \sum_{i=1}^{n} IEIQ_i \bullet S_{if} \qquad (9.2)$$

where:

$CEIQ_f$ = environmental impact quotient for pesticide compound f
$IEIQ_i$ = environmental impact quotient for ingredient i
S_{if} = amount of ingredient i in a standard (per hectare) dose of compound f

This aggregation procedure rests on the assumption that there are no cumulative effects from mixing different active ingredients. It also ignores the possible influence of adjuvenants in the formulated product on the effects of active ingredients. There is no readily available scientific information to take account of such contingencies.

9.4.4   Ecotoxicology Load Indicators

While the Environmental Impact Quotient aggregates the environmental hazards embodied in a given pesticide, Ecotoxicology Load (ETL) indicators measure the contribution of different pesticides to specific environmental categories (for example toxicity to birds). Thus, an ETL indicator is an environmental pressure index showing the average load of a given category of toxicity from all types of pesticides used during a certain period of time (Clausen, 1998). Risk measures are calculated on a per weight basis. For example, acute toxicity is defined as the amount of ingredient required to kill half the test population of a given species. The notation is:[9]

$$ETL_{kj} = \frac{\sum_{i=1}^{n} \left(S_{ij} / r_{ik} \right)}{TA_j} \qquad (9.3)$$

where:

ETL_{kj} = indicator of toxicity load (number of toxicity doses) of type k per hectare in year j at the national level
S_{ij} = amount (kg) of active ingredient i sold nationwide in year j
r_{ik} = measure of type k toxicity/environmental fate property of ingredient i
TA_j = total arable area in year j

The indicator ETL_{kj} increases in both toxicity levels[10] and the (registered) amount of active ingredients sold to farmers. Reductions in the farmed area will increase

ETL_{kj}, everything else being equal. The policy relevance of this type of indicator is limited if no procedure is available for integrating the single-criteria measures into a composite index. Without weighing factors it is impossible to determine the magnitude of the overall environmental achievements; or the path if only a single indicator points in the opposite direction from the rest.

9.4.5 Use Intensity Indicators

The indicators above focus on the physico-chemical properties of pesticides such as toxicology and persistence. As already noted, there are biodiversity and uncertainty aspects of pesticide usage which are not attributable to the intrinsic properties of pesticides alone. This has led to the conclusion that a reduction in the intensity of chemical pest control is a goal in its own right. That is, even if the ecotoxicology loads (ETL_{kj}) were reduced to the targeted levels through reductions in ingredient toxicity and persistence (r_{ik}), Danish pesticide policy would nevertheless require a reduction in the number of applications. This, in turn, calls for relevant pesticide intensity indicators.

9.4.6 Volume Intensity Indicator

The simplest – and according to OECD (1994) most frequently used – indicator of pesticide intensity is the total amount (kilo) of active ingredient applied per hectare of agricultural land:

$$IK_j = \frac{\sum_{i=1}^{n}\left(S_{ij}\right)}{TA_j} \tag{9.4}$$

where:

IK_j = amount (kg) of ingredients (of all categories) available per hectare at the national level in year j
S_{ij} = amount (kg) of active ingredient i sold nationwide in year j
TA_j = total arable area in year j.

The indicator IK is directly related to the (registered) amount of active ingredients sold to farmers and inversely related to agricultural area. Using ingredient weight as a proxy for environmental hazards from different pesticides is, of course, arbitrary. With the introduction in recent years of biologically more potent chemicals, not even the trend in pest control intensity is adequately measured by IK.

9.4.7   Treatment Frequency Index

Pest control intensity may be measured on a per application basis using a
Treatment Frequency Index (TFREQ). This indicator shows the number of
times the whole agricultural area can be treated with the amount of pesticides
(compound) sold nationwide, provided standard dosage is applied:

$$TFREQ_j = \frac{\sum_{f=1}^{n} \left(C_{fj} / d_f \right)}{TA_j} \tag{9.5}$$

where:

$TFREQ_j$ = number of standard dosages of all pesticides available per hectare
in year j at the national level

C_{fj} = amount (kg) of pesticide (compound) f sold nationwide in year j

d_f = standard/recommended dosage of pesticide f per hectare

TA_j = total arable area in year j.

The indicator TFREQ increases with the (registered) amount of active ingredients sold to farmers and reductions in standard dosage. In contrast to the
weight based indicator IK above, TFREQ measures pesticide intensity adjusted
for technological changes in the form of more potent chemical agents. TFREQ
is one of the two policy performance indicators identified in the Danish Pesticide
Action Plan.

However, TFREQ is not an ideal indicator of changes in farmers' behaviour
toward less chemical intensive pest control practices. This is due to the fact that
TFREQ does not include changes in cropping pattern. For example, the optimal
treatment frequency is considerably higher for winter wheat than for spring
barley. During the past couple of decades the cropping pattern in Danish agriculture has changed towards a substantially higher share of winter cereals and
less spring barley. Everything else being equal, this tends to increase the use
of pesticides. The agricultural organizations claim that the success of the
Pesticide Action Plan should be measured on the basis of farmers' efforts to
reduce pesticide usage, rather than the quantitative reduction in absolute terms.[11]
Following this line of reasoning the Pest Control Behaviour Indicator below
would be the relevant measure of policy achievements.

9.4.8   Pest Control Behaviour Indicator

The effect of changes in cropping pattern is included in the Relative Treatment
Frequency Indicator (*RFREQ*) in Equation 9.6 below. *RFREQ* relates actual

treatment frequency to the extrapolated treatment frequency (*EFREQ*). The latter is calculated by multiplying crop specific treatment frequency levels in the base period by the hectarage under the relevant crops in year *j*:

$$RFREQ_j = \frac{FREQ_j}{EFREQ_j} = \frac{\sum_{f=1}^{n}(C_{fj}/d_f)}{\sum_{l=1}^{m}(CFREQ_{l0} * CA_{lj})} \qquad (9.6)$$

where:

C_{fj} = amount (kg) of pesticide (compound) *f* sold nationwide in year *j*
d_f = standard/recommended dosage of pesticide *f* per hectare
$CFREQ_{l0}$ = treatment frequency for crop *l* in base period
CA_{lj} = area under crop *l* in year *j* ($3CA_{lj} = TA_j$).

RFREQ increases with the (registered) amount of active ingredients sold to farmers, reductions in standard dosage, and the share of pesticide intensive crops. Compared to *TFREQ* above *RFREQ* may be considered a better policy-performance measure of changes in farmers' behaviour towards lesser dependence on chemical pest control. This would make *RFREQ* a better indicator of the specific effects of a pesticide tax, for example.

9.4.9   A Comprehensive Pesticide Policy Indicator

From a societal perspective it seems relevant to base the pesticide policy on an aggregate measure of the environmental impact from pesticide usage. Oskam and Vijftigschild (1998) propose a use-weighted environmental impact indicator where the amount of active substance applied per hectare is multiplied by the corresponding environmental impact quotient. However, ingredient weight is not a good indicator of pest control intensity; for reasons noted above. From a Danish pesticide policy perspective it would be more relevant to integrate the inherent hazards of the chemicals used with treatment frequency. An applicable solution would be the introduction of a toxicity adjusted treatment frequency index. Such an index could be constructed by multiplying the Environmental Impact Quotient (*CEIQ*) from Equation 9.2 with the treatment frequency indicator (*TFREQ*) of Equation 9.5. This would result in the indicator (*QFREQ*):

$$QFREQ_j = \frac{\sum_{f=1}^{n}(C_{fj}/d_f * CEIQ_f)}{TA_j} \qquad (9.7)$$

where:

$QFREQ_j$ = number of toxicity adjusted standard dosages of all pesticides
                available per hectare in year j at the national level
C_{fj} = amount (kg) of pesticide (compound) f sold nationwide in year j
$CEIQ_f$ = environmental impact quotient for pesticide f
d_f = standard/recommended dosage of pesticide f per hectare
TA_j = total arable area in year j.

The problem is that aggregation of the hazard categories in the Environmental Impact Quotient is necessary to obtain a cardinal measure of the impact of a given pesticide. That is, one has to determine the size of the importance weights, α_k, of the pesticide hazard categories, t_{ik}, in Equation 9.1 above. Science does not have an answer as to how the importance weights should be quantified. Pesticide externalities are not technically or biologically commensurate. Compromises must be made between, for example, lower toxicity and higher leaching risk, low toxicity to humans and high fish toxicity and so on. This is a decision problem involving value judgements. The elicitation of weights (in physical terms) is a corollary to economic valuation of environmental goods where money is used as the measuring rod. In both cases decision makers reduce a higher dimensional problem to a lower dimensional one through trade-offs. The basic difference is that valuation in terms of money presumes that all decision problems can be reduced to a one-dimensional space where environmental resources and market goods are all substitutable. For reasons mentioned in Section 9.2 the monetary valuation approach may not be feasible. The importance weights, α_k, on the other hand, can be specified as environmental trade-offs in bio-physical terms. Limiting the weighting problem to bio-physical relationships does not mean that the establishment of trade-off relations becomes uncontroversial. How this decision problem may be solved is discussed in Section 9.5.3 below.

9.5   ACHIEVEMENTS OF THE DANISH PESTICIDE PROGRAMME

As already noted there is disagreement between different actors (farmers' organizations, environmentalists and political parties) about how to determine whether the Danish pesticide policy has realized its goals or not. In the following we will tentatively assess the achievements of the Danish pesticide programme using the indicators specified above.

9.5.1   Ecotoxicity Load and Environmental Fate Indicators

The aim of the Danish Pesticide Action Plan was to prevent the continued use of chemicals which are significantly toxic, carcinogenic, highly mobile in soil, slowly decaying or liable to cause embryogenic or genetic changes. The regulatory instrument introduced to realize this objective was a decision to re-register pesticides licensed under the old registration criteria.[12] By 1997, 213 out of the 218 active ingredients licensed in Denmark had been re-evaluated (Environmental Protection Agency, 1997b). As a result, 105 of the 218 active ingredients previously approved for sale in Denmark were removed (op. cit.). In most cases the products were withdrawn by the manufacturers.[13]

Unfortunately, the reduction in the number of permitted ingredients does not show to what extent environmental pressure has been reduced. This depends on the physico-chemical properties of the remaining pesticides and the intensity of use. The Danish Environmental Research Institute has established a comprehensive set of ecotoxicity load and environmental fate indicators for pesticide use in the period from 1981–5 to 1996 (Clausen, 1998). These indicators are of the type specified in Equation 9.3 above. They provide *ex post* measures of policy achievements towards the reduction in toxicity load or exposure potential. Measurement is at the single-criteria level such as toxicity to fish from all pesticides used in Denmark during a given period of time. The development in central toxicity and exposure indicators are reported in Table 9.1.

Table 9.1   Toxicological and exposure properties of pesticides used in Denmark from 1981–5 to 1996

Toxicity indicators

Acute toxicity: Decline in indicators for toxicity to mammals, birds, fish, earthworms and crustaceans – due mainly to the prohibition of parathion and other 'old' substances.

Reproductive and teratogenic indicators: Decline for mammals, birds and crustaceans (results are tentative because of missing data for many relevant substances).

Carcinogenic to mammals: Decline until 1989, then increase to initial level (in reference period 1981–5) due to more widespread use of isoproturone.

Algae: Growth regulators show declining toxicity. No significant decrease for fungicides (data for herbicides and insecticides are not representative).

Environmental fate determinants

*Degradation time and solubility in water (leaching ris*k): Significant decrease except for fungicides.

Coefficient of adsorption (leaching risk): Tendency is not clear due to missing data.

Bioconcentration factor in fish: Decreasing for fungicides and increasing for insecticides, the latter primarily due to increased use of pyrethroids.

Source: Clausen (1998)

Most of the computed indicator values point to a reduction in the load of toxicity per hectare of the agricultural area. However, the trend is not unambiguous. Such factors as carcinogenicity to mammals and bioconcentration factor in fish has increased. Nevertheless, it seems safe to conclude that the re-evaluation and monitoring programmes have contributed to an overall reduction in hazards from pesticide use in Denmark. But the noted deviations from the general trend emphasize the limited policy relevance of this type of indicator when no procedure is available for integrating the single-criterion measures into a composite index. Without weighing factors it is impossible to determine the magnitude of the overall environmental achievements.

9.5.2 Reductions in Pesticide Use Intensity

The Pesticide Action Plan called for a 50 percent reduction in pesticide application by 1997 compared to average pesticide use in the period 1981–5. Table 9.2 shows the quantity of active ingredients sold during the 1990s, as compared to the average sales in the reference period 1981–5. If ingredient weight were a relevant indicator of pesticide intensity then the Danish pesticide policy could be deemed a success. The quantity of active ingredients applied has dropped by close to 50 percent since the first half of the 1980s.

Table 9.2   Pesticide usage in Denmark – sales of active ingredients for agricultural purposes, metric tonnes

Year	Herbicides		Insecticides		Fungicides		Growth regulators		Total	
1981–5[1]	4636	100%	319	100%	1779	100%	238	100%	6972	100%
1990	3128	67%	259	81%	1396	78%	867	364%	5650	81%
1991	2867	62%	146	46%	1426	80%	189	79%	4628	66%
1992	2824	61%	128	40%	1333	75%	281	118%	4566	65%
1993	2632	57%	107	34%	1033	58%	331	139%	4103	59%
1994	2685	58%	95	30%	892	50%	247	104%	3919	56%
1995[2]	3281	71%	163	51%	1055	59%	310	130%	4809	69%
1996[2]	2915	63%	36	11%	631	35%	87	37%	3669	53%
1997	2726	59%	51	16%	794	45%	104	44%	3675	53%
Target 1997[3]	2318	50%	160	50%	890	50%	119	50%	3487	50%

Notes:
1. Reference period of the Danish Pesticide Action Plan.
2. Hoarding of pesticides, due to introduction of pesticide tax, created discrepancy between sales and usage figures in 1995 and 1996.
3. Danish Pesticide Action Plan's reduction target for 1997.

Source: Environmental Protection Agency (1997a, 1997b).

However, pesticide usage in Denmark was practically unchanged when evaluated against the application frequency reported in Table 9.3. This divergence between the two quantitative measures is due to the introduction of biologically more potent chemical agents which has significantly reduced the required amount of active ingredient per treatment. Thus, if the number of applications can be taken as a proxy for the intensity of pest control, there is no reason to believe that the indirect ecological effects of pesticides have diminished.

Table 9.3   Pesticide intensity in Denmark – calculated treatment frequency[1]

Year	Herbicides		Insecticides		Fungicides		Growth regulators		Total	
1981–5	1.27	100%	0.14	100%	0.81	100%	0.45	100%	2.67	100%
1990	1.34	106%	0.38	271%	0.84	104%	1.00	222%	3.56	133%
1991	1.28	101%	0.09	64%	0.83	102%	0.71	158%	2.93	110%
1992	1.28	101%	0.13	93%	0.71	88%	0.61	136%	2.73	102%
1993	1.24	98%	0.15	107%	0.57	70%	0.61	136%	2.57	96%
1994	1.28	101%	0.12	86%	0.53	65%	0.58	129%	2.51	94%
1995[3]	1.72	136%	0.15	107%	0.58	72%	1.04	231%	3.49	131%
1996[3]	1.28	101%	0.04	29%	0.38	47%	0.21	47%	1.92	72%
1997	1.65	130%	0.05	36%	0.46	57%	0.30	67%	2.45	92%
Target 1997[4]	0.64	50%	0.07	50%	0.40	50%	0.23	50%	1.34	50%

Notes:
1. Number of standard doses available per hectare of the agricultural area.
2. Reference period of the Danish Pesticide Action Plan.
3. Hoarding of pesticides, due to introduction of pesticide tax, created discrepancy between sales and usage figures in 1995 and 1996.
4. Danish Pesticide Action Plan's reduction target for 1997.

Source: Environmental Protection Agency (1997a, 1997b).

The relative treatment frequency indicator (*RFREQ*) in Equation 9.6 takes account of changes in cropping patterns toward more pesticide demanding crops. This indicator provides a measure of the change in farmers' behaviour toward less dependence on chemical pest control measures. Since the base period 1981–5 the cropping pattern adjusted treatment frequency has dropped by 23–25 per cent (Environmental Protection Agency, 1997b). Farmers' organizations claim that an environmental pressure adjusted treatment measure would be a more relevant policy performance indicator than the unadjusted treatment frequency in Table 9.3. The change in cropping pattern toward more winter cereals is required by another environmental policy; the nitrogen pollution programme. Thus, arguing from what might be termed a partnership or social

contract perspective farmers argue that the sector should be judged on a performance rather than a result-oriented basis. Even if *RFREQ* were accepted as
a policy achievement measure, agriculture has realized only about half the
targeted reduction in pesticide treatment frequency.

9.5.3 An Efficient Pesticide Taxation Scheme

By the mid-1990s it became clear that the regulatory measures introduced would
fail to realize the 1986 Action Plan's quantitative reduction targets. To strengthen
the incentives for farmers to reduce pesticide usage, an economic instrument
was introduced in the form of an eco-tax on pesticides.[14] The revenue from the
tax is reimbursed to the agricultural sector. It is the general assumption of environmental economics that the use of economic control instruments is justified
by allocative efficiency considerations, rather than enforcement efficacy.
However, Danish pesticide policy statements have made no reference to the
efficiency arguments offered by theoretical economics. Political willingness to
use the tax instrument seems to have been prompted primarily by the deficiency
of regulatory measures in achieving the specified reduction targets.

The Danish pesticide tax is levied *ad valorem*, initially with 37 percent on
insecticides and 15 percent on the remaining pesticides (herbicides, fungicides
and growth regulation products) (see Environmental Protection Agency, 1995).
In 1998 it was decided to double these tax rates. Using value as a taxation base
suggests that the more expensive compounds should also be considered the
most hazardous; which seems quite unrealistic. For example, the insecticide
Pirimor is a highly specific plant louse agent with little or no impact on beneficial
arthropods. It is also more expensive than the older, less specific substitutes
available. Consequently, the present taxation scheme gives farmers incentives
to use insecticides with more adverse side effects than the best available alternative. Administrative simplicity is the primary justification given by regulators
for choosing value as a taxation base (Taxation Ministry, 1995). With the recent
increase in pesticide tax rates the issue of efficiency in targeting this instrument
has become more pressing.

The Pesticide Committee (1999) suggests that the Danish pesticide tax should
be targeted to usage intensity rather than value. An intensity compatible tax
scheme could be implemented by imposing a (flat rate) charge per standard
dosage (Dubgaard, 1991). The relevant indicator would be the Treatment
Frequency Index specified in Equation 9.5. In essence this would be a tax on
pesticide application intensity adjusted for ingredient weight variations.
However, differences in toxic properties and so on would not be reflected by
the incidence of a standard dosage tax.

The targeting of the pesticide tax could be further improved by differentiat-
ing the tax rate in accordance with the environmental impacts of the different

pesticides. This would require a composite indicator to aggregate the relevant environmental attributes and place the different pesticides in risk categories. The toxicity adjusted treatment frequency indicator (QFREQ) in Equation 9.7 seems to offer an adequate basis for an efficient targeting of the pesticide tax; at least conceptually. To transform this indicator into an applicable policy instrument there is a need to elicit the pesticide hazard weights (α_k) in the Environmental Impact Quotient (see Equation 9.1).

It is unlikely that policy makers have well defined substitution preferences between the relevant risk categories. Still, by suggesting a set of tax rates the decision maker (implicitly) indicates trade-off relations among the risk criteria. The ratio between the tax rates s_1/s_2 epitomizes the implied substitution propensity between the risk factors 1 and 2. This framework may be applicable for the progressive articulation of preferences (Bogetoft and Pruzan, 1997). Central to this approach is the fact that the decision maker can successively express substitution preferences when confronted with different feasible alternatives. By increasing s_1 relative to s_2 policy makers signal stronger emphasis on the first risk criterion, for example toxicity to a given target species. Pease et al. (1996) outline how Multi-attribute Theory may be applied to elicit decision makers' trade-off ratios (weights) between different pesticide externalities. Levitan (1997) (quoting van der Werf and Zimmer, 1997) mentions the fuzzy membership functions approach as a means of avoiding sharply defined impact categories. The controversy among economists about the Contingent Valuation Method has brought new (non-monetary) preference elicitation techniques into focus. The method of paired comparisons seems a promising methodology for non-monetary valuation of environmental assets and damage (Rutherford et al., 1998). It is beyond the scope of this chapter to go into details about the application and merits of the respective elicitation methods. It will suffice to note that behavioural economics offers an array of methodologies to identify decision makers' preferences.

9.6 CONCLUSIONS

In recent years Denmark has implemented pesticide policy measures leading, among other things, to the removal of about half the substances previously permitted. This has undoubtedly led to a reduction in the overall toxicity load associated with pesticide usage. However, the pesticide programme's intensity reduction targets have not been realized.

It is the presumption of this chapter that the construction of composite pesticide impact indicators could help facilitate more efficient policy decision making. With about half the previously permitted substances already removed, future pesticide registration/cancellation decisions will probably involve more conflict; due to the fact that improvements along one dimension of environmental criteria will have to be achieved at the expense of deterioration in some other criteria. There is also a critical need for an efficient targeting of the pesticide tax. The present *ad valorem* tax gives farmers incentives to use pesticides which are more hazardous than the best available substitute. In both cases identification of efficient alternatives requires a weighting procedure which in turn involves the assignment of importance weights to the different environmental criteria.

According to Dushoff et al. (1994) the current understanding of pesticides and their effects is not sufficient to allow the environmental impact of a pesticide to be captured by a single number. This chapter does not dispute the scientific underpinnings of this statement. However, even in the absence of 'scientifically correct' hazard weights, policy makers have to make choices involving trade-offs. An explicit elicitation of importance weights may contribute to identifying a more consistent set of objectives and improve the cost-efficiency of pesticide policy. Recent developments within the field of behavioural economics seem to offer promising methodologies for the elicitation of scales of the relative importance of environmental changes.

NOTES

*   British usage and spelling retained where appropriate
** Acknowledgement: The author is grateful to Vibeke Østergaard, the Royal Veterinary and Agricultural University and employees from the Danish Environmental Protection Agency, who extracted a large portion of the chemical and judicial technicalities required for the preparation of this chapter. The author is of course solely responsible for any errors and misinterpretations that might prevail.
1. The marginal rate of substitution between the environmental good/bad and the composite alternative good (income) is not defined.
2. For an overview of applied examples see, *inter alia*, Pimentel et al., 1992; Higley and Wintersteen, 1992; Foster and Mourato, 1997; Oskam, 1998; Waibel, 1998.
3. For deliberations on the ethical problems associated with economic valuation of environmental goods, see for example Sagoff (1994); Hanley and Milne (1996); McConnel (1997).
4. Zilberman and Marra (1993, pp. 261–2) report survey respondents' rankings of risk according to the characteristics embodied in the risks such as uncertainty, observability of effect, controllability of exposure, catastrophic effects, and so on. Among a number of risk factors, for example smoking, pesticides came out among the factors characterized by a high degree of uncertainty and possible fatal or catastrophic consequences.
5. Pease et al. (1996) define hazards as 'threats,' while *risk* estimates are 'quantitative measures of hazard consequences'.
6. The registration procedure follows the standards specified in EU Council Directive 91/414 from 1991. Criteria and threshold values are specified in Environmental Protection Agency (1994).
7. Isoproturone is currently undergoing *ex post* evaluation after detection of residues from this chemical in groundwater.
8. The meaning and application of the precautionary principle is examined in O'Riordan and Cameron (1994).

9. The specification is essentially the same as the one used in the USDA ERS 'Chronic and Acute Risk Indicators of Pesticide Use' and in the German SYNOPS model (Levitan 1997).
10. For example, acute oral toxicity is measured as the amount of ingredient (mg per kg bodyweight) required to kill half the test population (for example rats) within a given period of time. Thus, the lower the lethal dosage (LD50), the more toxic the pesticide.
11. The justification given for this is a requirement by the Danish nitrate pollution abatement programme that two-thirds of the arable area must have autumn crop cover – such as winter cereals (cf. Section 9.2).
12. The Danish decision to re-evaluate 'old' pesticides preceded the EU Council Directive 91/414 from 1991 demanding a re-registration of all pesticides licensed before 1993. Up to now only a small number of the pesticides marketed in the EU have been evaluated by the Standing Committee on Plant Health and listed in Annex I of Directive 91/414.
13. Such a self-regulatory action seems to be the common strategy by agro-chemical companies when they know that a product will not be reregistered by regulators (Nadaï, 1994).
14. Strictly speaking an existing, purely fiscal, 3 percent *ad valorem* levy on pesticides was increased.

REFERENCES

Baumol, W.J. and W.E. Oates (1988), *The Theory of Environmental Policy* (2nd edition), Cambridge: Cambridge University Press.

Berson, V., L. Torstensson, M. van der Gaag and G. Matthess (1997), 'Report from an international expert panel on the evaluation of the Danish approval system for plant protection products with special regards to protection of groundwater', Copenhagen: Ministry of the Environment and Energy.

Bogetoft, P. and P. Pruzan (1997), *Planning with Multiple Criteria*, Copenhagen: Handelshøjskolens Forlag.

Buschena, D.E., and D. Zilberman (1994), 'What do we know about decision making under risk and where do we go from here?', *Journal of Agricultural and Resource Economics*, **19**, 425–45.

Clausen, H. (1998), 'Ændringer i bekæmpelsesmidlernes egenskaber fra 1981–85 frem til 1996' (Changes in pesticide characteristics from 1981–85 to 1996), faglig rapport fra DMU (scientific report), no. 223, Roskilde, Denmark: Danish Environmental Research Institute.

Dubgaard, A. (1991), 'Pesticide regulation in Denmark', in Hanley, N. (ed.) *Farming and the Countryside: An Economic Analysis of External Costs and Benefits*, Wallingford, UK: CAB International.

Dushoff, D., B. Caldwell and C.L. Mohler (1994), 'Evaluating the environmental effect of pesticides: a critique of the Environmental Impact Quotient', *American Entomologist*, Autumn.

Environmental Protection Agency (1994), 'Rammer for vurdering af plantebeskyttelsesmidler' (Framework for the assessment of pesticides), *Bekæmpelsesmiddelkontoret*, j.nr. 7016–0002, 30 August, Copenhagen, Denmark.

Environmental Protection Agency (1995), Danish tax on pesticides (act no. 416 of June 14, 1995), Miljøstyrelsen J.nr. M 7040–0004, October 10, 1995, Copenhagen, Denmark.

Environmental Protection Agency (1997a), Bekæmpelsesmiddelstatistik 1996 (Pesticides Statistics 1996), Orientering fra Miljøstyrelsen, no. 10 1997, Copenhagen, Denmark.

Environmental Protection Agency (1997b), Status for miljøministerens handlingsplan for nedsættelse af forbruget af bekæmpelsesmidler (Status for the pesticide reduction action plan), Bekæmpelsesmiddelkontoret, Miljøstyrelsen, November, Copenhagen, Denmark.

Foster, V. and S. Mourato (1997), 'Behavioural consistency, statistical specification and validity in the contingent ranking method: evidence from a survey on the impacts of pesticide use in the U.K.', CSERGE working paper GEC 97–09.

Hanley, N. and J. Milne (1996), 'Ethical beliefs and behaviour in contingent valuation surveys', *Journal of Environmental Planning and Management*, **39**(2), 255–72.

Heimlich, R.E. (1995), 'Environmental indicators for U.S. agriculture', in S.S. Batie (ed.), *Developing Indicators for Environmental Sustainability: The Nuts and Bolts, Proceedings of Resource Policy Consortium Symposium*, Washington DC, June 12–13.

Higley, L.G. and W.K. Wintersteen (1992), 'A novel approach to environmental risk assessment of pesticides as a basis for incorporating environmental costs into economic injury levels', *American Entomologist*, **39**, 34–9.

Kovach, J., C. Petzoldt, J. Degli and J. Tette (1992), 'A method to measure the environmental impact of pesticides', *New York's Food and Life Science Bulletin*, **139**.

Levitan, L. (1997), 'An overview of pesticide impact assessment systems', background paper prepared for the OECD workshop on pesticide risk indicators, Copenhagen 21–23 April (revised July 7), Department of Fruit and Vegetable Sciences, Cornell University, USA.

McConnel, K.E. (1997), 'Does altruism undermine existence value?' *Journal of Environmental Economics and Management*, **32**, 22–37.

Ministry of the Environment (1986), 'Miljøministerens handlingsplan for nedsættelse af forbruget af bekæmpelsesmidler' (Government action plan to reduce pesticide usage), Copenhagen, Denmark.

Nadaï, A. (1994), 'The greening of the EC agrochemical market: regulation and competition', *Business Strategy and the Environment*, **3**(2).

OECD (1994), 'The use of environmental indicators for agricultural policy analysis', Joint working party for the Committee for Agriculture and the Environment Policy Committee, 24 October Paris.

OECD (1997), 'OECD environmental performance reviews: a practical introduction', OECD working papers, vol. V, no. 17, Paris.

O'Riordan, T. and J. Cameron (1994), 'The history and contemporary significance of the precautionary principle', in O'Riordan, T. and J. Cameron (eds), *Interpreting the Precautionary Principle*, London: Earthscan Publications.

Oskam, A.J. (1998), 'External effects of agro-chemicals: are they important and how do we cope with them?' in G.A.A. Wossink and C.G. van Kooten (eds), *The Economics of Agro-Chemicals*, Aldershot, UK: Ashgate.

Oskam, A. and R. Vijftigschild (1998), 'Towards environmental pressure indicators for pesticide impacts', in F. Brouwer and B. Crabtree (eds), *Environmental Indicators and Agricultural Policy*, Oxford, UK: CABI Publishing.

Pearce, D. (1998), 'Environmental appraisal and environmental policy in the European Union', *Environment and Resource Economics*, **11**(3–4), 489–501.

Pease, W.S., J. Liebman, D. Landy and D. Albright (1996), 'Pesticide use in California: strategies for reducing environmental health impacts', Environmental Health Policy programme report, School of Public Health, University of California, Berkeley.

Pesticide Committee (1999), report of the main committee, the Committee for Full or Partial Phasing Out of the Use of Pesticides (the Bichel Committee), Copenhagen: Environmental Protection Agency.

Pimentel, D., H. Acquay, M. Biltonen, P. Rice, M. Silva, J. Nelson, V. Lipner, S. Giordano, A. Horowitz and M. D'Amore, (1992), 'Environmental and economic costs of pesticide use', *BioScience*, **42**(10), 750–60.
Rutherford, M.B., J.L. Knetsch and T.C. Brown (1998), 'Assessing environmental losses: judgments of importance and damage schedules', *Harvard Environmental Law Review*, **22**, 51–101.
Sagoff, M. (1994), 'Should preferences count?', *Land Economics*, **2**, 127–44.
Taxation Ministry (1995), 'Bemærkninger til lovforslag (nr. L 186) om afgift på bekæmpelsesmidler' (Motivations for introducing a bill about levies on pesticides), Skatteministeriet, j.nr. 8.94–231–90, Copenhagen, Denmark.
Van der Werf, H.M.G. and C. Zimmer (1997), 'An indicator of pesticide environmental impact based on a fuzzy expert system' [in April review], cited in Levitan (1997).
Waibel, H. (1998), *Kosten und Nutzen des Einsatzes chemisher Pflanzenschutzmittel in der deutchen Landwirtschaft aus gesamtwirtshaftlicher Sicht*, Kiel: Vauk-Verlag.
Zilberman, D. and M. Marra (1993), 'Agricultural externalities', in Calson, G.A., D. Zilberman and J.A. Miranowski (eds), *Agricultural and Environmental Resource Economics*, Oxford: Oxford University Press.

10. Conclusion

David E. Ervin, James R. Kahn and Marie Leigh Livingston

Rather than use our final chapter to summarize the conclusions of each individual contributed chapter, we will focus on some research needs that have become apparent in our thinking about the contributed chapters and the issues they raise.

First, although there has been a predominant focus on economic efficiency in these chapters (and in the environmental economics literature in general) our ability to conduct cost-benefit analysis and related evaluations remain limited. The reason for this shortfall is that economists still have a very limited ability to measure the economic values associated with both indirect use-benefits (such as existence values) and ecological services.

Many of the chapters in this book have made progress in this regard. For example, Barbier measures the value of the environment as an input to agricultural processes in Africa. Kahn, Hanley and Whitby, Dubgaard, and Archibald and Bochniarz all explore the ability of indices to incorporate these values, while McCauley looks at methods for measuring these values in Asia. However, there is a general paucity of this type of research in the literature and more work needs to be done in an effort to measure the economic efficiency implications of changes in ecosystems and changes in the flow of ecological services. Although innovate economic approaches are key to making progress on valuing such ecological benefits, economists must also collaborate with environmental scientists, environmental ethicists, and other types of social scientists. In addition, more research needs to be done in terms of measuring the economic efficiency implications of indirect uses of the environment, such as aesthetic values and existence values.

Second, our ability to develop indicators for the full suite of decision-making and assessment criteria is also extremely limited. Again, there are significant problems with ecological resources and the services they provide. However, the problem of lack of progress on the development of indicators is not limited to just ecological criteria. More progress needs to be made in terms of developing criteria for environmental justice, equity, ethical considerations, sustainability, and public participation. The compilation of a list of criteria in our introductory chapter is just a preliminary attempt. There needs to be extensive discussion about which criteria are most appropriate under different sets of circumstances, and then the appropriate indicators require further development.

Third, there is a great need to take advantage of the knowledge gained from replication. Replication in scientific inquiry leads to the observation of regularities and these regularities can be a very important source of knowledge in both current decision-making and in the assessment of past decisions.

The first important role that replication can play is in the process of benefit transfer. Benefit transfer is a technique for measuring the net economic benefits of an environmental change that avoids much of the time and expense associated with original environmental impact and environmental valuation research. Benefit-transfer methods take values from sites where valuation work has already been done (the reference sites) and apply these values to the site (referred to as the actual site) where there is a current need to develop value estimates. There are two basic methods to successfully apply benefit transfer methods. The first method looks at the whole constellation of valuation studies that have been done in the past and pulls out the set of reference sites that are most symmetric to the actual site. The estimates from these sites then serve as the basis for value estimates for the actual site. The second method looks at the whole constellation of valuation studies and seeks to determine statistical regularities between value estimates, the characteristics of the resource and the socio-economic characteristics of the users of the resource.

Either technique requires a large number of reference sites to be successful, but with few exceptions (recreational fishing, beach use and value of human life) there are simply not enough studies conducted over a broad enough spectrum of resource characteristics to facilitate this process. This must be kept in mind in the planning of future research. In particular, valuation researchers should be transparent in describing their methodology, and, in each of their studies, they should build in a certain amount of variation, so their research can fill in a span of the resource use spectrum.

The same need for replication exists outside the realm of economic efficiency in the quest for developing indicators of diverse decision-making and assessment criteria. In order to develop better indicators, we need to observe regularities, and in order to observe regularities, we need a full spectrum of observations. This is particularly important for criteria such as sustainability and ecosystem health/integrity. There needs to be additional research and development of accepted assessment design standards. A first step in the process is that the assessment or experimental design is transparent and follows accepted protocols of social science, natural science and survey research

Our fourth general observation is that while progress in improving assessment methods in the developed countries can help improve methods in developing countries, there is not a one-to-one correspondence between the methodological needs of developed countries and the methodological needs of developing countries. In particular, the informal sector in developing countries presents a different set of challenges and constraints in the assessment process. For example, in many developing countries, many people do not participate in the formal sector of the economy, such as those participating in subsistence agriculture. Consequently, willingness-to-pay survey methods are not meaningful unless the trade-offs are structured in commodity-based, time-based, or other non-market price-based terms.

Finally, perhaps the most glaring need in this area of research is the need to develop better methods for simultaneously evaluating multiple assessment criteria. Although there is a long-standing literature in the area of multi-objective maximization, this literature turns the assessment process from an information organizing process into a decision-making process.

Rather than attempting to resolve these problems here, we wish to raise several important related questions and issues. In particular, does economic efficiency have an elevated role among all other decision-making criteria? Should it have an elevated role, or should it be just one of a number of types of information that are used in the assessment and decision-making process?

If one answers this question by affirming the importance of multiple criteria, then this leads to an additional question of great importance. How does one process disparate types of information into a single quantitative or qualitative measure? Should weights be developed for each indicator or criterion, or should this information aggregation process be an explicit part of the policy debate? Can techniques be developed to narrow the range of choices or must all choices be explicitly considered at all junctures along the decision-making or assessment path?

It is our view that economists should be encouraged to recognize that economic efficiency is not the only assessment criterion. An interdisciplinary view is critical to address the problems associated with outcomes assessment. The chapters in this book provide a fine example of the use of interdisciplinary perspectives. Similarly, ecologists should be encouraged to think past the paradigms of ecological risk assessment, ecosystem health, and ecological integrity. In addition, a prominent role should be developed for public participation in both the assessment and decision-making processes, but the outcome of such a public participation process should not be the sole determinant of either the assessment or decision-making process.

We have made much progress in the last thirty years in terms of developing the ability to assess the potential outcomes of environmental policy, but we need to make more progress to resolve the issues highlighted in the contributed chapters and conclusion of this book. Along these lines, researchers are encouraged to think broadly in the development of assessment criteria and techniques to make these criteria and techniques as transparent as possible, and accessible to people from all disciplines and backgrounds. If we facilitate a full and open discussion we will make progress in this important area. However, if we remain trapped in our disciplinary research foci, the issue will remain unresolved for the foreseeable future.

Index